VOLUME 20

Studies in the History of Art

RETAINING THE ORIGINAL
Multiple Originals, Copies, and Reproductions

Center for Advanced Study in the Visual Arts
Symposium Papers VII

National Gallery of Art, Washington

Distributed by the University Press of New England
Hanover and London

This publication was produced by the Editors Office, National Gallery of Art, Washington
Printed by Schneidereith & Sons, Baltimore, Maryland
The type is Baskerville, set by VIP Systems, Inc., Alexandria, Virginia
The text paper is LOE Dull, with matching cover

Distributed by the University Press of New England, 17½ Lebanon Street, Hanover, New Hampshire 03755

Abstracted by RILA (International Repertory of the Literature of Art), Williamstown, Massachusetts 01267

ISSN 0091-7338
ISBN 0-89468-113-3

Proceedings of the symposium "Retaining the Original: Multiple Originals, Copies, and Reproductions," jointly sponsored by the Center for Advanced Study in the Visual Arts, National Gallery of Art, Washington, and The Johns Hopkins University, Baltimore, 8–9 March 1985

Cover: Ingres, *Raphael and La Fornarina*, 1814, Fogg Art Museum, Cambridge, Massachusetts, Grenville L. Winthrop Bequest

Frontispiece: Gilbert Stuart, *George Washington* (Vaughan-Sinclair portrait), 1795, National Gallery of Art, Washington, Andrew W. Mellon Collection

The volumes for 1967–1969 included the National Gallery of Art's annual report, which became a separate publication in 1970

CONTENTS

PREFACE

HENRY A. MILLON
Dean

IN 1982 the Center for Advanced Study in the Visual Arts and the department of the history of art at The Johns Hopkins University initiated a joint annual symposium intended to address broad issues in the history of art and related disciplines. The Center is grateful to the Arthur Vining Davis Foundation for making possible its part in these cosponsored gatherings. This publication, containing twelve papers presented in March 1985 plus a prologue, is the second of the Center/Hopkins programs to result in a volume within the symposium series of *Studies in the History of Art*.

Where does originality lie? This principal question raised during the sessions of "Retaining the Original: Multiple Originals, Copies, and Reproductions," generated quite a number of different responses, comparable, it now seems, to the variable function of copies of and after original works of art from antiquity to the present day. During the eighteenth century and earlier, making copies (including reproductive prints) constituted a major part of the artistic "enterprise"; copies were valued and costly. With these issues in mind, the chairman of the art history department at Johns Hopkins and the dean of the Center invited speakers to address two aspects of originality in the visual arts: first, copies of recognized works of art made, in some sense, to possess the original or replicate its iconic or cultural meaning; second, copies intended to be multiple originals that equally enable possession of the original while replicating and disseminating its image. Of parallel interest were those "replicas" in which the designer selected only what was thought to be the significant identifying feature of the original. In retrospect it may be said that the formulation of these issues, like that of the symposium title itself, was oversimplified, particularly in implying a constant distinction between original and copy. As became evident during the symposium, there are other dimensions of the complex problem of originality to be considered, such as copies made by an artist of his or her own works, which may be quite different (in form and function) from copies made by other artists.

The Center and Johns Hopkins would like to acknowledge the assistance of Egon Verheyen in preparing the papers for publication. We are also grateful to Rosalind Krauss for contributing a prologue to the volume in addition to her own symposium paper. As attentive readers will perceive, the prologue already has stimulated debate on approaches toward the concept and meaning of originality. It is our expectation that the papers gathered in this volume will contribute toward further consideration of notions of originality.

Retaining the Original?
The State of the Question

WHEN A 1985 symposium jointly organized by the Center for Advanced Study in the Visual Arts and the Johns Hopkins University focuses on the problems posed to the original work of art by copies and multiples and a session of the 1988 College Art Association meetings is called "Recycled Images: Citations and Appropriations of Style," something, clearly, is in the wind. That this wind should be blowing from the streets of the art world upward into the towers of academia such that the very objects of study the art historian takes up can be seen to be the *function* of contemporary artistic production may or may not be a welcome idea. But it is certainly not a new one.

Art history's porousness to the aesthetic issues current at any given moment is by now a story nearly worn out by its retelling. How Aloïs Riegl came to feel the necessity of a separate aesthetic value called "opticality" in relation to his own (contemporary) experience of the force of impressionist art or how the historical revivals of El Greco and Piero della Francesca took place against the backdrop of German expressionism on the one hand and the crystalline plenitude of Léger's pictorial style on the other, have become commonplaces of the discipline. The possibility that the discipline is now being buffeted by the winds of a postmodernist interest in "appropriation" should, therefore, seem strange to no one.

Yet it is strange, of course. A measure of this strangeness was to be found in the 1988 CAA paper by Roger Benjamin delivered in the session just referred to. This, while addressing the role of copying within modernism, tried to defend the traditional values of originality against the outré notion of appropriation. Modernist artists, it pointed out, certainly made copies from other materials: old master paintings (Matisse's copy after de Heem); prints (Van Gogh's copies after Millet, Doré, Japanese woodcuts); popular imagery (Cézanne's copies after fashion plates). But far from being viewed as an abdication of the powers of originality, so important to the claims of modernism in art, this copying was seen at the time as a vehicle for making the individuality of the artist in question reveal itself against the backdrop of the pirated image. Which is to say that under the pressures of a modernist definition of art as an act of originality, even copying the work of another is seen as the origination of something new, becoming, that is, an arrestingly distinct interpretive moment. And taking a stance of *plus ça change, plus c'ést la même chose*, the argument continued that "postmodernist" appropriation is simply another version of this modernist demand for orginality. Because if Sherrie Levine pirates Edward Weston photographs (rephotographing his photographs and presenting the "new" prints as her own work) or Mike Bidlo does a stroke-for-stroke replica of *Guernica*, these are acts that nonetheless register as original moments in that subgenre of modernism known as conceptual art.

Yet, against this argument that refuses to relinquish the value of originality—even to images plagiarized by means of mechanical reproduction—since art is almost unthinkable without it, there is the evidence of current art history itself. It is here that we find a registration of some kind of changed experience of the object—and this is reflected in a new set of problems for historical analysis, problems that the *modernist* practice of copying never seemed to force on the historian.

And if the art-historical field is displaying symptoms of a deeper change than that of mere fashion, we have only to look to art history's sister disciplines within the humanities to see the effects of a massive reorganization of thought that has been occurring over the last forty years. With that unsettling displacement within the humanist's anthropocentric universe, by which the "individual" is supplanted by language (a language understood, that is, as both preceding and exceeding the individual), structuralism and its radical, poststructuralist revision opened severe challenges to each of those entities that humanism took to be unimpeachable. One of these entities was that of *origin:* the individual's intention as the origin of his acts, utterances, meanings; the experience in the present as the origin of (future) memories and thus the possibility of a (historical) retrieval of that present-as-origin; (human) nature as the origin of man, and thus the dream of a positivist conquest of the realms of psychology, sociology, cultural studies.

Authorship—one such derivation of the notion of *origin*—is dear to art history, for within the value system of our discipline authorship brings with it a host of privileges. It promotes the work's emergence from the anonymity of shop or craft practice, securing its relation to the actions of an individual. It underwrites the hermeneutic activity with regard to the work, since the individual is seen as the source of an intention toward meaning. Investing the work with market considerations of scarcity, it also uncovers all those traces through which the author registers his individuality, a set of marks that only the original object can bear. If poststructuralism works against this interest in authorship, it does so by positing the "death of the author," reducing him or her to something referred to as an *effect*—as in author-function, author-effect—of other structures, and by exchanging the idea of the work (created by the author) for the

concept of text (which generates the author-effect). Even further, if we think of the conceptual pair within which authorship is secured for art history—the pair original/copy—poststructuralism tends to overturn the conventional art-historical hierarchy through which the original's value is secured as superior. Poststructuralism is suspicious of the ease with which this hierarchy is maintained. Like the psychoanalyst wondering about the repressed ideas that are at work beneath the patient's pronouncements of his *idées réçues* as *truth,* the poststructuralist tends to ask what kind of psychic or cultural or ideological *work* is being done by this devaluation of the copy.

Poststructuralism and postmodernism share this interest in the copy, then. The question about which one influenced the concerns of the other or whether both are related to yet a third set of historical conditions cannot be our concern here. Rather, art history's registration of the *problem* of the copy—and its experience of that problem as something that exceeds the modernist and humanist capacity to reinvest the copy with the values of authorship—emerges from the various symposia and conferences lately convened to examine the matter.

In this regard "Retaining the Original: Multiple Originals, Copies, and Reproductions" is a title intended to hedge its bets. By opening up the question of "multiple originals," the conference's banner seems to welcome the newly blowing wind. But in inviting its participants to wonder about "retaining the original," it allows for the countercurrent that, against the dispersal of authorship into author-function, the author can be retained and can be made to rise, like some kind of strange conceptual phoenix from the very ashes of the copy.

Indeed, the contributions to the conference represent the full range of these possibilities, a range that can be indicated in relation to two readings of the same work, my own and that of Richard Shiff, that place us at opposite ends of the spectrum I have been describing. This work, Ingres' *Raphael and La Fornarina*, we both take as illuminating the practice of classicism in the nineteenth century, which we both assume in turn to be illuminated by another practice, namely, that of photography. Operating at many levels in relation to the issue of *origin* or *original*, this painting depicts Ingres' Renaissance forebear, Raphael, seated before a portrait he has just finished of the woman (the portrait's *original*) he is clasping in his arms. Yet in this represented scene neither Raphael's model nor his canvas can escape the fact that in Ingres' rendering of them, Raphael's style or mode of depiction has been infiltrated by Ingres' own, something that both saps their status as originating in Raphael as the author of their production and admits to the way Raphael is a powerful origin of Ingres' art.

In Shiff's reading the painting is to be seen as a model of classicism, of its calm relation to the question of repetition, with classicism underscored as a system of developing certain norms or standards for the representation of reality and of transmitting these from generation to generation by means of their reproduction through the copy. For Shiff this system is acknowledged in two ways in the painting in question. First, Ingres' unproblematic entry into Raphael's style demonstrates the naturalness of the relation between "original" and "copy" within classicism: unproblematic because within a tradition these priorities lose their rigidity. So Ingres could say of Raphael (as he would of himself), "Raphael, in imitating endlessly, was always himself." Second, in the chain of classical representation as depicted in Ingres' painting, the features of the Fornarina as she sits on Raphael's lap and as she appears inside the painting on the easel are indistinguishable: they have not been shown to have been idealized in their transfer from real woman to her depicted, classical copy. This synonymy, Shiff argues, is also part of the system of classicism, within which a given representation is esteemed to the degree that it is considered true or adequate to its model, which in turn serves as the basis for its becoming standardized within the system of classicism. This is not an argument for the freakishness of realism's "evidence" but for the standardization or commonplaceness of classicism's "truth."

Shiff is describing, then, an unproblematic relation between original and copy (both at the level of representation and of dissemination) within classicism. He claims, further, that this relation only came to be obscured for us by another form of reproduction—a more mechanical one—that of photography. Given photography's higher degree of verisimilitude and its documentary nature, classicism could only be seen as a form of idealization, of abstraction, of a high degree of metaphorization of its real-life models, rather than being, as it was for itself, a form of true standardization of reality. And too, Shiff argues, as we lose touch with classicism's "realism," we likewise lose our connection to the naturalness of the workings of its system of transmission, from one master to another.

From the point of view of the range of positions on the notion of authorship, it must be seen that Shiff's discussion of the unproblematic nature of original and copy within classicism is conducted in front of a single painting, within the unique field of which the vectors of the system are described. But Ingres did four *Raphael and La Fornarina* pictures, as he did many versions of each of his major works, and often these auto-repetitions are not variations of a theme but replications of it. Serial repetition is not classical repetition, for in the classical system of *adequatio* there is always an original against which the adequateness of the copy can be tested. Within the system of seriality, however, we come up against the freakish problem of a proliferation of identical copies with no original to underwrite their accuracy, their goodness, their truth. As a form of mechanical reproduction photography belongs to this system of seriality, of "the multiple without an original." And it is, I would (and do) argue, in Ingres' peculiar participation in the creation of the replica—four *Raphael and La Fornarina*s, eleven *Paolo and Francesca*s, etc.—that we see the system of photography working *within* nineteenth-century classicism to render its assumptions problematic at every possible level.

One of these levels seems to control Ingres' very choice of theme. Often these scenes to which Ingres is repeatedly drawn are, like *Raphael and La Fornarina*, tableaux displaying the power of copies to form a series among themselves that has no need of an original or origin in nature. His mistress may be in his arms, but Raphael is depicted turning away from the living model, riveted instead on the series of representations aligned in his studio and formed within his art—the *Fornarina*, the *Madonna della Sedia*, and others—these establishing a kind of infinite regress of image-types for which there is *no* original.

These two readings would fall, then, on either side of the colon in the conference's title, with Shiff's "Phototropism (Figuring the Proper)" on the side of "Retaining the Original," and my "You Irreplaceable You" on the side of "Multiple Originals, Copies, and Reproductions." For the former the system of authorship remains unaffected by the multiple; for the latter it is seen to be breached from within by the appearance of the author-effect.

Against the neoclassical backdrop of this debate over the status of the original, the question of the Roman copy takes on particular importance. Indeed, as Miranda Marvin points out in "Copying in Roman Sculpture: The Replica Series," the explanatory theory for the production of Roman copies, securely in place until just recently, was very like the idea of neoclassicism as a continuous tradition of aesthetic choice. The copy theory supposed on the part of Roman sculptors and patrons alike a veneration for the Greek original expressed through a desire to make or purchase copies that would prolong and extend the experience of the original: the original master, the original style, the original access it opened onto beauty.

Against this, however, there has emerged evidence for what Marvin calls a "programmatic" theory, supported by texts and by evidence internal to the replica series themselves. This theory hypothesizes that sculpture was installed within specific building types as a kind of scenic announcement of the building's use: bath, forum, basilica, theater, hippodrome. "The visual equivalent of clichés," this sculpture was valued for its recognizability in terms of subject rather than its style, master, or even Greek origin. These programmatic values created social decors, as in the example of Cicero's villa in Tusculum, where his purchase of sculpture to line the porticoes of his "Academy" (named after the gymnasium in Athens where Plato had taught) was meant to put in place the features of a space conducive to a particular activity. His purchase, then, was of "the 'generic brand' of gymnasium statuary. He sought to create not a literal copy of Plato's Academy but what he saw as its essential character as a place of philosophic discussion—what he remembered from his student days—the long porticoes, the walking up and down, the earnest conversation, and a marble blur of statuary as they passed."

Sharply distinct from the eighteenth-century use of classical statuary as decor, the programmatic theory explicitly rules out the aestheticization of these choices. And thus it also rules out a practice that can be assimilated to the notion of authorship with regard to the "original." Since the function of the object within a replica series was that it be instantly recognizable, much of its value or capacity to fill this function lay in the image's fame. But this fame need not have been attached to names like Praxiteles or Myron, although this, of course, was a possibility. The objects that functioned as points of origin for various replica series "may have become popular after they arrived in Rome, perhaps because they were set up in a particularly conspicuous place. Others may have achieved notoriety through association with famous donors or because they played a role in Roman religious life. Still others of the many replica series that survive today may not refer to any Greek original at all but may simply be the version of the, say, Venus Pudica produced by a popular workshop, which was then imitated by other workshops and entered the repertory of well-known types." Within this argument, the assumption of a Roman admiration for the greatness of Greek art, limited to a canonical list of artists, and thus defined by either its authors or their originality, becomes a merely modern aesthetic prejudice projected backward onto Rome.

Other contributions to "Retaining the Original" put forward similar arguments, albeit for different periods and cultures, for this atomization of the author into a social or religious practice in which neither authorship nor originality have any function. Indeed, as is the case in the example Gary Vikan discusses in his "Ruminations on Edible Icons," Byzantine pilgrim tokens function at the deepest level as multiples without originals. Of course, within the tradition he is concerned with—or that of the medieval illuminated manuscript as in the case of Jonathan J. G. Alexander's essay "Facsimilies, Copies, and Variations"—the forms of both anonymity and repetition built into the very system of production would seem to preclude any question of authorship. Yet both of their discussions point to the way that the art-historical method itself has tended to bring the author back into play by trying to locate *some* originating authorial point from which to view the elaboration of the work.

Yet to transfer authorship from artist, where it is understood to be located in most practices after the Middle Ages (although architecture, with its use of pattern books continuing up to modern times, forms a vast exception), to bishop or abbot or sacrist is not to invoke what I earlier referred to as the author-effect or the author-function. It is, some would argue, to create an author retroactively within conditions where the application of such a term can seem, as it does for Vikan, inappropriate. Rather, this effect can only work against the background of a secular and modern (Renaissance and post-Renaissance) conception of authorship, which both produces and is produced by the textual practices that are understood as the operations of authors. Thus it is to those later periods that we must look for the activity of the author-effect as it operates contemporaneously with the production of art. For this, the literature of connoisseurship makes riveting reading.

That a concern over the way copying could undermine the authority of the original was not a nineteenth-century invention—a function of the industrial age—but had deeper roots within artistic production, emerges if one examines the literature of connoisseurship during the seventeenth and eighteenth centuries. This is what Jeffrey M. Muller does in "Measures of Authenticity," in which he presents us with the writing addressed to the "threat of the copy" (in the sense of forgery or fake) and the overcoming of that threat through modes of detection. The connoisseur, as the one who could distinguish the authentic work of art from its imitations, was interested, naturally enough, in isolating those marks within the work that would provide a reliable warrant that it was the original, marks that would be, that is, inimitable. Believing that it was spontaneity that could be copied only with greatest difficulty, the marks of this improvisation and freedom were seen to be carried by open brushwork and expressive, rapid drawing. And because these marks were believed to be so invested, they came to lead an almost independent life in the condition of authorship. Thus works of Rubens' students became authentic works of the master if he merely put his finishing touches on them or works by Sebastiano del Piombo completely based on drawings by Michelangelo were declared in the eighteenth century to be *by* Sebastiano because the logic of the connoisseur contemporaneously invested authorship in the "handling" of the paint rather than in the "thought" of its draftsman.

Within this logic the self-confirming hypothesis that develops is a wonderful illustration of the author-function, for if certain marks express the originality of the original more clearly than others, it only follows that these marks can be used to generate what looks like, and thus what will be taken for, originality. And if this is true, then this set—which can be used to produce an "author"—will constitute the author-function. That the connoisseur is part of a system for *producing* authors rather than certifying the work of ones that exist already is an argument that could be made from the material Muller assembles.

These are certain terms and issues that might serve to locate the various contributions to this collective meditation on "Retaining the Original," contributions of a variety and richness impossible to describe within the space of a brief introduction. All the essays—whether Brunilde S. Ridgway's "The Greek Period," Caroline Karpinski's "Historiographic Perspective" on printmaking, Beverly Louise Brown's "Replication and the Art of Veronese," or Alan Gowans' "Anglican Church Architecture of the Fifteen Colonies"—bring the unique considerations of a particular field to bear on the problem. Which side of the conference title's colon they fall on, or whether likc intellectual colossi they straddle it, the reader of this collection will determine.

ROSALIND E. KRAUSS
Hunter College and the Graduate Center,
City University of New York

April 1988

Defining the Issue: The Greek Period

BRUNILDE S. RIDGWAY
Bryn Mawr College

IN APPROACHING THE topic of Greek copying—understood as the intentional reproduction of a work of art either immediately or at some remove in time—I am keenly aware that I have already discussed the issue elsewhere, and, therefore, it may be said that I have "shot my bolt."[1] I was then, however, primarily concerned with establishing what was being copied, while I now wish to concentrate on the intent behind the copying. To be sure, our knowledge of such motives for the Greek period is quite limited; inevitably, therefore, some of my suggestions are founded on speculation and should be considered tentative, especially in view of the slanted nature of the Greek material. It may bear pointing out, for instance, that in the realm of Greek sculpture we have great gaps. After numerous examples from the archaic period (c. 650–480 B.C.) and even the severe period (c. 480–450 B.C.) our extant originals dwindle to the point that our evidence for the classical period (broadly intended as ranging approximately from 450 to 330 B.C.) is largely confined to architectural sculpture, which, if often of excellent quality and always competently carved, was nonetheless not the primary expression of the best sculptors of the time. As for the Hellenistic period (c. 330–30 B.C.), the picture is still confused and we cannot claim to distinguish with confidence between Hellenistic originals and sculptures made during the Roman period in Hellenistic style. Throughout this chronological span, if we extend our consideration to other forms of art, we are confronted with regional preferences and discontinuous or ambiguous evidence that we have not yet learned to interpret.

I nonetheless have the advantage of discussing the relative beginning of the Western artistic tradition, the time when the first originals were created. By this statement I do not wish to imply, of course, that there were no other civilizations whose artistic forms preceded or coexisted with the Greeks' and from which the Greek artists drew inspiration. Yet the Greeks managed to assimilate and transform whatever influence they absorbed from elsewhere into their own distinctive creation. It is the Greek legacy that had the strongest impact on the Romans and eventually on the whole of Western art. Leaving aside the early phases of Greek art after the Dark Ages, I can, therefore, focus on what has occasionally been called the Greek miracle: the apparent flowering of a fully formed artistic expression as distinctive and sudden as the birth of Athena, who burst fully armed from the head of Zeus.[2]

Because Greek art has always been greatly admired, it has been difficult to accept the notion that copying could exist within its repertoire. It has long been held that the Greek artistic personalities, so highly praised by the Romans, could only produce original works, creating art along the lines of a logical stylistic development that was forever building on the established premises. The Romans, in their great appreciation for Greek achievements, only copied preexisting monuments, mostly because they lacked the imagination for creating original works beyond their realistic portraits and their historico/funerary monuments. Even some scholars who hold a more balanced view of ancient art tend to discredit copying among the Greeks, if for no other reason than their belief that the appropriate technology had not yet been developed and that accurate reproduction could, therefore, not be attained. Such copying, defined in mechanical terms and measured by its degree of faithfulness to the original, could only be considered less creative than spontaneous production and, therefore, inferior to it.[3]

Such tenets are deeply embedded in most handbooks on the history of art, and it is essential that we disregard them if we want to approach our topic with objectivity and a receptive mind.

To be sure, no Greek word for *copy* is known, but only two terms are used in relevant context: *mimēsis* (imitation) and *paradeigma* (example or model). The first, significantly, was applied primarily to the theatrical arts, from which it extended to the sphere of sculpture and painting. Although we cannot consider this point at any length, we would do well to remember that a play in ancient times was as much a visual as an auditory experience (*theatron*, a place where one *sees; orchestra*, from *orcheomai*, the place where the *choros* [rhythmical dancers] danced). In this sense every performance could be seen as a *copy* of an original play, which, however, would carry no stigma and would still offer some scope for personal expression. Conversely, actors wore masks, again a form of reproduction based on standard (that is, recognizable) types, which to some extent prevented individual recognition and limited originality.[4]

It is also important to realize that our concept of originality is relatively modern and may not have applied during Greek times. To speak of originals in terms of permanent, immutable works of art, we must first accept the concept of originality—the unique expression of an artist that defines a personal style and can be shared by no others. Insofar as it is unique, personal style cannot be duplicated and its creations are limited in time and number; dissemination can only be obtained through faithful reproduction—hence the need for copying. But these conclusions are based on the premise of artistic

personality and imply not only individual talent but also a striving for personal expression. The focus is, therefore, on the artists as much as on their productions. In Greek times, however, art for art's sake did not exist; most monumental art—if not literally all—had religious purposes, and far from being shunned, imitation was pursued as a means of ensuring recognition of forms. Such forms, significantly, were not even directly copied from nature but were based on abstract theoretical principles that are largely responsible for the idealizing nature of classical art. Only with the Hellenistic period is a shift in approach observable, so that human beings are shown "not as they were, but as they appeared to be" in their outward physical identity rather than as essences of humanity.[5] Hellenistic anecdotes suggest that artistic personalities began to emerge, according to modern concepts, during the fourth century B.C. at the earliest. Ancient writers, however, are so likely to distort or interpret the evidence according to their own times that great caution must be used in accepting their truthfulness: most accounts probably are fabrications for rhetorical or moralistic purposes.[6]

It would, therefore, appear that no true copying, in terms of faithful and mechanical reproduction meant for the dissemination of the original, can be credited to the Greeks until late Hellenistic or even Roman times. If, however, we include in our consideration other forms of duplication, made for different purposes and aiming at varying degrees of similarity, then the Greeks can be shown to have practiced various types of copying. Some occurred as early as the archaic period and are especially obvious in sculpture, although architecture and painting also present a few examples. The reasons for copying may largely be technical and practical, but additional motivation seems to have been provided by iconographic conventions, religious conservatism, and even outright admiration. I have, therefore, divided my analysis into categories, according to what I believe to have been the possible causes for the practice, and I have followed a roughly chronological order to suggest a certain development and expansion of the concept of copying throughout the Greek period.

Duplication to Suggest Association

I begin with this category because a major sculptural find made on Samos during the summer of 1984 has enriched it with a spectacular example. The well-known "Hera of Samos," one of the art treasures of the Louvre since its discovery in 1875, has now gained a double, regrettably also headless but almost identical.[7] Like the Louvre statue, this second image carries an inscription identifying it as the dedication of a certain Cheramyes; it thus joins another female figure in Berlin and a fragmentary but colossal male leg still in Samos, both inscribed by the same dedicant. Before this recent discovery the three votives had been given different dates, the Louvre's "Hera" being considered the earliest, around 570–560 B.C., the Berlin kore (Aphrodite?), about 560 and probably by a different master, and the kouros, 550–540.[8] The new find suggests that all four gifts may have been simultaneous, part of a single monument in which the two identical figures stood side by side, their relationship expressed by their similarity as much as by their juxtaposition. The Berlin kore differs in being shorter and in holding a hare against the chest (the Louvre and the Samos korai may have been empty-handed), but she wears the same attire as the other two and is an unmistakable product of the same stylistic approach to the female figure.

One such group was already known from the same sanctuary on Samos, made by the sculptor Geneleos (as attested by his signature), probably around the same time, 560–550 B.C.[9] It consists of a long base set up along the Sacred Way, on which three korai and a kouros once stood at attention, between the seated mother at one end and the reclining father at the other. Only two of the korai are well enough preserved to bear stylistic analysis, and again they are strikingly alike, although some variation occurs in details. Their relationship could not have been missed, given their juxtaposition but especially given their similarity. Familial ties are equally expressed by the much cruder Dermys and Kittylos from Tanagra in Boiotia or by the Delphic twins, whether Kleobis and Biton, as they used to be identified, or the Dioskouroi, according to a more recent interpretation.[10] In this last case only modern technology has been able to demonstrate some proportional differences between the two statues, which suggest that each was made by a different sculptor; the example is, therefore, all the more striking in that intentional duplication, rather than style, is responsible for the seemingly identical appearance of the two pieces.

Similarity Determined by Technique

Sculpture. In discussing the archaic kouroi, we must take into account the method by which they were made, for it may ultimately be responsible for their basic affinity. It is widely accepted that the Greeks inherited from the Egyptians not only the type of the standing male statue but also the canon of proportions and with them the

technique for applying a proportional grid to the quarry blocks from which such statues were to be carved.[11] Much preliminary carving took place in the quarries to eliminate excessive weight in shipping; thus the basic features of the kouroi were already established before they reached the intended sculptor, unless one assumes that masters traveled to the source of marble for each commission. Given the great consistency of the kouros formula (which has been defined as a straitjacket stifling archaic creativity and imagination),[12] the role of the quarrymen during the entire sixth century B.C. should not be underestimated. In this particular case, however, it is appropriate to speak of formulaic rendering rather than of copying, since scope for variation, albeit limited, still existed within the parameters of the kouros type.

The same comments may apply to the female counterpart of the kouros, the archaic kore, although greater variation in attire and pose was possible. In particular, a certain type of kore wearing chiton and diagonal himation and holding a bird against the chest occurs in such close examples at Samos, Miletos (figs. 1–2), and even

Figs. 1 and 2. Korai found at Miletos, marble. Staatliche Museen, Berlin, inv. 1791 and 1577.

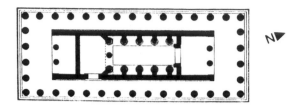

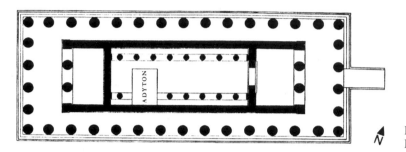

N

Fig. 3. Plans of the Temple of Apollo Epikourios, Bassai, and the Temple of Apollo, Delphi.

Theangela in Karia (that is, non-Greek territory) that the theory of a specific prototype, perhaps "created" at Miletos, seems plausible.[13] Whether hieratic meaning should be attached to the similarity and, therefore, be seen as the intent behind the reproduction is a question that cannot be answered at the present state of our knowledge.

Architecture. Technique and methodology may also be responsible for some architectural similarities. If a workshop had developed a system of proportions for a building, as well as a module or unit of measurement for its component parts, it stands to reason that the system would be applied to different commissions to expedite construction and minimize risky experimentation, especially at a time when adherence to architectural orders and plans was considered desirable rather than unimaginative. As an example, I can cite the sixth-century Apollonion and Olympieion at Syracuse, two temples within the limits of the greater city, although in different districts, probably erected by the same workers, with minimal variations.[14]

Similarity Suggested by Religious Conservatism or Symbolism

Architecture provides several examples of imitation based on religious association or symbolism, but they are less definite and rest more on modern speculation than on ancient statements. Yet there is no doubting the importance of the Temple of Apollo at Delphi, the seat of one of the most influential oracles of the ancient world. It has been suggested that the archaic Delphic plan, with six columns across the front and fifteen on the long sides, was deliberately repeated in other Greek temples also dedicated to Apollo, so that buildings whose cult is not presently known have been attributed to that god solely on the basis of their six-by-fifteen plan.

In effect such elongated forms were being built long after the archaic period, even when new systems of proportions were preferred and would have dictated a shorter plan. Various solutions were adopted for modernization. For instance, the Temple of Apollo Epikourios at Bassai, Arkadia, retained the six-by-fifteen peristyle, but an ingenious internal arrangement created the impression of a cella shorter than that required by the excessive length of the structure (fig. 3).[15] At Delphi itself, the temple was rebuilt after the destructive fire of 373 B.C. along exactly the same plan and on the same foundations—perhaps in part for reasons of economy but primarily for religious conservatism. The only concession to modernity was made in the elevation, which incorporated the slender proportions, lighter entablature, and rinceau sima with rampant antefixes typical of the fourth century.[16]

Bilateral Symmetry or Repetition of Many Elements

Architectural demands are responsible for much sculptural duplication, either intended as mirror reversal of two images or as a series of equal elements within a building. Examples of the first kind include not only obvious features like lateral akroteria—ranging from single figures such as sphinxes to complex equestrian groups or kidnapping scenes—but also pairs of sculptures framing funerary structures, for instance, lions or mourning servant figures.[17] Karyatids are also manifestations of the principle of bilateral symmetry, including the korai of the Erechtheion porch, although as many as three statues fall on either side of the central axis. It is important to note that although generally similar, the Erechtheion karyatids differ in individual details, and at least two models (*paradeigmata*) have been suggested for their execution.[18] Mirror reversal has been generally assumed for karyatids of which only one is extant, as in the Siphnian Treasury at Delphi, although a recent theory suggests that a nonmatching piece should be considered the second element of the Siphnian porch.[19] Conversely, freestanding statues in mirror image may be tentatively interpreted as architectural elements (as karyatids or akroteria) even if structural evidence is missing and iconographic reasons could be responsible for the rendering.[20]

The most obvious example of serial duplication is provided by waterspouts along the eaves of a building, not only those made of terracotta (fig. 4) and, therefore, easily repeated by use of the same mold, but also the more complex spouts carved from stone and of considerable size.[21] In the Temple of Zeus at Olympia, the first series of lion heads was carved with the rest of the ornamentation on the building and must have been produced by several sculptors, perhaps after a single model. Later damage forced the replacement of several waterspouts, and differences in the carving make apparent the change in contemporary styles or the inability of the repairers to observe a model at close quarters.[22] When variations occur within the original series, a certain spirit of independence should perhaps be attributed to the carvers, so that even this seemingly routine task can be appreciated as a demanding job of sculpting.

Need for Replacement

The same damage that required the replacement of waterspouts made much heavier demands on sculptural workshops when some of the corner figures on the west gable of the Temple of Zeus at Olympia had to be carved anew to substitute for the ruined originals. That such damage occurred at least as early as the fifth century B.C. is shown by pieces of the horizontal cornice reused as filling material in foundations of fourth-century buildings, which provide a terminus ante quem for at least one occasion in which the Temple of Zeus underwent repairs. There were probably others.[23] No certainty has been reached as to the date of the replacement figures, but such precision is irrelevant for our purposes. Far more important is to note that statues could be carved in plausible imitation of the severe style of the 460s. Differences in proportion, facial expression, and sharpness of folds alert us to the fact that we are viewing a classical rather than a severe sculpture, but the effect is credible and must have been convincing to the distant viewer.

Copying from Models Because of a Difficult Setting

The same pediment from the Temple of Zeus at Olympia provides one more example of possible copying, this time from models at a reduced scale. Considering the narrow shelf on which pedimental figures rested and the complexity of some pedimental groups (fig. 5), it is unlikely that architect and sculptor executed their work without some preliminary idea of how the finished pieces would fit into the available space. The size and weight of the

Fig. 4. Sima from the Temple of Casa Marafioti, Locri, terracotta. Museo Nazionale, Reggio di Calabria.

Fig. 5. Reconstruction of pediments from the Temple of Zeus, Olympia (from Curtius and Adler, eds.; G. Treu, *Olympia* 3).

Olympia sculptures would have prevented any but the most trivial modifications during installation, when the load was in suspension. Perspective drawing of the sculptures in position demonstrates the interlocking and overlapping of the groups, conditioned not only by the narrowness of the base line but also by the sloping frame of the triangular gable.[24] Some unfinished spots on a few pedimental heads have been considered possible measuring points used by the sculptors to transfer and magnify dimensions from small-scale models, perhaps of clay, to large stone blocks. Whatever the method, even a rudimentary copying system must have been adopted at Olympia as in other large temples with elaborate pedimental sculptures.[25]

Repetition of Patterns: The Use of Molds and Pattern Books

Architecture continues to suggest other forms of copying that straddle the distinction between true carving and mechanical reproduction as a form of handicraft. Yet it should be stressed that such distinctions between the so-called major and minor arts are purely artificial as applied to ancient times and were certainly not drawn by the Greeks themselves.

Archaic buildings were often decorated with terracotta plaques as simas, geisa, or other forms of architectural revetments. Many carried only abstract designs, but several created a kind of continuous figured frieze by the repetition of single representational units in a row. One such unit of great popularity, especially in Asia Minor,

was the racing chariot, with charioteer bent over in action, often accompanied by a coursing hare or dog beneath the galloping horses to convey the idea of great speed (fig. 6). It may seem at first that such repetition is a direct consequence of the use of the mold; yet it should be noted that the chariot frieze existed also in stone, which required that each block be painstakingly and individually carved (figs. 7–8). Moreover, the practice was not limited to the archaic period, when influence from the terracotta examples could be surmised, but continued as late as the mid-fourth century B.C., when a chariot frieze was employed on the famous Halikarnassos Mausoleum, probably on the base of the quadriga topping the pyramid.[26]

Molds were especially important for the dissemination of the prototype. From recent finds we now know that piece casting and the making of bronze statues by the indirect method were known by the early fifth century. Indirect casting permitted the preservation of the original model from which the molds were taken and would thus have allowed numerous reproductions of the same statue.[27] Extant ancient bronzes are, however, so few that we cannot demonstrate the practice beyond the potential for its occurrence. But we can prove it in the case of terracottas, both protomes or full figures in the round. We have several instances of the same type produced in two different clays and in different geographical areas, suggesting that molds traveled, either alone or in the baggage of itinerant coroplasts. Even more significant is the case in which "family trees" of terracottas can be established, like stemmata of manuscripts, each subse-

18

Fig. 6. Reconstruction of terracotta sima from Larisa. Nationalmuseum, Stockholm.

quent generation revealed by the smaller dimensions of the finished product.[28] This evidence suggests that the object itself must have traveled, presumably through trade. A new mold was then taken from it, with consequent shrinkage and reduced size for the matrix and its output. Given the relative anonymity of such creations, which were certainly not reproduced for their originality or stylistic value, we must assume that such copying was motivated by other purposes: perhaps convenience, economy, or even iconographic meaning. Yet it is impossible to place great emphasis on this last factor, since attributes and ornaments were often changed at will from place to place, thus lending identity to a basic generic type. Aesthetic appeal, however, should not be excluded as a possible motivation because many of these terracottas are large and very fine.

Transmission by terracotta molds finds a certain counterpart in the transmission by pattern books, although these elusive models have yet to be materially attested or excavated. Several archaic reliefs of identical dimen-

Above right: Fig. 7. Frieze block with charioteer, marble, Iasos.

Fig. 8. Reconstruction of architectural frieze from Myus. Staatliche Museen, Berlin.

Fig. 9. Ball Players Base, marble. National Museum, Athens, 3476.

Fig. 10. Funerary base from the Themistoklean wall, marble. Kerameikos Museum, Athens, P1002.

sions have been found in different areas; others, very similar, come from the same artistic district, the Athenian Kerameikos, and may have been the product of the same workshop. Of these, the best known is the so-called Ball Players Base (fig. 9), which has found a fragmentary but close counterpart in a recently excavated funerary base (fig. 10). This is low-relief sculpture, which, therefore, partakes more of the nature of drawing than of carving.[29]

Workshops of potters and vase painters may have used the same methods as the marble carvers' establishments nearby. That a single painter could repeatedly reproduce his own figures has now been shown by a group of fragments excavated from a single atelier,[30] but other examples exist. One is provided by the famous dice-playing scene between Ajax and Achilles on the Vatican amphora by Exekias (c. 540 B.C.; found at Orvieto, Italy), which is repeated, with variations and in bilingual form, on an amphora by the Andokides Painter, now in Boston (c. 525; from Vulci). Since the Andokides Painter has been considered one of Exekias' pupils, it could be inferred that such patterns were "copyrighted" by a specific workshop.[31]

Copying or Imitation from Monumental Painting (?)

Other vase painters may have derived inspiration not from their colleagues but from mural painters, although again the point cannot be demonstrated, given the almost total loss of monumental painting. The well-known Orvieto krater by the Niobid Painter (c. 460 B.C.), showing the Killing of the Niobids and another epic scene, should be considered imitative of wall painting not only because of its many ground lines suggesting a mountainous landscape but also because it is unique in the painter's repertoire. His typical production consists of smaller vases (pelikai) decorated with fewer figures on a single ground line and even showing different anatomical markings from those present on the Orvieto krater. Yet these very renderings form the primary basis for attributions to artists, according to the Morellian system followed by Beazley.[32]

Copying as Iconographic Quotation

Monumental painting, considered in antiquity the highest form of art, may have also influenced the sculptors who composed the west pediment of the Temple of Zeus at Olympia. The Theseus in that scene, wildly swinging his weapon in defense of the bride, has been connected with the Centauromachy painted in the Athenian Theseion, especially since virtually the same figure appears in the same context on a vase by the Painter of the Woolly Satyrs in New York.[33] More significant perhaps is the adoption of the same gesture and pose for the younger Tyrannicide in the bronze group made by Kritios and Nesiotes in 477 B.C. If the particular iconography was by that time already associated with the hero Theseus, its transference to Harmodios would automatically have bestowed on the young man the status of a hero comparable to the legendary king of Athens. The Centauromachy frieze over the west porch of the Hephaisteion could in turn depict a similar Theseus now back to back with a figure stretching out his mantle in a pose reminiscent of the older Tyrannicide of the Kritian group.[34] Iconographic meaning could thus become superimposed on a previous iconographic meaning, each enriching and redefining the other. Conversely, iconographic imitation may help identification. For instance, if Figure G on the Parthenon east pediment (fig. 11) truly imitates the so-called Running Girl from Eleusis (fig. 12; c. 490 B.C.) she should perhaps be identified as Hekate on the basis of a recent and convincing assessment of the archaic piece.[35]

A subcategory of iconographic quotation includes the copying of themes as specific allusions. It is significant that so many Amazonomachies and Centauromachies were carved as architectural decorations after the Parthenon and its Athena Parthenos had made the subjects famous. With the passing of time these mythical battles may have come to signify no longer the supremacy of the Greeks over the Persians, as traditionally believed, but simply the glory and civilization of Athens. It is perhaps in this sense that both myths were chosen for the Halikarnassos Mausoleum, the monumental tomb of a Karian ruler with strong Persian ties.[36] Yet it was in turn the fame of this major monument, one of the Seven Wonders of the World, which may have suggested the Amazonomachy for the decoration of a private tomb structure, the Kallithea Monument, named after its findspot near the Peiraeus—once again, a case of transference of meanings and allusions.[37]

Copying of Major Monuments for Their Fame

A specific statue in the round may occasionally have been copied not for its iconographic meaning but for its own renown or, although more doubtfully, for that of its maker. Several youths on the Parthenon frieze, for in-

Fig. 11. Figure G from the east pediment of the Parthenon, marble. British Museum, London.

Fig. 12. Running Girl, marble. Eleusis Museum.

Left: Fig. 13. Alxenor stele from Orchomenos, marble. National Museum, Athens.

Right: Fig. 14. Double stele of Deines from Apollonia, marble. National Museum, Sofia.

stance, exhibit poses and anatomical renderings clearly reminiscent of the Doryphoros of Polykleitos. Yet the Argive master, to our knowledge, was not connected with the workshops active on the Parthenon, which were allegedly supervised by the Athenian Pheidias. Nor can we be sure of the location of the original Doryphoros, yet the type is reproduced not only on Athenian but even on Cyrenaican funerary and votive reliefs—perhaps once again through the medium of pattern books.[38]

Typology

Gravestones offer significant examples of another form of copying: typological. In addition to the well-known

example of the Ilissos Stele reproduced in approximately reverse image by an obviously less-talented hand, there is the early classical case of the so-called man-and-dog stelai, which repeat the general type of a mature man leaning on a stick and offering a tidbit to a dog climbing against the narrow frame of the relief. Since one such gravestone was found at Orchomenos, in Boiotia, where it had been made by the Naxian Alxenor (fig. 13), and another comes from Apollonia on the Black Sea (fig. 14), it is obvious that the type itself was popular, regardless of individual style and authorship.[39]

In other cases the geographical range may be smaller and the type chosen may be adapted to suit different contexts, such as the female draped figure made by Chairestratos to represent the Themis of Rhamnous (c. 300 B.C.), for which a plausible prototype at larger scale has now been excavated in the Athenian Agora. A recent article has argued that the figure represents Demokratia (c. 335–330 B.C.), on the basis of a similar image appearing in relief as the *en-tête* of an engraved decree (337/336 B.C.) and identified by inscription—in itself another example of "copying" involving the same original in the round.[40]

"Doubles"

It is fortunate but unusual to possess both an original from which a copy was made and the copy itself. Most often only the copies remain, identifiable as such by the date of their manufacture, which is considerably later than the style of the prototype they reproduce. But in some cases there is evidence to suggest that the original in our hands could not possibly have served as the model from which the copies were made. We must, therefore, assume that another such "original" was available, close enough in appearance to qualify as a double, although we may never be able to prove its existence.

A case in point is the famous Penelope (c. 460 B.C.), excavated in scattered fragments from the ruined Treasury at Persepolis, where it had been buried since Alexander the Great conquered and destroyed the city in 330 B.C. (fig. 15). Yet several Roman replicas are known, made during imperial times (fig. 16), therefore, quite a few centuries after the destruction of Persepolis, presumably copying a double of the Penelope available in Greece or in Rome.[41] Another such case is the bronze Athena (c. 340 B.C.) accidentally found at Peiraeus within a cache of bronzes of different dates. It has been assumed that the statues were buried within a warehouse destroyed by Sulla during his attack on Athens in 86 B.C.

But a marble replica of the Athena, the so-called Mattei Athena in the Louvre, suggests that a double of the bronze was available to copyists during the second century after Christ, in Antonine times, and the casting technique may easily have allowed the making of more than one replica in the fourth century B.C. A second hypothesis would question the fourth-century date of the Peiraeus bronze and even the Sullan connection in the burying of the cache.[42] This uncertainty highlights the difficulty preventing more precise statements in most matters of ancient art.

Reproduction of Cult Images for Private Dedication or Devotion

Equally impossible to document is the Greek practice, which seems to have begun during the fifth century B.C., of reproducing at smaller scale divine images that were presumably cult statues in temples or sanctuaries. Because they are not mechanical or even identical copies, such works represent originals in their own right and may have been used as private dedications to the same deity whose cult image they imitated or as objects of private devotion in domestic shrines. Within this category the best known are the Grimani statuettes, now in Venice but originally from Crete; others have been found in Kos and on Crete itself.[43] Significant confirmation is provided by the fourth-century historian Xenophon, who states in his own works that he had erected at smaller scale for his estate at Skyllous a statue and even a temple like those of the Ephesian Artemis.[44]

The last two categories I will set forth represent special cases and could be said to mark the end of "specialized" duplication as I have defined it. By the end of the fourth century B.C. different approaches prevailed in Greek art, and made typological copying subordinate to morphological copying, with the intent of reproducing a given work not only in its general but also in its specific appearance.[45] Literary sources mention the brother of

Fig. 15. Penelope from Persepolis, marble. Teheran Museum.

Fig. 16. Penelope, marble. Vatican Museums, Rome.

Lysippos who made plaster casts directly from human limbs in order to obtain a close imitation of natural forms.[46] Lysippos himself is supposed to have devised a canon of proportions more directly comparable to physical reality, and although such ancient statements were written long after the fact, they may retain some sense of the actual events.

It is only with the mid-second century B.C., however, that definite evidence becomes available—and it involves primarily the reproduction of cult images for official purposes. Perhaps the trend was sparked by the fact that Damophon of Messene was asked to repair the Pheidian Zeus at Olympia. Perhaps a wave of nostalgia for the classical past of Athens was responsible. Certainly around 150 B.C. several replicas of Pheidian statues were made, occasionally at proportionately reduced scale but still colossal in general size: a Zeus Nikephoros for Antioch, an Athena Parthenos (akrolithic) for the mid-fourth century Temple of Athena at Priene, another for a temple at Notion, and a third for the Library at Pergamon—for a location, therefore, that subtly changed the meaning of the divine image from a warlike defender into a patroness of learning.[47] The Pergamene sculpture, preserved almost in its entirety, allows us to note that its style betrays the Hellenistic times in which it was made. The intent, however, was to copy the Pheidian original closely enough to insure immediate recognition. In the same vein Attalos II (r. 159–138 B.C.) sent Kalas and Gaudotos to Delphi to copy the Polygnotan paintings.[48]

By the first century B.C. stylistic developments encompassed another, and subtler, form of copying: the imitation of a definite earlier style in a retrospective vision that involved no specific prototype. Archaistic sculpture had existed since the fifth century B.C., but it acquired new impetus in late Hellenistic times.[49] In addition, a "severizing" trend began that can be chronologically pinpointed at least in the works of Stephanos, a student of Pasiteles in the first century B.C. Stephanos' master, moreover, seems to have incurred great danger because of his naturalistic tendencies, moving too close to some African wild animals he was sketching in the harbor of Naples.[50] Such direct copying from nature would have been unthinkable during classical times.

During the first century B.C. we also find the first instances of sculptural copying in the strict sense of the term. The Diadoumenos from Delos, found in a pre-88 or 69 B.C. context, the Herakles of the Farnese type recovered from the Antikythera shipwreck, which foundered around 80 B.C., the playful satyriskos from the Mahdia wreck of somewhat earlier date, which finds its counterparts in three youthful statues from Sperlonga, all clearly indicate that the copying industry had begun in earnest to supply the Roman patrons.[51] This is, however, the beginning of the Roman story rather than the end of the Greek account and by definition lies outside the scope of my survey.

NOTES

1. Brunilde S. Ridgway, *Roman Copies of Greek Sculptures: The Problem of the Originals* (Ann Arbor, 1984), especially 6–9; see also Volker M. Strocka, "Variante, Wiederholung, und Serie in der griechischen Bildhauerei," *Jahrbuch des Deutschen archäologischen Instituts* 94 (1979), 143–173.

2. See, for example, Waldemar Deonna, *Du miracle grec au miracle chrétien* (Basel, 1945–1946). This position, however, is no longer so firmly held.

3. Similar concepts had already been expressed by some Greek philosophers, notably Plato, who considered art imitation twice removed and, therefore, even more imperfect than natural forms, themselves only copies of the ideas. For these theories see the useful summary by Jerome J. Pollitt, *The Ancient View of Greek Art: Criticism, History, and Terminology* (New Haven and London, 1974), 41–49.

4. For *mimēsis* and *paradeigma* see Pollitt 1974, 37–41 and 23, respectively; see also Nikolaus Himmelmann, "Zur Entlohnung künstlerischer Tätigkeit in klassischen Bauinschriften," *Jahrbuch* 94 (1979), 127–142. On the terminology of the Greek theater see Erika Simon, *Das antike Theater* (Heidelberg, 1972).

5. The citation is from Pliny *Natural History* 34.61, apropos of Lysippos.

6. See Pollitt 1974, 52–55; see also Filippo Coarelli, "Introduzione," in *Artisti e artigiani in Grecia: Guida storica e critica*, ed. Filippo Coarelli (Bari, 1980), vii–xxx. For anecdotes about artistic personalities see F. Preisshofen, "Phidias-Daedalus auf dem Schild der Athena Parthenos?" *Jahrbuch* 89 (1974), 50–69.

7. At the symposium "Retaining the Original" held at the Center for Advanced Studies in the Visual Arts, National Gallery of Art, Washington, March 1985, I was able to show a photograph of the new find through the great courtesy of the director of the German Archaeological Institute in Athens, Dr. Helmut Kyrieleis. The first news of the discovery appeared in the Greek newspaper *Kathēmerinē*, 21 October 1984. The official publication of the sculpture is by Helmut Kyrieleis, "Neue archaische Skulpturen aus dem Heraion von Samos," *Archaische und klassische griechische Plastik*, ed. Helmut Kyrieleis (Mainz, 1986), 1:35–43, especially 41–43, pls. 20–22; it includes a section of the base that makes the similarity to the Geneleos Monument (see below) even stronger.

8. On the archaic sculpture from Samos see Brigitte Freyer-Schauenburg, *Samos* 11. *Bildwerke der archaischen Zeit und des strengen Stils* (Bonn, 1974): "Hera" (Musée du Louvre, Paris), 21–27, no. 6; kore with hare (Berlin), 27–31, no. 7; kouros, 95–96, no. 49A/B. The dates given in my text are those suggested in Freyer-Schauenburg 1974.

9. Freyer-Schauenburg 1974, 106–130, nos. 58–63.

10. For Dermys and Kittylos see Gisela M. A. Richter, *Kouroi: Archaic Greek Youths* (London, 1970), no. 11, figs. 76–77. For Kleobis and Biton see Richter 1970, nos. 12A, 12B, figs. 78–83. For identification as the Dioskouroi see C. Vatin, "Monuments votifs de Delphes," *Bulletin de correspondance Hellénique* 106 (1982), 509–525. For the proportional differences see Eleanor Guralnick, "The Proportions of Kouroi," *American Journal of Archaeology* 82 (1978), 461–472; Eleanor Guralnick, "Profiles of Kouroi," *American Journal of Archaeology* 89 (1985), 399–409. If Vatin is correct in his reading, the two statues in Delphi were signed

by the sculptors Polymedes and Theodotos of Argos, but his readings have not yet found confirmation and acceptance.

11. For the use of the Egyptian canon of proportions see Guralnick 1978 and 1985 and others mentioned in her bibliography. For preliminary carving in the quarries see Sheila Adam, *The Technique of Greek Sculpture in the Archaic and Classical Periods* (London, 1966), 7–8.

12. This position is held by Anthony Snodgrass, *Archaic Greece: The Age of Experiment* (London, Melbourne, and Toronto, 1980), 179–180.

13. For the kore with bird in Samos see Freyer-Schauenburg 1970, 43–48, no. 20, with pertinent comments. For the korai from Miletos and Theangela see Gisela M. A. Richter, *Korai: Archaic Greek Maidens* (London, 1968), no. 161, figs. 512–515, and no. 167, figs. 532–535, respectively.

14. See Hans Riemann, "Die Plannung des ältesten sizilischen Ringhallentempels," *Mitteilungen des Deutschen archäologischen Instituts: Römische Abteilung* 71 (1964), 19–59. See also Dieter Mertens, *Der Tempel von Segesta und die dorische Tempelbaukunst der griechischer Westens in klassischer Zeit* (Mainz, 1984), especially 177–179 on the workshop of Akragas.

15. On the "quotation" represented by the Temple of Apollo at Bassai see, for example, Helmut Berve, Gottfried Gruben, and Max Hirmer, *Greek Temples, Theatres, and Shrines* (New York, 1962), 351; see also 417, 424 for other plans.

16. On the archaic and classical temples of Apollo at Delphi see Fernand Courby, *Fouilles de Delphes* 2.1 (Paris, 1927), 1–117; see also Berve, Gruben, and Hirmer 1962, 331–333 and figs. 20–24 for the contrast in elevations.

17. For a discussion of akroteria during the archaic period, already including complex groups, see Marilyn Goldberg, "Archaic Greek A-kroteria," *American Journal of Archaeology* 86 (1982), 193–217. For group akroteria of the classical period see, for example, the Locri Dioskouroi in the Reggio di Calabria Museum (Ernst Langlotz and Max Hirmer, *The Art of Magna Graecia* [London, 1965], pls. 122–123). For servant figures see Carl Blümel, *Die klassisch griechischen Skulpturen der Staatlichen Museen zu Berlin* (Berlin, 1966), 44–45, no. 45, figs. 62–69; for funerary lions see Ridgway 1984, pls. 5–6.

18. On the Erechtheion karyatids see Hans Lauter, "Die Koren des Erechtheion," *Antike Plastik* 16 (1976). Some of the present variations in details may be due to later repairs and recutting (see Maria Bruskari, "Bemerkungen über die vierte und fünfte Karyatide des Erechtheion," *Jahreshefte der Österreichischen archäologischen Instituts* 55 [1984], 55–62).

19. This would be the so-called ex-Knidian head; for the suggestion see Francis Croissant, *Les protomés féminines archaïques: Recherches sur les représentations du visage dans la plastique grecque de 500 à 480 av. J.-C.* (Paris, 1983), 72 n. 1. A new fragment of the Siphnian karyatids seems to have been found some years ago, but it is still unpublished except for a brief mention in the "Chronique" of the *Comptes rendus de l'Académie des inscriptions et belles lettres* (1984), 534.

20. See, for instance, two archaic korai from the sanctuary of Apollo at Cyrene: Enrico Paribeni, *Catalogo delle sculture di Cirene* (Rome, 1959), 10–12, nos. 8–9, pls. 12–15. For two more korai from the same site, quite similar but not in mirror image, see John G. Pedley, "The Archaic Favissa at Cyrene," *American Journal of Archaeology* 75 (1971), 39–46, especially 42–46, pls. 6–8. Arrangements of costume reversed from the norm may serve as clues even when only one statue from a possible pair is preserved; the architectural function of the famous Lyons Kore I had suggested on such grounds has now been confirmed by the technical treatment of its top surface, as observed by John R. Marszal, "An Architectural Function for the Lyons Kore," *Hesperia* 57 (1988), 203–206.

21. For a glance at several such spouts see, for example, Mertens 1984, pls. 82–83; one series is in terracotta, others are in stone, from different buildings and sites.

22. Franz Willemsen, *Die Löwenkopf-Wasserspeier vom Dach das Zeustempels*, Olympische Forschungen 4 (Berlin, 1959). See also Himmel-mann 1979, supranote 4.

23. A series of repairs is suggested by Willemsen 1959; for additional comments, especially on the replacement figures, see Bernard Ashmole and Nicholas Yalouris, *Olympia: The Sculptures of the Temple of Zeus* (London, 1967), 179 (A, B, and U), see also 21–22.

24. See, for example, the comments by Bernard Ashmole, *Architect and Sculptor in Classical Greece* (New York, 1972), 58, and note the drawings of the rear view of many sculptural groups from the pediments: figs. 47, 49, 57, 70. For a perspective drawing of the west pedimental shelf with the statuary in position see Peter Grunauer, "Der Westgiebel des Zeustempel von Olympia: Die Münchener Rekonstruktion—Aufbau und Ergebnisse," *Jahrbuch* 89 (1974), 1–49, especially 18, fig. 17.

25. See, for example, Ashmole and Yalouris 1967, 20, pls. 90, 58–61, 147–148. For comments pertinent to the pediments of the Temple of Asklepios at Epidauros and other areas see Himmelmann 1979.

26. On chariot friezes, both in terracotta and stone, see Brunilde S. Ridgway, "Notes on the Development of the Greek Frieze," *Hesperia* 35 (1966), 189–204, especially 193–195; also *The Archaic Style in Greek Sculpture* (Princeton, 1977), 259 and n. 7; Clelia Laviosa, "Un rilievo arcaico di Iasos e il problema del fregio nei templi ionici," *Annuario della Scuola archeologica di Atene* 50–51, n.s. 34–35 (1972–1973, published 1975), 397–418; Emanuela Fabbricotti, "Fregi fittili arcaici in Magna Grecia," *Atti e memorie della Società Magna Grecia* 18–20 (1977–1979), 149–170.

On the chariot frieze of the Halikarnassos Mausoleum see, for example, Ashmole 1972, 159–163, figs. 182–187. There is still some uncertainty about the position of the chariot frieze on the Mausoleum; for a recent opinion that would place it elsewhere (putting the Centauromachy frieze around the base of the quadriga) see Kristian Jeppesen and Jan Zahle, "Investigations on the Site of the Mausoleum, 1970/1973," *American Journal of Archaeology* 79 (1975), 67–79, especially 76. For a line drawing of the elevation of the Mausoleum as reconstructed in the light of new finds see Geoffrey B. Waywell, *Freestanding Sculptures of the Mausoleum at Halikarnassus in the British Museum* (London, 1978), 58–59, figs. 8–9.

27. For a general discussion of bronze casting in antiquity, with helpful bibliography, see, for example, Suzannah Doeringer, David G. Mitten, Arthur Steinberg, eds., *Art and Technology: A Symposium on Classical Bronzes* (Cambridge, Mass., and London, 1970). See also Carol C. Mattusch, "Bronze- and Ironworking in the Area of the Athenian Agora," *Hesperia* 46 (1977), 340–379; Edilberto Formigli, "Note sulla tecnologia nella statuaria bronzca greca del V sec., a.C.," *Prospettiva* 23 (October 1980), 61–66.

28. See R. V. Nicholls, "Type, Group, and Series: A Reconsideration of Some Coroplastic Fundamentals," *Annual of the British School in Athens* 47 (1952), 217–226; for an actual example of busts made in different places from a single prototype see Malcolm Bell III, *Morgantina Studies I: The Terracottas* (Princeton, 1981), 3–4, 142–143, no. 113; see also pl. 32 (no. 113a) and pl. 147 (fig. 17).

29. For the Ball Players Base and its "copy" see Ridgway 1984, 7, pls. 7–8, and Strocka 1979, supranote 1, 166. For other examples of reliefs known through doubles or copies see not only Strocka but also the bibliography cited in Ridgway 1984, 12 nn. 14–17. To the Telemachos Monument discussed by Luigi Beschi a new fragment has now been added (see Luigi Beschi, "Il rilievo di Telemachos ricompletato," *Athens Annals of Archaeology* 6, no. 1 [1982]: 31–43).

30. The workshop of the Painter of the Athens Dinos (active c. 425 B.C.) was discussed by John H. Oakley, "An Athenian Red-figure Workshop from the Time of the Peloponnesian War" (paper delivered at the Seventy-third College Art Association Meeting, Los Angeles, 16 February 1985).

31. For Exekias' Vatican amphora see, for example, John Boardman, *Athenian Black Figure Vases* (New York, 1974), 57, fig. 100; for the Boston bilingual amphora and for comments on the Andokides Painter

see John Boardman, *Athenian Red Figure Vases: The Archaic Period* (New York and Toronto, 1975), 17 and fig. 2.1-2. Conversely, Boardman ("Exekias," *American Journal of Archaeology* 82 [1978], 11–25, especially 18) has pointed out that the dice-playing scene recurs in more than 150 vases in the half-century after the Vatican amphora. For copies in vases see also Peter J. Connor, "Representations in Greek Vase-Painting: The Work of the Painter of Louvre F 6," *Bulletin van de Vereeniging tot Bevordering der Kennis van de Antike Beschaving* 56 (1981), 37–42.

32. On the Orvieto krater and its scenes see, for example, Evelyn B. Harrison, "Preparations for Marathon: The Niobid Painter and Herodotus," *Art Bulletin* 54 (1972), 390–402; for comments on the anatomical renderings by the Niobid Painter see John P. Barron, "New Light on Old Walls," *Journal of Hellenic Studies* 92 (1972), 20–45; general comments in Martin Robertson, *A Shorter History of Greek Art* (Cambridge, Mass., 1981), 72–73 and fig. 108. Note that also the much earlier Chigi vase (a proto-Corinthian olpe, c. 640 B.C., found in Etruria) has been considered a reflection of monumental painting for its treatment of space and unusual polychromy (see Robertson 1981, 13 and fig. 18).

33. On the krater by the Painter of the Woolly Satyrs see, for example, Ashmole and Yalouris 1967, fig. 20, opposite p. 180, and see also figs. 21–22; additional comments in Robertson 1981, 72–73, fig. 109, and see also 87.

34. See Evelyn B. Harrison, "The South Frieze of the Nike Temple and the Marathon Painting in the Painted Stoa," *American Journal of Archaeology* 76 (1972), 353–378, especially 353 and pl. 73. I am indebted to my colleague Gloria F. Pinney for discussing with me some of her ideas on this topic.

35. See Charles M. Edwards, "The Running Maiden from Eleusis and the Early Classical Image of Hekate," *American Journal of Archaeology* 90 (1986), 307–318.

36. A discussion of the possible meaning for the choice of themes on the Mausoleum can be found in Kristian Jeppesen, "Zur Gründung und Baugeschichte des Maussolleions von Halikarnassos," *Mitteilungen des Deutschen archäologischen Instituts: Abteilung Istanbul* 27/28 (1977/1978), 169–211, especially 210–211. For different comments see Ashmole 1972, 164–165.

37. The Kallithea Monument, an elaborate funerary structure for Nikeratos of Istria and his son Polyxenos, is still virtually unpublished. See, however, Elias K. Tsirivakos, "Vorläufiger Bericht über eine Grabung in Kallithea," and "Nouvelles de Callithéa," *Athens Annals of Archaeology* 1 (1968), 35–36, 108–109, 212 (erratum). See also Ursula Knigge, "Marmorakroter und Fries von einem attischen Grabbau?" *Mitteilungen: Athenische Abteilung* 99 (1984), 217–234.

38. Brunilde S. Ridgway, *Fifth Century Styles in Greek Sculpture* (Princeton, 1981), 142–143, with bibliography on 157; see also 202 n. 14, and cf. 7, with figs. 43–44, for Polykleitan influence on the Parthenon.

39. Brunilde S. Ridgway, "The Man-and-Dog Stelai," *Jahrbuch* 86 (1971), 60–79, figs. 1–2; Hilde Hiller, *Ionische Grabreliefs der estern Hälfte des 5. Jahrhunderts v. Chr.*, Istanbuler Mitteilungen, *beiheft* 12 (Tübingen, 1975), 129, 137–139.

Another group of reliefs linked by strong typological affinities is that of the so-called Funerary Banquet (Totenmahl-) Reliefs; see, most recently, Jean-Marie Dentzer, *Le motif du banquet couché dans le Proche-Orient* (Rome, 1982).

40. For the Agora statue and its typology see Olga Palagia, "A Colossal Statue of a Personification from the Agora of Athens," *Hesperia* 51 (1982), 99–113, see especially 111 and pl. 36c for the anti-tyranny relief. On the duplication of inscriptions see also the comment in Ridgway 1984, 7 and note 15.

41. For a discussion of the options available to solve the puzzle of the Penelope from Persepolis see Brunilde S. Ridgway, *The Severe Style in Greek Sculpture* (Princeton, 1970), 101–104, and Ridgway 1981, 232.

42. The Peiraeus Athena is not yet fully published; for a discussion see Olga Palagia, *Euphranor*, Monumenta Graeca et Romana 3 (Leiden, 1980), 21–23, where the issue of Greek original versus Roman copy is left open; that the bronze Athena may date after the Sullan sack has been tentatively suggested, for example, by Peter Bol, *Grossplastik aus Bronze in Olympia*, Olympische Forschungen 9 (1978), 45–46 and 45 n. 4. For a possible reconstruction of the historical events that may have led to the burial of the Peiraeus cache see George Dontas, "La grande Artémis du Pirée: Une oeuvre d'Euphranor," *Antike Kunst* 25 (1982), 15–34.

43. On the Grimani statuettes see Renate Kabus Jahn, "Die Grimanische Figurengruppe in Venedig," *Antike Plastik* 11 (1972); Ridgway 1981, 194–198, and bibliography on 219. That some cult images in the round may have been reproduced in relief format as part of private dedications is suggested by Gerhard Neumann, *Probleme des griechischen Weihreliefs* (Tübingen, 1979), 56–68. For reliefs duplicating the same image for emphasis on the divine power of the icon see Strocka 1979; and especially Theodora Hadzisteliou Price, "Double and Multiple Representations in Greek Art and Religious Thought," *Journal of Hellenic Studies* 91 (1971), 48–69.

44. Xenophon *Anabasis* 5.3.12; the Greek word used is *eoiken*. Skyllous is in Elis.

45. For this terminology see Luigi Beschi, reporting on the International Congress of Classical Archaeology held in Athens in September 1983, *Magna Graecia* 19, no. 1–2 (January–February 1984), 18.

46. For Lysippos' brother, Lysistratos, see Pliny *Natural History* 35.153; see also Ridgway 1984, 85.

47. For the most recent discussion on the cult image in the Temple of Athena at Priene see Joseph C. Carter, *The Sculpture of the Sanctuary of Athena Polias at Priene* (London, 1983), chap. 4; for comments on other cult images at this time see 236. For the Athena Parthenos at Pergamon see Ridgway 1984, 9, and Michelle Gernand, "Hellenistische Peplosfiguren nach klassischen Vorbildern," *Mitteilungen des Deutschen archäologischen Instituts: Athenische Abteilung* 90 (1975), 1–47.

48. See, for example, *Enciclopedia dell'arte antica, classica, e orientale*, s.vv. "Kalas" and "Gaudotos."

49. For the latest discussion of the archaistic style see Mark D. Fullerton, "Archaistic Draped Statuary in the Round of the Classical, Hellenistic, and Roman Periods" (diss., Bryn Mawr College, 1982) and "Archaistic Statuary of the Hellenistic Period," *Mitteilungen des Deutschen archäologischen Instituts: Athenische Abteilung* 102 (1987), 259–278, with additional bibliography; see also Ridgway 1977, chap. 11, with bibliography.

50. For the term *severizing* see Ridgway 1970, chap. 9, and 135–139. See also the extensive discussion in Paul Zanker, *Klassizistische Statuen: Studien zur Veränderung des Kunstgeschmacks in der römischen Kaiserzeit* (Mainz, 1974). The ancient source about Pasiteles' sketching from nature is Pliny *Natural History* 36.39.

51. On the Delos Diadoumenos see Ridgway 1984, 9, 50, with notes and bibliography. On the Herakles Farnese from Antikythera see Peter Bol, *Die Skulpturen des Schiffsfunds von Antikythera*, Athenische Mitteilungen, *beiheft* 2 (Berlin, 1972), 48–49; also Ridgway 1984, 9. On the Sperlonga children and Mahdia satyriskos see Bernard Andreae, "Schmuck eines Wasserbeckens in Sperlonga—Zum Typus des sitzenden Knäbenleins aus dem Schiffsfund von Mahdia," *Mitteilungen: Römische Abteilung* 83 (1976), 287–309.

Copying in Roman Sculpture: The Replica Series

MIRANDA MARVIN
Wellesley College

ROMAN SCULPTURE TODAY is chiefly esteemed for the splendor of its portraits and the power of its historical reliefs. In its mythological/decorative statuary (what the Germans call *Idealplastik*), however, a certain lack of originality is conspicuous. The same images of major and minor gods, athletes, personifications, and culture heroes are reproduced century after century from one end of the Mediterranean to the other. All these "ideal" works, moreover, are Greek in style.

This repetition is explained as a peculiarity of Roman patronage. Since the Romans were unstinting in their admiration for Greek sculpture, and in particular for the works of a handful of fifth- and fourth-century artists recognized as supreme masters, Roman purchasers are thought to have wanted to decorate their private dwellings and public places not with original contemporary sculptures but with the closest possible replicas of the works of those Greek artists most admired by Roman writers. To own an acknowledged masterpiece, even in a surrogate version, is thought to have been the goal of most Romans when buying sculpture.[1]

There is little direct information about the intentions of Roman patrons. On the whole, their goals must be deduced from their purchases. The one exception is that prolific correspondent, M. Tullius Cicero. In his letters a wealthy Roman can be observed in the process of buying statuary for a villa. The picture of a Roman patron that emerges from these letters is strikingly unlike the one posited for Roman purchasers in traditional theory. It is, however, completely congruent with the discoveries about Roman art and its relationship to the Greek past made by recent scholars.[2] Following their lead, it becomes possible, starting with Cicero, to develop a new explanatory hypothesis for the presence in Roman contexts of so many replicas of familiar works. Accepting this hypothesis leads in turn to consideration of the terms used to describe Roman sculptors and to a realization that the nature of Roman ideal sculpture needs to be redefined.

In a series of ten early letters to T. Pomponius Atticus, his intimate friend who lived much of the time in Athens, and a much later letter to another correspondent, Cicero discusses in some detail the sculptures he is buying for his villa in Tusculum.[3] This correspondence is the best testimony available for the frame of mind with which at least one Roman buyer approached the purchase of works of art. The letters to Atticus dating between November 68 B.C. and the early summer of 65 B.C. (in the arrangement of D. R. Shackleton Bailey) are the earliest to survive from their long correspondence. Some earlier letters are clearly lost since the first to survive refers to a project already in motion by which Atticus in Athens is to buy sculptures for the villa Cicero recently purchased in Tusculum. As the correspondence proceeds, it gradually becomes clear what sort of sculptures Cicero wants and where he intends to put them.

Two things are notable in the first letter (see Appendix). There is, to begin with, the loose definition of Atticus' assignment. He is to provide for the Tusculan villa not just the works Cicero had specified but whatever he recognizes as suitable for the place. Cicero's confidence in Atticus' ability to choose correctly is absolute. Second, there is the immediate association made between the purchases and the villa as the place where Cicero can "rest from all troubles and toils."

The second letter introduces the Greek term that will be the closest Cicero will come to defining just what sort of sculptures he has in mind. He wants decorations (*ornamenta*) that will be *gymnasiode*, or "appropriate for a *gymnasium*."[4] Gymnasia, beginning as places where athletes trained, by Cicero's day had become known equally well as places where young men went to study philosophy.[5] Wealthy Romans, moreover, following Hellenistic precedents, delighted in naming parts of their extensive gardens after Greek building types. Gymnasia (interchangeably called *palaestrae* by the Romans) were especially popular, thanks to their philosophical and aristocratic associations. Most of the Roman versions seem to have been peristyle gardens.[6] In the villa at Tusculum Cicero had two "gymnasia," and to each he gave a specific name. One he called the Lyceum and the other the Academy after the two gymnasia in Athens, where, respectively, Aristotle and Plato had taught.[7]

The Lyceum in Athens has not been excavated, but the Academy has, and although the building has been robbed down to its foundations, the plan is recoverable (fig. 1).[8] The design is characteristic of most Greek gymnasia: a large rectangular open area (once filled with shade trees) surrounded by porticoes with a set of rooms on one side, originally containing the athletes' bath complex, dressing rooms, equipment storage, and other necessary facilities. By Cicero's day the structure was given over to students of philosophy, who, as was the ancient practice, strolled up and down in their earnest debates.

Cicero himself in his twenties studied philosophy in Athens where he spent a good deal of time with Atticus who was already living there.[9] Cicero's philosophical dialogues often reflect a nostalgia for those golden months. One of his most evocative references is specifically to the Academy. For the setting of the *De Finibus*, he imagines or remembers walking out there with Atticus and a group

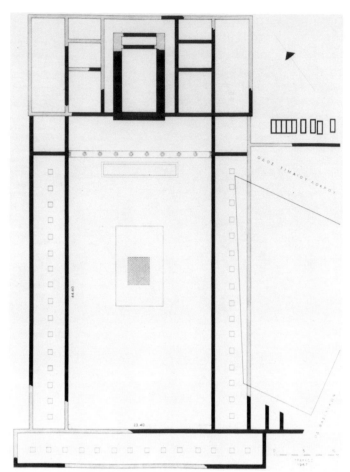

Fig. 1. Plan of the gymnasium at the Academy, Athens. From John Travlos, *Pictorial Dictionary of Ancient Athens.*

of other friends one afternoon and finding that the place itself, deserted at that time of day, brought Plato more vividly to their minds than did simply reading or hearing about him and made them realize the power of places to stir the imagination.[10] Cicero's nostalgia was deep, and his affection genuine. Rather touchingly he writes much later to Atticus (*Att.* 115.26) that he hears Appius Claudius Pulcher is building a propylon for the sanctuary of Demeter at Eleusis, and he wonders if "it would be out of the way if I did the same for the Academy? . . . I am really very fond of Athens, the actual city. I want to have some memorial there."[11]

Whether Cicero's Tusculan Academy looked like the Athenian Academy is not known since Cicero's villa has not been excavated. Cicero's writings, however, make it clear that he liked to think of himself as using his gymnasia as their prototypes were used, as the sites for philosophical discussions.[12] He sets one of his dialogues in his Lyceum, for example, telling the reader that the discussion took place when he and his brother had gone there "for a stroll" (*ambulandi causa*).[13] The Academy was the place where, he would have us believe, he and his friends spent every afternoon walking up and down discussing philosophy.[14] The likelihood is, therefore, very great that Cicero's gymnasia too consisted of long porticoes surrounding tree-shaded areas dotted with seats to drop into when the conversation became intense.[15]

As letter two continues, Cicero associates the villa again with happiness and peace of mind, as he does in the third letter, of February 67 B.C. Here he introduces a new theme: the purchase of a library. Apparently, this too had been promised by Atticus, who has, it would seem for the first time, actually made some purchases for Cicero. It is not until the fourth letter, however, that it is clear that these were Megarian statues and cost HS 20,400.

The fourth letter contains a rather perplexing reference. Since Cicero describes the herms with bronze heads that Atticus had bought him (from letter six it is clear that they were Herakles heads) as Pentelic, it would be reasonable to suppose that the "Megarian" statues were made of Megarian marble. Megara, however, was never famous for statuary marble and was little known as a center of sculpture production.[16] The city is, however, very close to Athens, and Kim Hartswick and John Pollini have suggested that perhaps the statues were not newly made but were purchased by Atticus in Megara as antiques.[17] The price is very high, but since we do not know how many statues were bought, the sum is useful only as a reminder of how much Cicero was prepared to spend on works of art.[18]

The fourth letter positively bubbles with enthusiasm as Cicero again urges Atticus not to stop at the Megarian statues and the herms but to buy more ornaments, "as many and as soon as possible," objects that would be "suitable to a gymnasium and xystus" (*gymnasi xystique*). The term *xystus*, which originally meant a running track, was in Roman usage employed for an open-air garden.[19] Here, no doubt, it is to be distinguished from the covered porticoes of the gymnasium. The two were often paired in garden planning.

As he waits impatiently for the opening of the spring sailing season, Cicero is at last in letter five explicit about where he plans to put the sculptures—in his Academy.[20] The instructions to Atticus remain the same, to spare no expense but to send anything "suitable for the Academy." Works that are *gymnasiode* are what he wants.

Cicero writes the sixth letter, he reports, sitting in the Academy itself, so that the very place reminds him of its need for sculptures. Being in Tusculum (this is the first letter from there) seems to provoke new ideas about decorating the villa, and Cicero requests some reliefs for the walls of the "little atrium" ("in tectorio atrioli") and two well heads decorated with reliefs ("putealia sigillata duo").[21] These are the only references in this group of letters to sculptures for any place other than the Academy. He mentions again the library first brought up in letter three.

The seventh letter is written from Rome and is infused with his affection for Tusculum. He once more immediately associates the Academy with the books he plans to buy, a pattern suggesting that he might be intending to house them there. Elsewhere he refers, however, to a library in the Lyceum.[22] Either he plans two libraries for the villa or perhaps the two gymnasia were parts of the same complex.

The two following letters let us know that the works have finally arrived safely, although Cicero has been unable to see them, and that Atticus has made one further purchase for the villa, a herm of Athena.

Cicero's satisfaction with the Minerva (Athena) herm is usually taken to refer to Cicero's own inclinations. Shackleton Bailey's note puts it deftly "as a giver of wit and wisdom Minerva was the natural protectress of Cicero's Academy and of Cicero himself."[23] In this case, however, more than such a general suitability seems to be meant. Cicero and Atticus, both familiar with the Academy in Athens, knew that it contained a sanctuary of Athena, who was one of the tutelary deities of the place. It is this association that makes the Athena herm so appropriate and explains the allusion in the tenth and final letter of the series, which notes that the Athena has been so nicely placed that the whole gymnasium appears like a votive offering to her.[24]

After a brief note telling Atticus of the birth of a son, the correspondence ceases for almost four years, since Atticus comes to Rome. We never hear Cicero's reaction, therefore, to the rest of the sculpture that Atticus bought for him nor how the decoration of the villa continued.

Nevertheless, there is enough information in these ten letters to give some sense of Cicero as a purchaser.[25] Cicero tells Atticus what sort of sculpture to buy, not by describing the artist or the style or the scale or the material or the subjects that he wants him to look for, but by describing the location where the works are to be placed. Atticus knows the villa, knows what Cicero uses it for, knows the mood Cicero wants to evoke there—or rather, as Cicero says in letter six, what the place itself reminds him that it needs ("me locus ipse admoneret")—and does not require any further information to make an appropriate purchase except the welcome assurance that money is no object.[26] That additional letters giving more specific instructions are not missing is clear from Cicero's delight that the new herm Atticus had found should have turned out to be an Athena—the perfect choice—but not one that Cicero had anticipated.

It is interesting that Cicero mentions nothing about the Athena herm except its subject. Atticus has either not told him anything about the style or the material or the artist or Cicero is not interested enough in that information to mention it. Even after the work has arrived and been set in place, Cicero's thanks include nothing about the quality or appearance of the work, only its effect on the architecture around it. Perhaps this is simply Cicero patting himself on the back. (Who, after all, chose that judicious placement?) Perhaps it is his good manners concealing a disappointment with Atticus' selection. It seems most likely, however, to be a straightforward reflection of what was important to Cicero when he bought art. This supposition is confirmed in a much later letter to a different correspondent.

In 46 B.C. Cicero writes to M. Fabius Gallus about some sculptures that Gallus had bought for him, which were not as welcome as those Atticus had acquired. In this rather testy letter good manners and tact are clearly not responsible for Cicero's failure to discuss the works' quality, material, scale, style, or artist. His principal objection is to the cost of the statues. His irritation is intensified, however, by being asked to pay so much for works that he would not have chosen at any price. Not knowing where Cicero intended to put the statues, Gallus has bought works that are not *gymnasiode*. Their subjects are, in fact, so contrary to Cicero's image of himself that he can think of no suitable place anywhere on his property for them ("Bacchis vero ubi est apud me locus?") and wants only to find someone to take them off his hands. He claims to have seen the Maenads (Bacchantes), to know them well ("novi optime et saepe vidi"), and to think them pretty (*pulchellae*).[27] This does not make him like them any better, and he irritably points out that he would have asked for specific works if he had wanted them. What he does want yet again are works he can use to decorate "a place in my palaestralike gymnasia." Here the language strengthens the supposition that his two gymnasia are part of one complex (*locum*). It is noteworthy that Cicero claims he would have objected less to the group of Muses that Gallus had mentioned since they at least could find a home in his library.

Cicero's interest, in other words, is still exclusively in the role that statuary can play in creating a special kind

of atmosphere.[28] In these particular letters he is interested specifically in using it to evoke Plato's Academy.[29] He has no desire for an exact replica of the place, however. He had, after all, spent six months in Athens and knew it well. Atticus lived in Athens and could go to the Academy every day. It would have been possible for him to reproduce its architecture and sculpture point for point. In the case of the architecture we have no evidence of what he may have done, but we do know that he did not attempt to copy the sculptures exactly. The Athenian Academy contained quite a number of statues, and we know what some of them were. There was a portrait of Plato, for instance, and statues of the Graces, which stood in a sanctuary of the Muses dedicated by Plato.[30] In addition to the sanctuaries of Athena and of the Muses there were altars (some at least with images) to Eros, Prometheus, Hermes, Zeus, and Herakles as well as a memorial of the hero Akademos after whom the Academy was named.[31] The excavations there also produced many fragments of sculptures.[32]

Cicero did not ask for replicas of specific works, only for the "generic brand" of gymnasium statuary.[33] He sought to create not a literal copy of Plato's Academy but what he saw as its essential character as a place of philosophic discussion—what he remembered from his student days—the long porticoes, the walking up and down, the earnest conversation, and a marble blur of statuary as they passed. The sculptures played their part not by exactly duplicating any particular work but by awakening the associations Cicero thought proper. It was not the appearance of the Academy that he wanted to reproduce but his feelings about it. The sculptures, therefore, had to be agreeable to a mood of philosophic tranquillity and suggest only the prime use of the space in which they were set. Plato may have erected a shrine of the Muses in the Academy, but Cicero could imagine placing statues of Muses only in a library, where their function was comfortingly predictable. Sculptures evoking the wrong associations (Mars, Maenads) were manifestly impossible, handsome though they might be. What emerges strongly in these letters is Cicero's sense of the power of sculpture to affect the meaning of the architecture around it. Admitting statues of Maenads into his villa might turn his philosophic retreat into a Dionysiac garden, and the Athena herm, after all, redefines the space in which it is placed so that "the whole gymnasium appears to be its votive offering."[34]

An analogy is sometimes drawn between Cicero's acquisition of sculpture for Tusculum and the filling of English country houses in the eighteenth century with classical statuary.[35] Cicero's willingness to let Atticus make decisions for him is not unlike the dependence of these English patrons on the discretion of the Roman dealers who supplied them with marbles. Their use of statuary, however, was very different.[36]

One of the finest of the neoclassical country houses, Syon House, remodeled in 1762 by Robert Adam for Sir Hugh Smithson, is typical. It contains in its entrance hall a collection of replicas after the antique. These are dominated by the Dying Gaul at one end of the room and the Apollo Belvedere in the other. The walls between are lined with a heterogeneous mix of figures.

In two notable ways this assemblage differs from anything thought desirable by Cicero. There is, first, the juxtaposition of incongruous subjects. What has Apollo to do with a dying Gaul (or gladiator as it was known in the eighteenth century)? What is a dying barbarian doing in the country estate of an English landed proprietor anyway or what are pagan gods doing in the house of a Christian gentleman? (Cicero's tones of outrage are audible even today.) Smithson and Adam's use of these classical replicas depend on their being considered exclusively as works of art, as two of the canonical antiquities admired by every person of taste. Their significance is reduced to general notions of "the antique," "the sublime," and "the noble."

The ability thus to trivialize the content of representational works depends on the viewer's feeling distant from the culture that produced them. Such uses of classical sculpture occur in Roman contexts but only in later periods when the world Cicero lived in and the values he cherished were remote.[37]

Second, these sculptures do not define the function of the space around them. The hall stands at the entrance to Syon House. It is the place where as they came in visitors handed their overcoats to the footman. The statues here, if anything, attempt to disguise the rather mundane use of the room, to suggest that it is instead what Cicero's villa is often quite wrongly said to be, a museum.[38]

In one way Smithson is very comparable to Cicero. He clearly shares Cicero's concern that sculptures reflect their owner. Smithson was known as a man of "perfect taste" and wanted his visitors to know that the minute they walked in his door. Reducing the content of his works to generalities, however, limited the meaning they conveyed. They no longer functioned in the sharply programmatic way that Cicero's did, a way that was typically Roman.

Writing in the first century B.C., Cicero is a very early example of a Roman purchaser. The attitudes of later, Imperial, patrons and of Republican patrons other than Cicero must be deduced from brief written references and from modern reconstructions of excavated material. From this evidence it is clear that Cicero's creation of evocative spaces in the grounds of his villa was typical. It is also clear that the patrons and architects who laid out the private domains of the rich indulged in personal taste and took pride in learned interests. Cicero's visitors were clearly assumed to be well-educated, well-traveled, cultured men capable of making sophisticated associations—an image of Athena—Cicero's Academy—Plato's Academy. Not every wealthy patron, however, shared Cicero's conservatism and conventionality. The unfortunate Gallus clearly had notions vastly different from Cicero's of what sort of sculpture might appropriately decorate his villa. Pliny's account shows that the taste and interests of Asinius Pollio, to cite a famous contemporary of Cicero, resulted in a very different display of statuary.[39]

The same principle of laying out the grounds of villas as clearly defined units redolent with specific meanings continued into the empire.[40] The finds from the Villa of the Papyri, for example, suggest that its owner chose and arranged his sculptures in agreement with the Epicureanism demonstrable in his library.[41] The transformation of a grotto at Sperlonga into a landscape of heroic mythology is even better known.[42] The sculptures from the largest and most elaborate villa of all, the Villa of Hadrian at Tivoli, have recently been published and show that the principle of using sculpture in an architectural and landscape setting to make a special world for the visitor is retained in the second century A.D.[43] In the spreading acreage of Tivoli the emperor and his guests could apparently wander from rustic shrines to evocations of a Hellenistic hunting park to a romantic Egyptian dreamland. It was the sculptures that helped to give each setting its distinctive identity.

The same guiding principle, that the function of sculpture is to suggest the character of the space in which it is set, dominates public as well as private displays of statuary. Vitruvius makes this plain in a comic anecdote about the people of Alabanda, who

> were considered bright enough in all matters of politics, but that on account of one slight defect, the lack of a sense of propriety, they were believed to be unintelligent. In their gymnasium the statues are all pleading causes, in their forum, throwing the discus, running, or playing ball. This disregard of propriety in the interchange of statues appropriate to different places has brought the state as a whole into disrepute.[44]

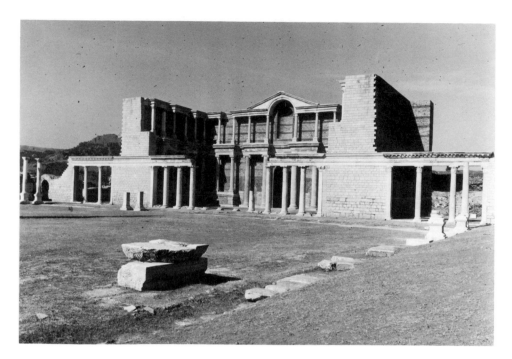

Fig. 2. The "Marble Court," or Entrance to the Bath-Gymnasium Complex, Sardis.

Analysis of the sculptural programs of Roman public buildings is just beginning, but it is already clear that most cities tried to maintain a "sense of propriety."[45] Even the plundered Greek works displayed in public places in Rome itself are now seen to have been chosen more with a view to the propaganda messages they could convey than to the names of the artists associated with them.[46]

Most users of these public buildings were uneducated, untraveled, familiar with very few works of art, and capable of making no arcane associations. Yet since it was the function of the sculpture to help define the character of the space around it, here too patrons had instantly to be made to recognize the special nature of the space they were in, whether it was a bath, forum, theater, basilica, or hippodrome. All public buildings were enriched with statues and depended in part on them to convey the messages of the place to the user. By necessity the designers of such buildings confined themselves to works whose associations were familiar, unambiguous, and immediately recognizable. They came to rely on a handful of works whose meaning was instantly clear to everyone, the visual equivalent of clichés.

In this requirement perhaps lies the explanation for that curiosity of Roman sculpture, the absolute dominance in the production of "ideal" statuary of a few familiar types, endlessly repeated. What is known as the "replica series"—a set of replicas that, although differing in material, scale, quality, and iconographic detail, can

Fig. 3. "Septizodium," Rome.

Fig. 4. Theater, Sabratha.

Fig. 5. Library of Celsus, Ephesus.

be seen as deriving from a common type—accounts for most of the market in these statues.

The designers of Roman buildings needed instantly recognizable sculptures, and for public places they needed them in quantity. It is no coincidence that the great age of replica production coincided with the spread throughout the empire of what has been called the Marble Style in architecture.[47] The most imposing feature of this style, apart from the glittering material that gives it its name, was the erection of elaborate facades decorated with superimposed recesses and projections framed by columns supporting continuous architraves or little individual triangular or arcuated pediments. Once thought to be a second-century phenomenon, recent finds from Aphrodisias demonstrate that in Asia Minor, the heartland of the style, these columned facades appear in a building that may be Julio-Claudian.[48] The varieties of design were many, but the general effect was uniform: ascending rows of pavilions framing statues. These are almost all lost today, but often empty bases testify to where they once stood. Such facades characterized buildings of the most diverse types, the *scaenae frontes* of theaters, temple precincts, swimming pools in baths, public libraries, city gates, fountains, and palaces; by the mid-second century and into the early third the style had

become almost inevitable for certain types of pretentious civic structures (figs. 2–6).[49]

This similarity of appearance among buildings of such different functions is one of the puzzles of the Marble Style. For architects to whom the idea of appropriateness was as important as it was to the Romans, it looks like an anomaly. When their sculptural decoration was in

Fig. 6. North Agora Gate, Miletos.

place, however, these facades must have seemed less uniform as the choice of subjects suitable for each place would have more clearly differentiated them from each other than is now apparent.[50]

It was, of course, not merely the facades of these buildings that were filled with sculpture. Standing on the floors or set in niches in the walls, statues abounded in the public buildings of the empire.[51] When to these massed displays is added the great bulk of statues used in smaller numbers in private contexts and less flashy public buildings, the effect of "mass production" given by the most popular statuary types is understandable.

The explanation suggested for a large replica series is that it represents a tribute to the usefulness of the type in a variety of Roman sculptural programs.[52] Figures such as, for example, Aphrodite or Herakles, who have a role both in the life of the state and in popular affection and who find themselves at home in a number of con-

Fig. 8. "Medici Venus." Galleria degli Uffizi, Florence.

Fig. 7. Copy of the Aphrodite from Knidos by Praxiteles. Vatican Museums, Rome.

texts, are the subjects that survive today in the greatest numbers. The particular sculptural types chosen were those capable of conveying the desired meaning most clearly, those everybody knew.

How certain images of favorite subjects came to represent those subjects to the popular imagination is an important and difficult question. In many cases the types were replicas of well-known statues by the great Greek artists of the past, and it was the fame of the original work that inspired the copies. The best example of this phenomenon is perhaps the Aphrodite of Knidos, of which Pliny says that "with that statue Praxiteles made Knidos famous" (fig. 7).[53] In 1933 Christian Blinkenberg counted fifty-one replicas, and more have appeared since.[54]

Fig. 9. "Capitoline Aphrodite." Capitoline Museum, Rome.

More interesting is the large number of adaptations and variations on the Knidia that appeared after Praxiteles. The two best known today are the Medici and Capitoline Venus types (figs. 8–9). Replica lists for these were assembled in 1951. Thirty-three versions of the Medici were recorded, and 101 of the Capitoline.[55] The dates when these types were created are fiercely debated; no artists' names can be plausibly associated with them.[56] They state richly and unequivocally, however, the Venus Pudica theme, which had, thanks to Praxiteles, come to represent the goddess at her most characteristic.[57] They were as satisfactory a depiction of that theme as was a copy of the Knidia herself and were equally, or in the case of the Capitoline possibly even more, acceptable to

Roman purchasers looking for a traditional image of Aphrodite.[58] The meaning of the figure could hardly escape the most inattentive or ignorant viewer.

Other popular works are difficult to connect even at secondhand with a famous original. The Crouching Aphrodite, for example, is another very familiar image of the goddess (fig. 10). Now that doubts have been cast on the attribution to Doidalsas, she has become a foundling, dumped by the Romans' affection for her on the doorstep of art history.[59] The failure to establish secure connections for the type with known schools or artists may simply be a failure of modern scholarship that time will correct. It is not, however, absolutely necessary for a work to be connected with a great artist for it to become famous.

A modern analogy comes to mind. Undoubtedly the most famous American painting of the nineteenth century is the work universally known as Whistler's Mother (fig. 11). Painted in 1871, the work had become so famous by the 1930s that it was used, untitled, as a Mother's Day commemorative stamp. Although the Romans had

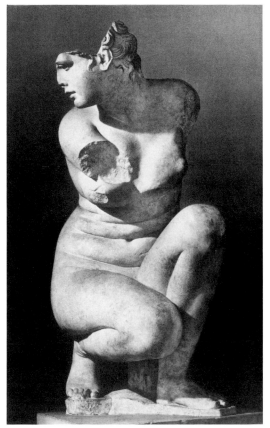

Fig. 10. Crouching Aphrodite. Museo Nazionale Romano.

Fig. 11. James McNeill Whistler, "Whistler's Mother" (*Arrangement in Gray and Black, No. 1: "Portrait of the Artist's Mother"*), 1872. Louvre, Paris.

neither Mother's Day nor postage stamps, there are nevertheless aspects to the fame of this work that are not irrelevant to the problem of the replica series. First, although the name of the artist is locked into the title by which the work is popularly known, its celebrity is independent of the reputation of his other works or even of his personal notoriety. Second, greater and more famous artists, even including Rembrandt, have painted better portraits of their mothers, which have no fame outside the world of art. In the case of Rembrandt this is particularly striking since his is one of the names that resonates to the modern public as Pheidias or Praxiteles did to the Romans. Finally, there is almost nothing in this painting that suggests the feelings the Post Office would reasonably be expected to associate with Mother's Day. Mrs. Whistler sits isolated and withdrawn, exuding neither warmth, nor nurturance, nor selfless, maternal love. Hers is not a lap to snuggle in. It is, in fact, hard to imagine any quality other than fame that could have made this work a symbol of motherhood.

The point is that the process that turns works of art into clichés takes place for many different reasons, not all of which are immediately apparent. Once, however, a work becomes familiar, then it will be reproduced again and again simply on the strength of its notoriety. Works

of art, like human celebrities, can be famous for being famous.

The moral to be drawn for Roman art from this digression into the anomalies of fame in the twentieth century is that it is no easier to predict what factors made a work successful in the Roman art market than in the modern one. Works brought from Greece, for instance, may have become popular after they arrived in Rome, perhaps because they were set up in a particularly conspicuous place.[60] Others may have achieved notoriety through association with famous donors or because they played a role in Roman religious life.[61] Still others of the many replica series that survive today may not refer to any Greek original at all but may simply be the version of the, say, Venus Pudica produced by a popular workshop, which was then imitated by other workshops and entered the repertory of well-known types.

Works of art may also have symbolic meanings that are not visually obvious. As Mrs. Whistler could represent motherhood, so surprising works could symbolize Roman values. Joachim Raeder has suggested, for example, that the wounded Amazons from the Euripus at Hadrian's villa symbolize Virtus (valor), pointing out how close the standard Virtus iconography is to representations of Amazons, despite the connection of the word with "manliness" (fig. 12).[62] If he is right and if that is what those particular Amazons could mean to the Romans, then the popularity of the types can be understood independently of their connections to particular fifth-century Greek artists.[63]

This explanation for the preponderance of the replica series in Roman sculptural production is not commonly offered. A large replica series is usually considered to indicate that a major work by a famous Greek artist must lie behind it. Gisela Richter put it clearly in *The Sculpture and Sculptors of the Greeks* (1970), saying of the Herakles Farnese that "the original . . . must have been an important work, to judge by the number of extant copies."[64] Accounting for large replica series in this way is, of course, only one aspect of a theory of Roman copying developed in the nineteenth century and most characteristically expressed at its end by Adolf Furtwängler. Speaking of the sculptures that emerged in such numbers from the great excavations of that century, he wrote:

> The original sculptures from Greece are . . . works of the second or even inferior rank. The Roman copies, on the other hand, have preserved that pick from the masterpieces of the classical epoch which pleased ancient taste and connoisseurship in the times of highest culture. It is the pick of the best and the most famous that antiquity possessed.[65]

Furtwängler's enthusiastic belief that from Roman works he could trace the careers not merely of Pheidias, Myron, Polykleitos, and Praxiteles but of figures like Kresilas and Euphranor as well is now seen as overly optimistic; and many of the works he thought of as copies are recognized as Roman classicizing creations. Nevertheless, the fundamental principles he articulated still dominate contemporary surveys of classical art.[66] The Romans are still thought to have copied the works they most admired because they judged them to be "the best and the most famous that antiquity possessed."

One possibility that must be considered, however, is that in making the assumption that the Romans' undoubted love of Greek art led them also systematically to copy the greatest works of the greatest artists, scholars are throwing back on the Romans a point of view that properly belongs to modern art history. Contemporary art historians, conditioned by a discipline devoted to a chain of infinite regress in formal development and to the methodical sorting out of the influence of one artist on another, are naturally eager to know just what the great works of Pheidias, Praxiteles, Lysippos really looked like. We expect, as it were, to read our Pliny with illustrations. It is only modern technologies of reproduction (particularly the camera) that make these methodologies possible and expectations reasonable.[67] The expectations of the Romans, however, are the issue, and it is not entirely clear that an accurate knowledge of works of art they had never seen was one of them.

In yet another sense Furtwängler's view can be seen as a historical artifact. It is not surprising that it emerged from the nineteenth century, the great age of sculptural reproduction, the heyday of the plaster cast. The taste for surrounding oneself with replicas of great works, aristocratic in eighteenth-century England, came to be universal a century later. In an illuminating study of mid-Victorian taste in America, Michelle Bogart has demonstrated how owning reproductions of esteemed works lent status and refinement to the household displaying them. She quotes Clarence Cook in *House Beautiful* (1878):

> All is, to choose something for the living room mantel piece that shall be worth living with; it ought to be something that is good alike for young and old . . . there is hardly anything that better rewards trouble than a fine cast of a really noble or lovely piece of sculpture. Who would ever get tired of seeing on the wall, over his mantel piece, as he sat with his wife or friend before his sea coal fire, the mask of either one of Michelangelo's captives on one side, and the Naples Psyche on the other.[68]

Fig. 12. Villa of Hadrian, Tivoli.

In such an environment, in which a heterogeneous mixture of "noble or lovely" works distinguishes not just the formal spaces of the rich but the parlors of the middle class, it becomes easy to understand how the Romans could be thought to have desired replicas in the same way if not for the mantelpiece, at least for the garden.[69]

In recent years, principally among scholars in Germany and Italy, and in this country most notably by Brunilde S. Ridgway, a reexamination of the evidence for the Romans' attitude toward Greek sculpture has confirmed their enthusiasm for it, but has suggested that they collected, copied, and imitated it for reasons of their own.[70] This revised view compels a comprehensive reexamination of the problem, from the Romans' motives for choosing Greek works as war booty to careful formal analyses of period styles in classicistic works.[71] The increased emphasis on the Roman contexts in which sculptures are found and the meaning of the sculptures to Roman viewers is one part of this development.

To understand the specific issue of the replica series it is helpful to state the problem in a form borrowed from the philosophy of science. Two hypotheses have been put forward to explain the replica series. One could be called the "copy" and the other the "programmatic" hypothesis. The traditional or copy hypothesis holds that behind every large Roman replica series stands an important Greek original, copied by the Romans as a tribute to that original and a sign of their desire to own literal reproductions of acknowledged masterpieces. Recent studies can be seen as tests of that hypothesis that have demonstrated its weakness.

The alternative or programmatic hypothesis put forth here explains the existence of the replica series as a tribute to the usefulness of its base type in Roman contexts and its dependence on an original Greek work as true for some series but not for all. The letters of Cicero can be seen as a test strongly supporting that hypothesis since one Roman purchaser at least can be clearly shown to have been interested in sculptures appropriate for specific settings but to have left no evidence of wanting copies of particular Greek originals.

Certain logical consequences must be admitted to flow from accepting the new hypothesis as a model for Roman sculptural practice. If a direct connection to a specific work by a Greek artist is not needed to account for the popularity of a type, then the possibility that original Roman works also could generate replica series becomes not remote but likely. In fact, the principle of Occam's Razor would seem to dictate that a Greek original should be posited for a Roman sculpture only when there is

external evidence to suggest that the type was in existence before the date of the earliest Roman replica.

A second consequence must be a rise in the perceived status of many Roman sculptors. The traditional approach admits the makers of portraits and historical reliefs to be artists but degrades the makers of ideal types to "copyists." The term is properly functional, belonging to any sculptor at work on a copy. When the work is not a mechanical reproduction but an imitation or adaptation, a work "after the antique," its maker is better described as a neoclassical sculptor, and Roman ideal sculpture should be recognized for what it is, the first neoclassicism.

Fundamentally different from their European successors in most respects, Roman neoclassical artists and patrons were like them in the way they unreservedly admired antique art and diligently set themselves to imitate it.[72] Like them, they intertwined practice and theory. Like them also, they created original works from the raw material of a classical art. Modern art historians, however, have to struggle to recognize these Roman originals.

It is easy to separate the relationship to ancient statues found in Canova's *Venus Italica* from that of his *Three Graces* or *Perseus*, because his models are extant.[73] It is much more difficult to sort out whether a Roman work is, like the *Venus*, a close imitation of a single work, or, like the *Graces*, a freer adaptation, or, like the *Perseus*, a novel creation drawing on a variety of sources, when the only evidence for those sources is the appearance of the derivative work.[74]

The current willingness to make the effort and interest in looking directly at these Roman sculptures in Greek style as works of art in themselves rather than through them for evidence of their putative originals are signs that the programmatic hypothesis too is a historical artifact. In the later twentieth century neoclassical sculpture is again admired. Signaled by the Council of Europe's mammoth exhibition of 1972 (whose catalogue covers are front and rear views of Canova's *Three Graces*), the revival of neoclassicism has become an established fact of the contemporary art market.[75] The tastes and interests of our own time are making it possible to give Roman neoclassicism the attention and respect it has been for so long lacking.

APPENDIX
Selections from Cicero's Letters

The letters to Atticus are from D. R. Shackleton Bailey, *Cicero's Letters to Atticus*, vol. 1 (Cambridge, 1965). The letter to Gallus is from D. R. Shackleton Bailey, *Cicero: Epistulae ad familiares*, 2 vols. (Cambridge, 1977). Translations of the letters to Atticus from *Cicero's Letters to Atticus* and of the letter to Gallus from *Cicero's Letters to His Friends* (Harmondsworth, 1978) are also Shackleton Bailey's.

1. To Atticus
Letter One
1.7. November 68 B.C.

Epiroticam emptionem gaudeo tibi placere. quae tibi mandavi et quae tu intelleges convenire nostro Tusculano velim, ut scribis, cures, quod sine molestia tua facere poteris. nam nos ex omnibus molestiis et laboribus uno illo in loco conquiescimus.

I am glad you are pleased with your purchase in Epirus. Yes, do please look after my commissions and anything else that may strike you as suitable to my place in Tusculum, so far as you can without putting yourself to too much trouble. It is the one place where I rest from all troubles and toils.

Letter Two
2.2. November 68 B.C.

Haec habebam fere quae te scire vellem. tu velim, si qua ornamenta γυμνασιώδη reperire poteris quae loci sint eius quem tu non ignoras, ne praetermittas. nos Tusculano ita delectamur ut nobismet ipsis tum denique cum illo venimus placeamus. quid agas omnibus de rebus et quid acturus sis fac nos quam diligentissime certiores.

That is about all I have to tell you. If you succeed in finding any *objets d'art* suitable for a lecture hall, which would do for you know where, I hope you won't let them slip. I am delighted with my place at Tusculum, so much so that I feel content with myself when, and only when, I get there. Let me know in full detail about everything you are doing and intending to do.

Letter Three
3. February 67 B.C.

Apud matrem recte est eaque nobis curae est. L. Cincio HS $\overline{\text{XXCD}}$ constitui me curaturum Id. Febr. tu velim ea quae nobis emisse ⟨te⟩ et parasse scribis des operam ut quam primum habeamus. et velim cogites, id quod mihi pollicitus es, quem ad modum bibliothecam nobis conficere possis. omnem spem delectationis nostrae, quam cum in otium venerimus habere volumus, in tua humanitate positam habemus.

All is in order at your mother's and I am not forgetting her. I have arranged to pay L. Cincius HS 20,400 on the Ides of February. I should be grateful if you would see that I get the articles which you say you have bought and have ready for me as soon as possible. And please give some thought to how you are to procure a library for me as you have promised. All my hopes of enjoying myself as I want to do when I get some leisure depend upon your kindness.

Letter Four
4.2. February 67 B.C.

L. Cincio HS CCIƆƆ CCIƆƆ CCCC pro signis Megaricis, ut tu ad me scripseras, curavi. Hermae tui Pentelici cum capitibus aëneis, de quibus ad me scripsisti, iam nunc me admodum delectant. qua re velim et eos et signa et cetera quae tibi eius loci et nostri studi et tuae elegantiae esse videbuntur quam plurima quam primumque mittas, et maxime quae tibi gymnasi xystique vedebuntur esse. name in eo genere sic studio efferimur, ut abs te adiuvandi, ab aliis prope reprehendendi simus. si Lentuli navis non erit, quo tibi placebit imponito.

I have paid L. Cincius the HS 20,400 for the Megarian statues in accordance with your earlier letter. I am already quite enchanted with your Pentelic herms with the bronze heads, about which you write to me, so please send them and the statues and any other things you think would do credit to the place in question and to my enthusiasm and to your good taste, as many and as soon as possible, especially any you think suitable to a lecture hall and colonnade. I am so carried away by my enthusiasm for this sort of thing that it's your duty to help me—and other people's perhaps to scold me. If a ship of Lentulus' is not available, put them aboard any you think fit.

Letter Five
5.2. March or April 67 B.C.

Signa Megarica et Hermas de quibus ad me scripsisti vehementer exspecto. quicquid eiusdem generis habebis dignum Academia tibi quod videbitur, ne dubitaris mittere et arcae nostrae confidito. genus hoc est voluptatis meae. quae γυμνασιώδη maxime sunt, ea quaero. Lentulus navis suas pollicetur. peto abs te ut haec cures diligenter.

I am eagerly expecting the Megarian statues and the herms you wrote to me about. Anything you may have of the same sort which you think suitable for the Academy, don't hesitate to send it and trust my purse. This is how my fancy takes me. Things that are specially suitable for a lecture hall are what I want. Lentulus promises his ships. Please attend to this carefully.

Letter Six
6.3–4. c. May 67 B.C.

Signa nostra et Hermeraclas, ut scribis, cum commodissime poteris, velim imponas, et si quid aliud οἰκεῖον eius loci quem non ignoras reperies, et maxime quae tibi palaestrae gymnasique videbuntur esse. etenim ibi sedens haec ad te scribebam, ut me locus ipse admoneret. praeterea typos tibi mando quos in tectorio atrioli possim includere et putealia sigillata duo. bibliothecam tuam cave cuiquam despondeas, quamvis acrem amatorem inveneris; nam ego omnis meas vindemiolas eo reservo, ut illud subsidium senectuti parem.

Yes, I should be grateful if you would ship when you most conveniently can my statues and Heracles herms and anything else you may discover that would be *convenable* you know where, especially things you think suitable to a palaestra and lecture hall. In fact I am sitting there now as I write, so that the place itself is a reminder. Further please get me some bas-reliefs which I can lay in the stucco of the small entrance hall and two figured puteals. Mind you don't engage your library to anyone, no matter how ardent a wooer you may find. I am putting all my little gleanings aside to pay for this stand-by for my old age.

Letter Seven
7.3. August 67 B.C.

Tu velim quae nostrae Academiae parasti quam primum mittas. mire quam illius loci non modo usus sed etiam cogitatio delectat. libros vero tuos cave cuiquam tradas; nobis eas, quem ad modum scribis, conserva. summum me eorum studium tenet, sicut odium iam ceterarum rerum; quas tu incredibile est quam brevi tempore quanto deteriores offensurus sis quam reliquisti.

Please send the things you have got for my Academy as soon as possible. The very thought of the place, let alone the actual use of it, gives me enormous pleasure. Mind you don't hand over your books to anybody. Keep them for me, as you say you will. I am consumed with enthusiasm for them, as with disgust for all things else. It's unbelievable in so short a time how much worse you will find them than you left them.

Letter Eight
8.2. End of 67 B.C.

Signa quae nobis curasti, ea sunt ad Caietam exposita. nos ea non vidimus; neque enim exeundi Roma potestas nobis fuit. misimus qui pro vectura solveret. te multum amamus quod ea abs te diligenter parvoque curata sunt.

The statues you acquired for me have been disembarked at Caieta. I have not seen them, not having had an opportunity of leaving Rome. I have sent a man to pay the freight. I am most grateful to you for taking so much trouble and getting them cheaply.

Letter Nine
9.3. First half 66 B.C.

Quod ad me de Hermathena scribis per mihi gratum est. est ornamentum Academiae proprium meae, quod et Hermes commune est omnium et Minerva singulare est insigne eius gymnasi. qua re velim, ut scribis, ceteris quoque rebus quam plurimis eum locum ornes. quae mihi antea signa misisti, ea nondum vidi; in Formiano sunt, quo ego nunc proficisci cogitabam. illa omnia in Tusculanum deportabo. Caietam, si quando abundare coepero, ornabo. libros tuos conserva et noli desperare eos ⟨me⟩ meos facere posse. quod si adsequor, supero Crassum divitiis atque omnium vicos et prata contemno.

I am very grateful for what you say about the Hermathena. It's an appropriate ornament for my Academy, since Hermes is the common emblem of all such places and Minerva special to that one. So please beautify it with other pieces, as you promise, as many as possible. I have not yet seen the statues you sent me earlier. They are in my house at Formiae, which I am now preparing to visit. I shall take them all up to Tusculum, and decorate Caieta if and when I begin to have a surplus. Hold on to your books and don't despair of my being able to make them mine. If I manage that, I am richer than Crassus and can afford to despise any man's manors and meadows.

Letter Ten
10.5. Shortly before 17 July 65 B.C.

Hermathena tua valde me delectat et posita ita belle est ut totum gymnasium eius ἀνάθημα videatur. multum te amamus.

I am quite delighted with your Hermathena. It's so judiciously placed that the whole hall is like an offering at its feet. Many thanks.

2. To Gallus
To M. Fabius Gallus. December 46 B.C.
(Shackleton Bailey 1977, no. 209)

sed essent, mi Galle, omnia facilia si et ea mercatus esses quae ego desiderabam et ad eam summam quam volueram. ac tamen ista ipsa quae te emisse scribis non solum rata mihi erunt sed etiam grata. plane enim intellego te non modo studio sed etiam amore usum quae te delectarint, hominem, ut ego semper iudicavi, in omni iudicio elegantissimum, quae me digna putaris, coemisse. sed velim maneat Damasippus in sententia; prorsus enim ex istis emptionibus nullam dcsidcro. tu autem, ignarus instituti mei, quanti ego genus omnino signorum omnium non aestimo tanti ista quattuor aut quinque sumpsisti. Bacchas istas cum Musis Metelli comparas. quid simile? primum ipsas ego Musas numquam tanti putassem atque id fecissem Musis omnibus approbantibus, sed tamen erat aptum bibliothecae studiisque nostris congruens; Bacchis vero ubi est apud me locus? at pulchellae sunt. novi optime et saepe vidi. nominatim tibi signa mihi nota mandassem si probassem. ea enim signa ego emere soleo quae ad similitudinem gymnasiorum exornent mihi in palaestra locum. Martis vero signum quo mihi pacis auctori? . . .

Ista quidem summa ne ego multo libentius emerim deversorium Tarracinae, ne semper hospiti molestus sim. omnino liberti mei video esse culpam, cui plane res certas mandaram, itemque Iuni, quem puto tibi notum esse, Aviani familiarem. exhedria quaedam mihi nova sunt instituta in porticula Tusculani. ea volebam tabellis ornare. etenim, si quid generis istius modi me delectat, pictura delectat.

But everything would be straightforward, my dear Gallus, if you had bought what I needed and within the price I had wished to pay. Not but what I stand by these purchases you say you have made, indeed I am grateful. I fully understand that you acted out of good-will, affection indeed, in buying the pieces which pleased you (I have always regarded you as a very fine judge in any matter of taste), and which you considered worthy of me. But I hope Damasippus doesn't change his mind, for, frankly, I don't need any of these purchases of yours. Not being acquainted with my regular practice you have taken these four or five pieces at a price I should consider excessive for all the statuary in creation. You compare these Bacchantes with Metellus' Muses. Where's the likeness? To begin with, I should never have reckoned the Muses themselves worth such a sum—and all Nine would have approved my judgement! Still, that would have made a suitable acquisition for a library, and one appropriate to my interests. But where am I going to put Bacchantes? Pretty little things, you may say. I know them well, I've seen them often. I should have given you a specific commission about statues which I know, if I had cared for them. My habit is to buy pieces which I can use to decorate a place in my palaestra, in imitation of lecture-halls. But a statue of Mars! What can I, as an advocate of peace, do with that? . . .

For the sum you have spent I should really have much preferred to buy a lodge at Tarracina, so as not to be continually imposing on hospitality. To be sure, I realize that my freedman is to blame (I had given him quite definite commissions), and Junius too—I think you know him, Avianius' friend. I am making some new alcoves in the little gallery of my house at Tusculum, and I wanted some pictures for their decoration—indeed, if anything in this way appeals to me, it is painting.

I wish to thank the American Academy in Rome for its hospitality as I prepared this manuscript, George Heard Hamilton for his peerless knowledge of Whistler and of postage stamps, my colleague Katherine Geffcken for erudite aid, and Brunilde S. Ridgway for the joy of invigorating discussions.

1.   See Brunilde S. Ridgway, "The State of Research on Ancient Art," *Art Bulletin* 68 (1986), 22.

2.   Ridgway 1986 reviews recent literature (see her 9–15 and notes therein).

3.   See Appendix for texts and translations of the relevant passages in the letters. Unless otherwise noted, all references to Cicero's letters are from the editions of D. R. Shackleton Bailey cited in the Appendix.

4.   Paul Zanker, "Zur Funktion und Bedeutung griechischer Skulptur in der Römerzeit," *Entretiens Hardt* 25 (1978), suggests that the term *gymnasiode* refers to a standard "line" available in contemporary workshops. These letters alone cannot support such a hypothesis.

Shackleton Bailey consistently translates *gymnasium* as "lecture hall" and *gymnasiode* as "suitable to a lecture hall" (Appendix, letters 2, 4–6). As will become clear, Cicero refers to a peristyle in his garden, not an auditorium. I have, therefore, kept the word *gymnasium*, finding no easy English equivalent.

5.   The most comprehensive study of gymnasia is Jean Delorme, *Gymnasion* (Paris, 1960).

6.   Some examples: a villa of Crassus in Tusculum (*De Or.* 1.98) and Bauli (*Acad.* 2.9). The fundamental study remains Pierre Grimal, *Les jardins romains,* 2d ed. (Paris, 1969). See Paul Zanker, "Die Villa als Vorbild des späten pompejanischen Wohngeschmacks," *Jahrbuch des Deutschen archäologischen Instituts* 94 (1979), 460–523.

7.   *Div.* 1.8 (on the Lyceum). See Appendix for the Academy.

8.   See John Travlos, *Pictorial Dictionary of Ancient Athens* (New York, 1971), s.v. "Akademia." See also Pausanias 1, 30:1–2; *Real-Encyclopädie* 1, 1132–34, "Akademia" (Wachsmuth).

9.   D. R. Shackleton Bailey, *Cicero's Letters to Atticus* (Cambridge, 1965), 4.

10.   *De Finibus* 5.1.1–2 and 5.2.4.

11.   The translation is Shackleton Bailey's.

12.   See Michael Ruch, *Le préambule dans les oeuvres philosophiques de Cicéron* (Paris, 1958), 81–82. See also Filippo Coarelli, "Discussione," *Dialoghi di archeologia,* 3d ser., 2 (1984), 152–153. I wish to thank Professor William Harris for calling this reference to my attention.

13.   *Div.* 1.8.

14.   *Tusc.* 2.9, 3.7.

15.   Cicero, *Brutus,* ed. A. E. Douglas (Oxford, 1966), 17, notes that the word *consedimus* is "the customary indication in a Ciceronian dialogue that the main discussion is about to begin" (*Brut.* 24).

16.   Ronald P. Legon, *Megara* (Ithaca, 1981), 25; Pausanias 1, 40:4; H. Stuart Jones, *Select Passages from Ancient Writers . . . Greek Sculpture,* rev. ed. A. N. Oikonomides (Chicago, 1966), 142; Alfred Philippson, *Die griechischen Landschaften* (Frankfurt, 1952), 1, pt. 3:940–964; Emanuel Loewy, *Inschriften griechischer Bildhauer* (Leipzig, 1885), 78–79, no. 99, and 107, no. 140.

17.   This suggestion was made in discussion at the symposium "Retaining the Original" held at the Center for Advanced Study of the Visual Arts, National Gallery of Art, Washington, March 8, 1985, when this material was originally presented.

18.   To give a general sense of the worth of HS 20,400: Varro claims that a farm of two hundred *iugera* (about 130 acres) should produce an annual income of about HS 30,000 (Varro *Rust.* 3.2.15). See also Patrizio Pensabene, "Osservazioni sulla diffusione dei Marmi e sul loro Prezzo," *Dialoghi di archeologia,* 3d ser., 1 (1983), 55–63.

19.   Vitruvius explains the difference between the Greek and Roman xystus, 5.11.4 and 6.7.5.

Shackleton Bailey translates *xystus* as "colonnade," following the Greek usage. Since Cicero differentiates it from *gymnasium*, which was a peristyle colonnade, he clearly intended its Latin meaning.

20.   Some of the urgency in the letters can be explained by the closing of the Mediterranean shipping routes in the winter. The period 27 May to 14 September was considered the best time to transport goods by sea. The dates could be extended to between 10 March and 10 November but no further with safety (Lionel Casson, *Ships and Seamanship in the Ancient World* [Princeton, 1971], 270).

21.   These are Shackleton Bailey's "bas-reliefs which I can lay in the stucco of the small entrance hall and two figured puteals."

22.   *Div.* 2.8.

23.   Shackleton Bailey 1965, 1, 288 *ad.* 3: *singulare.*

24.   Shackleton Bailey 1965, 1, 296, discusses the textual difficulties with 5.2, *eius* ἀνάθημα.

25.   The basic studies of Cicero as a purchaser of works of art are Giovanni Becatti, *Arte e gusto negli scrittori latini* (Florence, 1951), especially 89–92, and Hans Jucker, *Vom Verhältnis der Römer zur bildenden Kunst der Griechen* (Frankfurt, 1950), especially 37–45. More recently see Andrew Stewart, "Sculpture in a Classical Landscape," in Mario del Chiaro, *Classical Art: Sculpture* [exh. cat., Santa Barbara Museum of Art] (Santa Barbara, 1984), 86–94, especially 92; Filippo Coarelli, "Il commercio delle opere d'arte in Età tardo-repubblicana," *Dialoghi di archeologia,* 3d ser., 1 (1983), 45–53 (principally about the practicalities of shipment); Zanker 1978, 284–285; Grimal 1969, 357–362; Delorme 1960, 223. For bibliography on Cicero's view on art see Magrit Pape, *Griechische Kunstwerke aus Kriegsbeute* (Hamburg, 1975), 101 n. 3c.

26.   See, however, letter eight and the letter to Gallus.

27.   In this case the statues seem very clearly to have been "previously owned" (as Kim Hartswick and John Pollini propose for the Megarian statues bought twenty years earlier).

28.   I consider Cicero's final comments about painting in his letter to Gallus to be more a function of his momentary bad temper than a considered aesthetic judgment.

29.   The use of the word *palaestra* leads Shackleton Bailey (*Cicero: Epistulae ad familiares,* 2 vols. [Cambridge, 1977], 2:372) to suppose that the letter refers to Cicero's house on the Palatine, in which he had a *palaestra* (*Att.* 24.7). Vitruvius, however, simply uses *palaestra* as a term for spacious peristyle gardens (6.5.3), and Cicero interchangeably uses it with gymnasium (*De Or.* 1.98). The reference to Tusculum later in the letter, therefore, must be allowed to keep its natural meaning and identify the place for which Cicero intended the decorations.

30.   Diog. Laert. 3.25, 4.1; Cicero owned a portrait of Plato (*Brut.* 24). The setting of the *Brutus* is vague, but it was not in Tusculum (*Brut.* 20,300). The portrait of Plato, therefore, was in one of his other properties.

31.   Pausanias 1, 30:1–2; Schol. *O.C.* 56 (= *FGrH.* 244 frag. 147); Ath. 13.609d.

32.   Travlos 1971. These sculptures remain mostly unpublished, and so it is not clear which ones may have been there in Cicero's day.

33.   This could be an alternative explanation for the plural gymnasia in the letter to Gallus. Cicero could be indicating that he wants to decorate his Academy with sculptures as gymnasia generally were decorated. His interest in re-creating the Athenian Academy might have lessened over the years.

34.   Shackleton Bailey's translation (Appendix, letter 10) makes Cicero appear to believe that Herms had feet. The Latin text implies nothing of the kind.

35.   Cornelius C. Vermeule, *Greek Sculpture and Roman Taste* (Ann Arbor, 1976), 6.

36.   On, for example, Matthew Brettingham's purchase for English patrons, see Seymour Howard, *Bartolomeo Cavaceppi* (New York and London, 1982), 32–49. On the dependence of the Marquis of Lansdowne on Gavin Hamilton see Adolf Michaelis, *Ancient Marbles in Great*

Britain (Cambridge, 1882), 104–106.

37. Miranda Marvin, "Freestanding Sculpture from the Baths of Caracalla," *American Journal of Archaeology* 87 (1983), 371–372.

38. See Delorme 1960, 223; Ruch 1958, 82.

39. Giovanni Becatti, "Letture Pliniane," in *Studi in onore di A. Calderini e R. Paribene*, 3 vols. (Milan, 1956), 3:199–210.

40. See note 6 above; Henner von Hesberg, "Einige Statuen mit bukolischer Bedeutung," *Mitteilungen des Deutschen archäologischen Instituts, römische Abteilung* 86 (1979), 297–317; Joachim Raeder, *Die statuarische Ausstattung der Villa Hadriana bei Tivoli* (Frankfurt, 1983).

41. Dimitrios Pandermalis, "Zum Programm der Statuenausstattung in der Villa dei Papiri," *Mitteilungen des Deutschen archäologischen Instituts, athenische Abteilung* 86 (1971), 173–209.

42. Two recent studies include earlier bibliography: Andrew Stewart, "To Entertain an Emperor," *Journal of Roman Studies* 67 (1977), 76–90; Manfred Leppert, "Domina Nympha," *Archäologischer Anzeiger* 93 (1978), 554–573.

43. Raeder 1983, 287–315.

44. Vitruvius 7.5.6 in *Vitruvius,* trans. Morris Hicky Morgan (Cambridge, Mass., 1914), 212.

45. Some studies of Roman public buildings: Marvin 1983, 347–384; Hubertus Manderscheid, *Die Skulpturenausstattung der kaiserzeitlichen Thermenanlagen* (Berlin, 1981); Giorgio Bejor, "La decorazione scultorea dei teatri romani nelle provincie africane," *Prospettiva* 17 (1979), 37–46; Filippo Coarelli, "Il complesso Pompeiano," *Rendiconti della Pontificia accademia romana* 44 (1971–1972), 99–122. Nymphaea are well documented. The basic study is Balázs Kapossy, *Brunnenfiguren der hellenistischen und römischen Zeit* (Zurich, 1969). See also A. Schmidt-Colinet, "Skulpturen aus dem Nymphäum von Apamea/Syrien," *Archäologischer Anzeiger* (1985), 119–133. A fine study of an alternative type of program is Renate Bol, *Das Statuenprogramm des Herodes-Atticus-Nymphäums,* Olympische Forschungen 15 (Berlin, 1984), 83–97. Note the different sculptural programs that were thought to be appropriate for this single building type. Additional references in Ridgway 1986.

46. If it is an original Greek work, a fine new example would be the sculpture from the Temple of Apollo Sosianus (Eugenio La Rocca, *Amazzonomachia* [Rome, 1985], 89–90). The statues in the Temple of Apollo on the Palatine are discussed in Barbara Kellum, "The Temple of Apollo on the Palatine," in *The Age of Augustus: The Rise of Imperial Ideology* (in press).

47. Compare J. B. Ward-Perkins, *Roman Imperial Architecture* (Harmondsworth, 1981), 391. The phenomenon has been often noted; see, for example, Zanker 1978, 293–295.

48. Kenan Erim, "Aphrodisias 1982," *Anatolian Studies* 33 (1983), 231–232; "Aphrodisias Excavations," *New York University Bulletin* 84/5-1 (April 1985), 3.

49. Visible at a glance in the illustrations to Ward-Perkins 1981. For example, figs. 66 (Rome, screen wall), 164 (Stobi, theater), 189 (Ephesus, library), 191 (Ephesus, bath), 192 (Miletus, nymphaeum), 204–205 (Baalbek, temple), 213 (Petra, rock-cut sandstone tomb), 249 (Sabratha, theater), 260 (Lepcis Magna, nymphaeum). For further illustrations and examples see Margaret Lyttelton, *Baroque Architecture in Classical Antiquity* (London, 1974).

50. In the newly discovered Julio-Claudian "precinct of Aphrodite Prometer" at Aphrodisias (Erim 1985, 3), for example, the inscribed bases include the names of Gaius, Lucius, Drusus (son of Tiberius), Aeneas, and Aphrodite Prometer (*Anatolian Studies* 33 [1983], 231–232). Other finds include an inscription mentioning Valerian and Gallienus. The difficulty of guaranteeing that the excavated sculptures represent the original program is characteristic for these structures, which were objects of civic pride, long maintained and often remodeled.

51. Baths were particularly rich in sculpture. See Marvin 1983 and Manderscheid 1981.

52. I am speaking of large-scale replicas. Figurines, statuettes, and other small statuary represent a separate issue, for which see Elizabeth Bartman, "Miniature Copies" (Ph.D. diss., Columbia University, 1984).

53. Pliny *Natural History* 36.21.

54. Christian Blinkenberg, *Knidia* (Copenhagen, 1933), 230–232; Barbara Vierneisel-Schlörb, *Klassische Skulpturen,* vol. 2 of Glyptothek münchen Katalog der Skulpturen (Munich, 1979), 333–348.

55. B. M. Felletti Maj, "Aphrodite Pudica," *Archeologia classica* 3 (1951), 61–65. (These lists include some statuettes.)

56. For a summary of much earlier literature see Dericksen M. Brinkerhoff, "Figures of Venus, Creative and Derivative," in *Studies Presented to George M. A. Hanfmann,* ed. D. G. Mitten, J. G. Pedley, J. A. Scott (Mainz, 1971), 9–16.

57. "Cypris [Venus], seeing Cypris in Cnidus, said 'Alas! Alas! Where did Praxiteles see me naked?'" in *The Greek Anthology,* trans. W. R. Paton, 5 vols. (London and New York, 1926), 5:255 (16.162).

58. The numbers in the replica counts are of absolutely no statistical value beyond indicating in a general way that these types were extremely popular.

59. A. Linfert, "Der Meister der 'kauernden Aphrodite,'" *Mitteilungen des Deutschen archäologischen Instituts, athenische Abteilung* 84 (1969) 158–164. See also Dericksen M. Brinkerhoff, "Hypotheses on the History of the Crouching Aphrodite Type in Antiquity," *Getty Museum Journal* 6–7 (1978–1979), 83–96.

60. Pape 1975, Appendix 1 (143–193), lists the buildings in Rome in which Greek works of art were kept. They included major temples, the Area Capitolina, the Horti Luculliani and Serviliani, colonnades, baths, and other frequented places. See also Zanker 1978, 291–292.

61. Pape 1975, Appendix 2 (194–208), lists donors; her list of sites (143–193) includes twenty-three temples.

62. Raeder 1983, 309.

63. For examples of the variety of meanings a single type could assume, depending on its context, see Zanker 1978, 295–296. Martha Weber, "Die Amazonen von Ephesos II," *Jahrbuch des Deutschen archäologischen Instituts* 99 (1984), 75–126, cites the extensive earlier bibliography on these disputed figures. Brunilde S. Ridgway, *Roman Copies of Greek Sculpture: The Problem of the Originals* (Ann Arbor, 1984), 99–100, still doubts a Greek origin for any of them.

64. Gisela M. A. Richter, *The Sculpture and Sculptors of the Greeks,* 4th ed. (New Haven and London, 1970), p. 226.

65. Adolf Furtwängler, *Masterpieces of Greek Sculpture,* ed. Eugénie Sellers (London, 1895), viii.

66. Most recently in English, Martin Robertson, *A History of Greek Art* (Cambridge, 1975), xiv–xv.

67. Compare Walter Benjamin, "The Work of Art in the Age of Mechanical Reproduction (1936)," in *Illuminations,* trans. Harry Zohn, ed. Hannah Arendt (New York, 1969), 218–222. I wish to thank Professor Zirka Filipczak for reminding me of the relevance of this passage.

68. Cited in Michelle Bogart, "Attitudes toward Sculpture Reproduction in America, 1850–1880" (Ph.D. diss., University of Chicago, 1979), 72.

69. Some variation on this approach may well have governed the collection, presumably of replicas, described in Lucian *Philopseudes* 18.

70. The most succinct statement of the new position is Zanker 1978. Ridgway 1984 contains not only her own stimulating and controversial views but a thorough bibliography of earlier literature.

71. Pape 1975; Paul Zanker, *Klassizistische Statuen: Studien zur Veränderung des Kunstgeschmacks in der römischen Kaiserzeit* (Mainz, 1974).

72. Compare Felix Preisshofen and Paul Zanker, "Reflex einer eklektischen Kunstanschauung beim Auctor ad Herennium," *Dialoghi di archeologia* 4–5 (1970–1971), 100–119; R. Wünsche, "Der Jüngling von Magdalensberg," *Festschrift für Luitpold Dussler* (Munich, 1972).

73. David Finn and Fred Licht, *Canova* (New York, 1983), color pls. 32 *(Perseus),* 42 *(Venus Italica),* 43 *(Three Graces).*

74. See the poignant comments of Ridgway 1986, 11 n. 28.

75. *The Age of Neo-Classicism* [exh. cat., Council of Europe] (London and Harlow, 1972).

Ruminations on Edible Icons: Originals and Copies in the Art of Byzantium

GARY VIKAN
The Walters Art Gallery

THE ART OF Byzantium is distinguished perhaps above all else by its remarkable conservatism. A Saint Sergios of the sixth century is basically like one of the fourteenth; a Christ Pantocrator in a dome mosaic is, save for size and medium, virtually identical with one of an ivory triptych or a gold coin. This essay will address a few of Byzantium's most characteristic model-copy relationships in terms of the presumed motives for the copying processes; it will also examine the underlying values and beliefs implied by that process and product.

This discussion will begin with the relatively common, basically quite simple model-copy relationship epitomized by the juxtaposition of two miniature paintings, one of the twelfth century (fig. 1) and one dating around 1300 (fig. 2).[1] At least a portion of the iconography of Byzantium was transmitted from generation to generation substantially unchanged along rootlike stemmata very much like those governing the transmission of texts.[2] This process is most clearly traced in cycles of narrative text illustration to books of the Bible. The hypothetical scenario is straightforward. At some point a scribe or illuminator iconographically rendered the biblical text using a set of narrative, cartoonlike vignettes such as these. This first narrative picture cycle (the "archetype") in turn served as the root of a centuries-long family tree comprising copies, and copies of copies, usually within the context of manuscript illumination but occasionally in other media as well. The result was that Byzantine narrative iconography maintained its integrity and momentum, even after having been physically separated from its text of origin.

Illustrated in figures 1 and 2 are miniatures from a pair of well-known picture cycles occupying the same branch of the stemmatic family tree to which belong the illustrated Byzantine Octateuchs.[3] This particular vignette illustrates several verses from chapter sixteen of Numbers, the fourth of the eight Old Testament books comprising the Byzantine Octateuch. The episode describes how three among the congregation of Israel rebel against the leadership of Moses and Aaron and as punishment for that rebellion are swallowed up by the earth along with all their household. Two of the three, Dathan and Abeiram, are clearly distinguished atop the heap of humanity, livestock, and buildings disappearing into a cleft in the earth at the lower right; the younger of the two raises an arm over his head to shield himself against the powerful rays emanating from the hand of God at the top center. Moses passively stands at the left, gesturing as though to condemn the doomed rebels, while the righteous elders of his congregation appear at the

Fig. 1. *The Punishment of Dathan and Abeiram*, twelfth century, tempera on vellum. Vatican Library, Vatican City (cod. gr. 746, fol. 340v).

center in various agitated poses; one seems to be pleading with Moses, another is clearly weeping, and a third throws up his arms in despair.

In overall composition and minute details of gesture, clothing, and color selection these two miniatures are virtually identical. Indeed the later miniature, along with its entire picture cycle, was directly copied from the twelfth-century picture cycle;[4] a comparable level of fidelity of copy to model may thus be traced through the scores of scenes they share. That both model and copy survive is quite unusual. The model-copy process to which these two miniatures attest, however, was in no way unusual; this was the modus operandi for the production of much of Byzantium's narrative iconography. This process was, moreover, the basis for its own art-historical methodology, which for several decades Kurt Weitzmann taught at Princeton University. His students first learned of the basic existence of iconographic stemmata and then of an essentially philological method of picture criticism whereby it could be documented. The goal of such analysis, beyond mere documentation, was threefold: first, to establish genealogical relationships among all surviving representatives of a given tradition (assuming that fidelity to text was gradually lost over time through copying and that cycles with "better iconography," therefore, had priority in the family tree); second, to identify innovative qualities characteristic of any one picture cycle

within that tradition and to interpret those innovations against the culture and history of their time; and third, to reconstruct as much as possible from all surviving representative picture cycles the breadth and detail of the lost archetype.

This methodology was painstaking, and for some, not easily mastered. In gaining an understanding of this methodology, however, one can easily overlook a fundamental question posed by the very evidence this approach was designed to master; namely, the question of motive. Why were the copies made in the first place? Why, when it came to narrating the biblical story in pictures, did the Byzantines so consistently choose imitation over invention? For the art historian's counterpart, the biblical philologist, this question simply does not exist; the text of the Book of Numbers was copied and recopied with absolute fidelity because it was believed to have been given by God to Moses on Mount Sinai. But these picture cycles, of course, were not, and any number of different ways of rendering the punishment of Dathan and Abeiram were possible, one no less iconographically valid than the other. For such major biblical books as Genesis there are multiple surviving recensions, each iconographically distinct from the other and possessing its own stemma. Moreover, within each of these iconographic stemmata is encountered a phenomenon unparalleled among sacred texts. Over time a significant portion of the original

Fig. 2. *The Punishment of Dathan and Abeiram*, c. 1300, tempera on vellum. Mount Athos (Vatopedi cod. 602, fol. 150r).

set of episodes will be reduced so that characteristically the further one descends through the roots of an iconographic tradition, the shorter its picture cycle becomes.[5] Pictures such as these clearly were not considered sacred and inviolable; there is little about them that would qualify as iconic, and they surely were not objects of veneration; yet they were copied and recopied over generations. Why?

Insofar as I ever attempted to answer this question, I did so assuming that such copying took place mainly for convenience' sake. I somehow imagined the manuscript illuminator working side by side with the scribe and, when obliged to illustrate a text, either copying over the scribe's shoulder or running off to a well-stocked library to find a manuscript with an appropriate model picture cycle. This same basic scenario I imagined for ivory carvers, mosaicists, and icon painters as well. After all, it saved them the trouble of reading the text themselves and inventing their own picture cycle, and it seems not to have offended the sensibilities of patrons. I assumed (and still assume) that whoever paid for the later manuscript (fig. 2) was fully satisfied in receiving a set of miniature paintings virtually identical to that in the earlier manuscript (fig. 1). In sum, then, my thinking was this: artists, working for patrons oblivious to modern notions of originality, acted out of convenience.

I would now like to consider quite a different sort of Byzantine model-copy relationship: the one posed by small objects of personal devotion like the one-inch-square cast-bronze icon of the Virgin and Child illustrated in figure 3.[6] Such pieces were typically designed in conscious imitation of iconic types otherwise familiar on grander scale and in more expensive media (for example, fig. 4).[7] They were usually manufactured in multiples, of bronze, lead, or glass, by means of reusable molds or dies.[8] This quite literally was Byzantine art in mass production and as such was a vastly more common and available part of daily life than were illustrated biblical manuscripts. Compared with their models, objects like these had two distinct advantages: they were portable and inexpensive. Since portability could easily be achieved in gold, enamels, and precious stones, it may be assumed that their primary advantage was economic, the goal being to produce as many such items as cheaply as possible. If so, one can legitimately impute to those who made and distributed such objects two quite different, although not necessarily contradictory motives. On one hand, there is the essentially Christian, democratic ideal of putting those things instrumental to religious experience into the hands of as many people as possible, irrespective of their wealth. There is evidence from the world of early Byzantine pilgrimage that the production of such small devotional objects was, in effect, a Church monopoly, and that they were distributed free, as a kind

Above: Fig. 3. *The Virgin Hodegetria*, eleventh–twelfth century, bronze. The Menil Collection, Houston.

Right: Fig. 4. *The Virgin Hodegetria*, eleventh–twelfth century, marble. Archaeological Museum, Istanbul (4730).

of "sacred dole."[9] The very abundance and variety of these mass-produced implements of piety suggest, however, that their primary point of distribution was not the church but the marketplace and that by implication the primary motivation was less one of idealism than of pure economics—of supply and demand.[10] But whether given away or sold, these objects were mass produced only because there was a great demand for them across a broad spectrum of Byzantine society. And this demand could only have existed as long as the consumer believed he was getting, in his cast-bronze, mass-produced copy, something of comparable spiritual value to the original on which it was based.

We are here finally beginning to penetrate the heart of the model-copy relationship in Byzantium, for we are moving beyond the realm of material evidence and beneath the layer of putative motives toward that substratum of shared values and beliefs on which both rest and of which both are necessarily the reflection. What bound the producer and consumer of the bronze plaquette together and what made the economics of their relation-

ship work was their shared conviction that the object was no less functional as an icon than was an object like that illustrated in figure 4. The Byzantines believed that the power and sanctity of revered iconic archetypes resided collectively and individually in all copies, regardless of medium, style, aesthetic merit, or expense.[11] The icon should thus not be considered in isolation but rather as the mediating vehicle between the venerating supplicant and the deity or saint represented. The Orthodox view was succinctly stated by Saint Theodore the Studite (ninth century):

Every artificial image . . . exhibits in itself, by way of imitation, the form [that is, *charakter*] of its model [that is, *archetupon*] . . . the model [is] in the image, the one in the other, except for differences of substance. Hence, he who reveres an image surely reveres the person whom the image shows; not the substance of the image. . . . Nor does the singleness of this veneration separate the model from the image, since, by virtue of imitation [that is, *mimesis*], the image and the model are one.[12]

50

In the eyes of Orthodoxy the icon as an art object virtually disappears. By virtue of mimesis it has become one and the same with the archetype, while by virtue of veneration it has become effectively transparent—that through which one gazes to gain access to the deity. Insofar as the palpability of the object is acknowledged, it is acknowledged as base substance whose "nature" must not be confused with that of the archetype. Theodore continues in his explanation of the essential insubstantiality of icons by introducing the metaphor of a signet ring:

> Or take the example of a signet ring engraved with the imperial image, and let it be impressed upon wax, pitch and clay. The impression is one and the same in the several materials which, however, are different with respect to each other; yet it would not have remained identical unless it were entirely unconnected with the materials. . . . The same applies to the likeness of Christ irrespective of the material upon which it is represented.[13]

For art historians there is much here to consider. First, the icon as an object, artistic or otherwise, is ignored. Second, there are no qualifications placed on what constitutes an icon. In the same text Theodore describes an icon as losing its quality as an icon through obliteration and thereby reverting to a state of base substance, but neither he nor apparently any other Byzantine ever addressed the fundamental question of what it took for a man-made object to become an icon in the first place. An icon was whatever was universally recognized to be an icon. A representation became an icon when it began to function as an icon, and at the same moment it effectively disappeared as a work of art.

A third point is worthy of note: there apparently is no qualitative hierarchy imposed among representations that have qualified as icons. There are no better or inferior icons; no originals or copies. This raises the fourth and most interesting point to emerge from Theodore's discourse; namely, that in his words "every artificial image . . . exhibits in itself, by way of imitation, the form of its model," and the archetype is "the person whom the image shows." Thus the real model behind a Byzantine icon—its archetype—was not and could never be another icon but rather must be the represented deity or saint. By their own definition every icon ever made in Byzantium necessarily was a copy. There could never be qualitative distinctions based on relative priority when one exemplar was by definition no less distant than another from the original—since each was, in effect, one and the same with it.

We seem to have come to a dead end in this iconophile dictum of Theodore the Studite; we are awash in a world of "substanceless" copies from which originals are excluded. In the real world of Byzantine piety, however, icons were not such pure and abstract entities. They were palpable objects to venerate and touch, which, despite their base substance and human manufacture, were often thought to possess and exercise miraculous powers. That this was true is substantially due to the fact that very early on, at least by the sixth century, the world of Byzantine icons intersected that of relics.[14] Consider again the bronze plaquette in figure 3. True, its archetype was the Virgin and Child, but its proximate prototype—its model in the art-historical sense—was a famous icon preserved in the Hodegon Monastery in Constantinople.[15] This particular icon was believed to have been painted from life by Saint Luke himself (fig. 5); according to legend, it was brought from Jerusalem to Constantinople in the fifth century by Empress Eudocia. Figures 3 and 5 tell the whole story: the theoretical archetype for both the bronze plaquette and the painted panel in the arms of Saint Luke was the Mother with Child posing before him, but the real model for both bronze worker and miniaturist—although surely at several removes—was a famous painted panel in their own city, around which

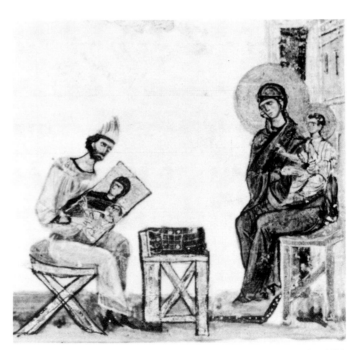

Fig. 5. *Saint Luke Painting a Portrait of the Virgin and Child*, tempera on vellum. Patriarchate, Jerusalem (Taphou cod. 14, fol. 106r).

had formed an acknowledged, conventional portrait type, precisely because it was revered as an icon and powerful relic. Thus the *Hodegetria* icon in the Hodegon Monastery was an original, insofar as it was unique and the art-historical source of multiple copies. This original *Hodegetria*, however, was revered not so much for its beauty or even for its "iconness" as for its "relicness."

According to Theodore the Studite's signet-ring metaphor, the holy image is insubstantial, existing between and independent of the sealing die and malleable medium into which the die is pressed. Not only does Theodore's definition of an icon allow for the production of an infinite number of identical copies, the very metaphor he chooses is one that presupposes such replication. But Theodore's world of icons becomes at once richer and more complex the moment relics are introduced. In the absence of relics an icon's sacred power derives solely from its representational identity with its archetype; the signet-ring metaphor, however, allows for a situation wherein the "forming agent," the die or its equivalent, was itself considered holy; that is, a relic, saint, or deity. The image produced would then have a double measure of sacred power, by virtue of iconic verisimilitude and physical contact with something or someone holy.

The most famous representatives of this special category of relic-icon are the holy textiles believed to have been miraculously imprinted with an image of Christ's face or body. Among the earliest is one formerly preserved in Egypt, at Memphis, and described there around A.D. 570 by an anonymous pilgrim from Piacenza:

> We saw there [in Memphis] a piece of linen on which is a portrait of the Saviour. People say he once wiped his face with it, and that the outline remained. It is venerated at various times and we also venerated it, but it was too bright for us to concentrate on since, as you went on concentrating, it changed before your eyes.[16]

The most famous holy cloth for the Byzantines was one "invented" about the same time for the city of Edessa, in Syria.[17] This cloth, which like the other seems to have shown only Christ's face, was taken to Constantinople in the tenth century by Emperor Romanos I and venerated as one of the city's prized relics (fig. 6).[18] It is with this now-lost cloth, the so-called Mandilion of Edessa, that some have mistakenly tried to identify the famous textile showing the entire body of Christ; namely, the Shroud of Turin (fig. 7).[19]

Since for our purposes what applies to one of these textiles applies to all, and since the Turin Shroud is the

Fig. 6. *King Abgarus with the Mandilion* (detail), tenth century, tempera and wood panel. Monastery of Saint Catherine, Mount Sinai (B58).

most famous one still to survive, I will direct my comments toward it. Certainly the Shroud had, and still has, sacred power, and certainly that power derives in part from the iconic likeness it bears. But much more than that, it is a world-famous object of veneration and miracle working precisely because it is believed to have touched the body of Christ. The Byzantines were always clear in their understanding of the implications of this, since for them (as for many still today) the sanctity of holy people, objects, and places was in some measure transferable through physical contact. In describing the True Cross, John of Damascus (active eighth century) could as well

Fig. 7. Shroud of Turin, linen. Duomo San Giovanni, Turin.

copy has a double portion of sanctity. There would again be no original, except for Christ himself, since each new shroud or mandilion would essentially be identical with and no less potent than the last.

Of course, no Christian believes that Christ more than occasionally wiped his face with a linen cloth, and there could only have been one burial shroud; yet divine impressions—whether of hands, feet, faces, or whole bodies—inevitably suggest mass production, and the general demand for copies of such powerful relic-icons must have been great. By the mid-sixth century an impression of Christ's body was to be seen on the Column of the Flagellation in the Church of Sion at Jerusalem.[21] According to the pilgrim from Piacenza, visitors to the church would mark off the dimensions of Christ's chest, fingers, or hands on little strips of cloth and then wear these strips around the neck as a means of combating disease. I know of no comparable textual or art-historical record of how the sacred power of the Mandilion of Edessa was made available to everyday Byzantine Christians, but I can offer by way of analogy a recent newspaper advertisement for the Shroud of Turin (fig. 8).

The basic idea is quite simple: Send twelve dollars to Richmond, Virginia, and someone there will send you a 2½-foot-long linen replica of the Turin Shroud (which, in fact, is more than fourteen feet long). This, the "Holy Shroud Miracle Cloth," will, in the words of the ad, "bring you everything in life that you desire and so rightly deserve." Drape it over your bed or fold it up in your wallet and "the same miraculous forces that brought about the creation of the Shroud . . . [will] . . . go to work for you," bringing you "remarkable cures, good luck, love, money, robust health and happiness," not to mention success "at bingo, the races, card games, the casino and other games of chance." One can get all this, "guaranteed or your money back," for just twelve dollars. From the point of view of Byzantine models and copies, there is something puzzling here. The ad itself bears a replica of a replica, a copy of a copy. What is it about the twelve-dollar Richmond replica that makes it so powerful, while the one at the center of this newspaper ad is apparently worthless? The ad makes no claim that what it offers for sale was ever blessed or that any contact was ever made with the real Turin Shroud; this object has, in other words, no real relic power.[22] What seems instead to be happening is that for purely economic reasons—that is, to encourage demand and restrict supply—a Richmond entrepreneur has chosen to impose his own, very un-Byzantine "threshold of verisimilitude," below which the sacred power of the archetype is apparently no longer

have been talking about the Shroud of Turin: "So, then, that honorable and most truly venerable tree upon which Christ offered Himself as sacrifice for us is itself to be adored, because it has been sanctified by contact with the sacred body and blood."[20] The implication of this for the question of originals and copies is basic: relic-icons like these, which the Byzantines called *acheiropoietai* (that is, "made without human hands"), derived both their sacred power and their imagery from the mechanical process that brought them into existence. It is as if Theodore the Studite's signet ring were itself holy; the mass-production metaphor still applies, but now each

Fig. 8. Advertisement from the *National Enquirer*.

accessible. The modern buyer must simply be convinced that 2½ feet and a linen backing make for a twelve-dollar difference; a Byzantine, of course, would have been fully satisfied with the newspaper clipping or with the image reproduced with this essay.

That is what could happen to icons when the "forming agent," the signet ring of Theodore's metaphor, was itself believed to be holy. Now imagine the other possibility; namely, that the medium into which the die was pressed was thought to possess sacred power.

One of the central phenomena of early Byzantine culture was pilgrimage, and among the central phenomena of pilgrimage was the eulogia.[23] Eulogia is the Greek word for "blessing," and to the pilgrim this meant the blessing received by contact with a holy place, object, or person. It could either be received directly and immaterially, as by kissing the wood of the True Cross, or it could be conveyed indirectly and materially, customarily by way of a substance of neutral origin that itself had been blessed by such direct contact—as, for example, through flasks of oil that had been touched against the True Cross. Substantive eulogiae like these were generally taken to be apotropaic and often specifically medicinal.[24]

Among the most popular pilgrim eulogiae of the early Byzantine period were Symeon tokens (fig. 9).[25] Symeon tokens are round bits of hardened reddish clay about the size of a quarter; they are named for Saint Symeon Stylites the Younger, a sixth-century Syrian ascetic who

Fig. 9. Symeon token, sixth–seventh century, clay. The Menil Collection, Houston.

spent more than six decades atop a series of ever-taller columns.[26] The ruins of Symeon's shrine (fig. 10) may still be seen atop the so-called Miraculous Mountain, which rises above the Mediterranean Sea, almost ten miles southwest of Antioch.[27] Included in the complex were a cruciform church, monastery, and Symeon's column, the surviving base of which appears at the center of figure 10. Symeon tokens customarily bear a stamped representation of the saint. Typically, as here, Symeon appears bust-length atop his column; a supplicant is often shown climbing a ladder toward the saint, angels fly forward to offer him crowns, and occasionally, as at the lower left of this token, a large jug is represented as well. Symeon tokens qualified as eulogiae not by virtue of that image but rather because they had been molded out of the red earth found near the base of the column, for this earth, by virtue of its physical contact with the column and thereby with the saint, was thought to be infused with sacred power. Specifically it was believed to be highly efficacious in the treatment of diseases.[28] In

Fig. 10. Remains of column within monastery, sixth century. Kutchuk Djebel Semaan (Miraculous Mountain of Saint Symeon, the Younger), Turkey.

chapter 255 of Symeon's *vita* his biographer describes the various ways in which the saint customarily worked healing miracles: "For many [the healing] was [accomplished] by [Symeon's words]; for certain others . . . by visions; and for others again, by the application of his holy dust."[29] This "holy dust," at once Symeon's token and the very stuff of his Miraculous Mountain, was usually consumed in the process of effecting its curative powers; that is, it would either be rubbed on the body or, with water, taken internally. For example, chapter 232 of the *vita* describes the healing of a certain praetorian prefect named Theodore Pikaridios, who suffered from an intestinal disorder. A monk from the Miraculous Mountain named Thomas offered Theodore a bit of Symeon's hair and some of "the dust of his eulogia" and then gave the following prescription: "take some, break them up in pure water, in faith drink them up, and [then] wash yourself with this water, and you will see the glory of God."[30]

Here at last is what seems to be the ultimate Byzantine copy: the edible icon. Here is an object that drew its miraculous powers in part from its stamped iconic image but mostly from the fact that its very medium has been "pre-blessed" with sacred power. Like the Shroud of Turin, the Symeon token is at once a relic and an icon, and, like the Shroud, it has been produced through the mechanical process of stamping. Unlike the Shroud, however, it truly presupposes mass production, and for two obvious reasons: first, because its medium (a mountain of red earth) and its means of production (from reusable, man-made dies) easily allowed for the manufacture of thousands of identical copies; and second, because its very function, which required that it be consumed, literally demanded serial production on a large scale.[31] Pharmaceutically speaking Symeon tokens were the "Bufferin of Byzantium," but at the same time they were Byzantine "art," albeit on its most plebeian level. As art they at first strike us as so many crude copies. But in truth this simply cannot be so, since none among them can be identified as the original, nor can the stamping die or its model, nor can the Magic Mountain or even Saint Symeon himself, since each token was essentially created anew at the moment when image and earth (icon and relic) converged. Either without the other would have been insufficient. In effect these tokens are at once copies without originals, and originals without copies.

What, then, are the common threads that draw together Symeon tokens, holy shrouds, *Hodegetria* icons, and Octateuch miniatures? First, it seems to me that there are basically just two categories of iconography here,

Fig. 11. *Sacra Parallela*, ninth century, tempera on vellum; with Saint Basil (above) and an icon painter at work (below). Bibliothèque Nationale, Paris (cod. gr. 923, fol. 328v).

nondevotional narrative illustration (figs. 1–2, 5–6) and devotional iconic imagery (figs. 3–4, 7–9), and for the latter there are two relic-related subgroups characterized by the likes of shrouds and tokens. Together, narrative illustration and iconic imagery account for a significant portion of the totality of Byzantine religious art. Moreover, they share much in common. The concept of archetype and principle of genealogical succession are intrinsic to both, and through time the history of each is characterized by extended model-copy "chains," the individual links of which essentially exist in function of the chain itself. That is, for narrative text illustration and iconic imagery the "tradition" will usually dominate the individual work of art—iconographic creativity and artistic personality will usually defer to the authority of the model.[32] The result for Byzantium is a millennium of art characterized by continuity through replication and dominated by mimesis, or imitation.

Why is that so? This is the question with which this essay began, and it is the one with which it will end. I am now prepared to offer at least a partial answer—and one that may encompass the spectrum of Byzantine models and copies, from Octateuch miniatures to Symeon tokens.[33] The motives that may be imputed from the evidence of surviving Byzantine art may be imputed as well from Byzantine texts (theological, historical, hagiographic, and liturgical), and these two categories of evidence in fact complement one another to form a single coherent, conceptual whole. From nonart sources it becomes clear that continuity through replication was not simply a workshop procedure governing the behavior of Byzantine painters and die-cutters, it was a religious ideal that in a much broader sense governed the actions and relationships of all Byzantine Christians. Christ was the ultimate archetype, and the individual Christian, by way of chains of replication through biblical heroes, martyrs, monks, and holy men, was his imitator.[34] No more clearly is this principle stated than in an early letter of Saint Basil written about A.D. 360:

> [In the scriptures] the lives of saintly men, recorded and handed down to us, lie before us like living images [that is, icons] of God's government, for our imitation [that is, mimesis] of their good works. And so in whatever respect each one perceives himself deficient, if he devotes himself to such imitation, he will discover there, as in the shop of a public physician, the specific remedy for his infirmity. The lover of chastity constantly peruses the story of [the Patriarch] Joseph, and from him learns what chaste conduct is. . . . Fortitude he learns from Job, who, when the conditions of his life were reversed . . . always preserved his proud spirit unhumbled.[35]

Basil's key words—icons and mimesis—are those familiar to us from the world of art, and this was not by accident, for just a few lines later he draws an explicit, intimate parallel between the proper behavior of artists and the proper behavior of Christians. It is this passage that is quoted and illustrated in the famous ninth-century *Sacra Parallela* manuscript now in Paris (fig. 11);[36] above, Saint Basil points toward the incipit, while below, in response to the text, a Byzantine artist is shown at work:

> Just as painters in working from models constantly gaze at their exemplar and thus strive to transfer the expression of the original to their artistry, so too he who is anxious to make himself perfect in all the kinds of virtue must gaze upon the lives of saints as upon statues, so to speak, that move and act, and must make their excellence his own by imitation *(dia mimeseos)*.[37]

It was the business of the Byzantine artist to copy—to imitate and thereby perpetuate his model—as it was the business of the Byzantine Christian to do likewise. For each, mimesis was an act of value in its own right, through which they might gain access to the sanctity and power of the archetype. Thus by necessity theirs was a world wherein copying was normative behavior.[38] It is no wonder that the manuscript painter who produced the illumination in figure 2 virtually copied his Octateuch model line for line; the artist was not acting out of convenience but out of a sense of conviction and in full conformity to the accepted, age-old rhythm of Byzantine pious behavior. This for the painter was something inherently good and at the same time the only natural and appropriate way of doing things. To have asked that miniaturist or the icon painter in the illumination in figure 11 why he chose to copy would have been as absurd as to ask Andy Warhol why he chose not to: the question would simply have been meaningless. As, I think, would most of my essay, since the questions it poses are substantially predicated on notions of artistic originality foreign to the Byzantine mind. So after all my ruminations—on models and copies, mass production, icons, sanctified dies, and sanctified media—all I have really concluded is that a Byzantine artist's art was an art of imitation just as a Byzantine Christian's life was a life of imitation. This for a Byzantine would only have been obvious; but perhaps that is the most that I could have hoped for.

NOTES

1. See John Lowden, "The Production of the Vatopedi Octateuch," *Dumbarton Oaks Papers* 36 (1982), 120, figs. 13–14.
2. See Kurt Weitzmann, *Illustrations in Roll and Codex: A Study of the Origin and Method of Text Illustration*, Studies in Manuscript Illumination 2, 2d ed. (Princeton, 1970).
3. For the Octateuchs in general see Lowden 1982, 115 nn. 1–14.
4. Lowden 1982.
5. For evidence of this for the Octateuchs, Books of Kings, and other biblical texts see Kurt Weitzmann, "The Illustration of the Septuagint," *Studies in Classical and Byzantine Manuscript Illumination*, ed. Herbert L. Kessler (Chicago and London, 1971), 53–57 (translated and reprinted from *Münchner Jahrbuch der bildenden Kunst* 3–4 [1952–1953], 96–120).
6. It bears the inscription: "Flesh, she holds the Word who existed

before the ages."

7. Reinhold Lange, *Die byzantinische Reliefikone* (Recklinghausen, 1964), no. 9.

8. For a contemporary diorite casting mold for the production of tiny lead icons of the Virgin and Child see Etienne Coche de la Ferté, *L'antiquité chrétienne au Musée du Louvre* (Paris, 1958), no. 58.

9. For example, at the healing shrine of Saints Cosmas and Damian, in Constantinople, "blessed" iconic tokens were distributed, apparently without charge, to infirm pilgrims during the all-night Saturday vigil (Ludovicus Deubner, *Kosmas und Damian* [Leipzig and Berlin, 1907], miracle 30). For more such evidence see Gary Vikan, "Art, Medicine, and Magic in Early Byzantium," *Dumbarton Oaks Papers* 38 (1984), 72 n. 43.

10. For clear evidence of the economic dimension to the production of pilgrim *devotionalia* in the late medieval West see Esther Cohen, "*In haec signa:* Pilgrim-Badge Trade in Southern France," *Journal of Medieval History* 2, no. 3 (1976), 193–214. In my forthcoming catalogue of more than seven hundred Byzantine small objects in the Menil Collection, Houston, substantial new evidence will emerge to show that the Byzantine bronze industry was largely dedicated to the production of inexpensive imitations of precious-metal originals. See also Gary Vikan and John Nesbitt, *Security in Byzantium: Locking, Sealing, and Weighing*, Dumbarton Oaks Byzantine Collection Publications 2 (Washington, 1980), 16.

11. For an excellent review of some of the most important primary texts relating to the Byzantine cult of images see Cyril Mango, *The Art of the Byzantine Empire, 312–1453: Sources and Documents* (Englewood Cliffs, N.J., 1972), 149–177. See also Norman H. Baynes, "Idolatry and the Early Church" and "The Icons before Iconoclasm," in *Byzantine Studies and Other Essays* (London, 1955), 116–143, 226–239; and Ernst Kitzinger, "The Cult of Images in the Age before Iconoclasm," *Dumbarton Oaks Papers* 8 (1954), 83–150.

12. Cited in Mango 1972, 173. The same principles applied as well to architecture. Robert Ousterhout, University of Illinois, Urbana-Champaign, in a forthcoming paper ("*Loca Sancta* and the Architectural Response to Pilgrimage," *The Blessings of Pilgrimage*), discusses two chapels in Constantinople laid out "eis mimesin tou naou tou taphou Christou" ("in imitation of the church of the tomb of Christ").

13. Cited in Mango 1972, 174.

14. See Kitzinger 1954, 96–115; and Gary Vikan, "Sacred Image, Sacred Power," *ICON* (Washington, 1988), 12–18.

15. See Victor Lasareff, "Studies in the Iconography of the Virgin," *Art Bulletin* 20 (1938), 46–65.

16. Translated in John Wilkinson, *Jerusalem Pilgrims before the Crusades* (Warminster, 1977), 88.

17. See Averil Cameron, "The Sceptic and the Shroud," *Inaugural Lecture in the Department of Classics and History, King's College, London, 29 April 1980* (London, 1980).

18. Kurt Weitzmann, *The Monastery of Saint Catherine at Mount Sinai: The Icons, Volume One: From the Sixth to the Tenth Century* (Princeton, 1976), no. B58.

19. Most notably Ian Wilson (*The Shroud of Turin: The Burial Cloth of Jesus Christ* [London, 1979]), whose thesis is effectively refuted by Cameron 1980.

20. Translated in *Fathers of the Church* (Washington 1958), 37:165 (Orth. Faith, 4.11).

21. See Wilkinson 1977, 60, 84.

22. Interestingly the word *Turin* does not appear in the ad.

23. For the meaning of eulogia see Gary Vikan, *Byzantine Pilgrimage Art*, Dumbarton Oaks Byzantine Collection Publications 5 (Washington, 1982), 10–20. For early Byzantine pilgrimage in general see that same publication as well as Wilkinson 1977, "Introduction," and 79–89; and Bernard Kötting, *Peregrinatio religiosa* (Regensburg, 1950).

24. For the medicinal, magical properties of the eulogia see Vikan 1984, 68–72.

25. On Symeon tokens see Vikan 1982, 31–39; and Vikan 1984, 67–74.

26. On Symeon the Younger, his *vita*, and his shrine see Paul van den Ven, *La vie ancienne de S. Syméon Stylite le Jeune (521–592)*, 2 vols. Subsidia hagiographica 32 (Brussels, 1962, 1970).

27. I wish to thank Dr. Elizabeth Fisher, Georgetown University, for permission to use her photograph.

28. See Vikan 1984, 68.

29. Cited in van den Ven 1962.

30. Cited in van den Ven 1962.

31. For Symeon stamping dies see Vikan 1984, 70, fig. 5.

32. There are, of course, exceptions, such as the famous Joshua Roll, where the Octateuch iconographic tradition, although clearly present, takes second place to the creative impulse for a specific, extraordinary work of art (see Kurt Weitzmann, *The Joshua Roll: A Work of the Macedonian Renaissance*, Studies in Manuscript Illumination 3 [Princeton, 1948]).

33. I owe much of what follows to the insight and scholarship of Susan Ashbrook Harvey, Brown University, and to an article by Peter Brown, "The Saint as Exemplar in Late Antiquity," *Representations* 1, no. 2 (1983), 1–25.

34. See Brown 1983, 5–8, 16–20. This is not to suggest that Christian mimesis was not an ideal in other cultures and at other times. What distinguished Byzantium in the realm of mimesis and icon veneration was the breadth and intensity with which a single belief molded artistic production and popular piety as well as more sophisticated theological debate (Kitzinger 1954).

35. *Saint Basil: The Letters,* trans. and ed. Roy J. Deferrari, Loeb Classical Library (Cambridge, Mass., 1961), 1:15–17 (letter written to Gregory Nazianzenus). Many other texts of various types and dates express the same conviction. The author of the *Martyrdom of Saint Polycarp*, for example, writes that "he was ... a conspicuous martyr, whose testimony, following the Gospel of Christ, everyone desires to imitate" (cited in Herbert Musurillo, *The Acts of the Christian Martyrs* [Oxford, 1972], 17). Similarly the author of the *vita* of Saint Anthony (c. 357) notes in his introduction that he is recording this information "so that you [that is, 'monks abroad'] may also lead yourselves in imitation of him" (see *Athanasius: The Life of Antony and the Letter to Marcellus*, trans. and intro. by Robert C. Gregg, with preface by William A. Clebsch [New York, 1980], 29).

For mimesis in the stational liturgy see John Wilkinson, *Egeria's Travels* (London, 1971), 124; in the behavior of the pilgrim see Gary Vikan, "Pilgrims in Magi's Clothing: The Impact of *Mimesis* on Early Byzantine Pilgrimage Art," in *The Blessings of Pilgrimage* (forthcoming); and in the Byzantine view of history see, for example, Averil Cameron, "Images of Authority: Elites and Icons in Late Sixth-Century Byzantium," *Past and Present* 84 (1979), 17, 21, 33.

36. Kurt Weitzmann, *The Miniatures of the Sacra Parallela, Parisinus graecus 923*, Studies in Manuscript Illumination 8 (Princeton, 1979), 213, fig. 569.

37. Here the Christian "anxious to make himself perfect" becomes the artist trying to replicate the biblical icon through behavior, while for John of Ephesos (c. 507–586) hagiographers are like artists, striving to:

draw, through obscurity, by means of the vile and common pigments of ... words, the pattern of their [saints'] likenesses for posterity ... [so that] ... souls entangled in the vanities of this world ... may be ... eager to imitate them, and to receive their patterns in themselves (*John of Ephesus: Lives of the Eastern Saints*, trans. and ed. Ernest W. Brooks, Patrologia Orientalis 17 [Paris, 1923], 1–2).

In both cases the model—the icon—is the immutable given, and precise replication the goal.

Applying the same basic metaphor but to quite a different end, Asterius of Amaseia (c. 400; Mango 1972, 51) argues against the wearing of image-bearing garments and recommends instead that Christians:

sell those cloths and honor instead the living images of God. . . . bear in your spirit and carry about with you the incorporeal Logos. Do not display the paralytic on your garments, but seek out him who lies in bed.

There is also the related theme of the saint being a mirror, at once the model for and reflection of the imitating Christian. The biographer of Antony (*Athanasius*, 37) noted that the saint: "used to tell himself that from the career of the Great Elijah, as from a mirror, the ascetic must always acquire knowledge of his own life."

38. Brown 1983, 6. For a less-pious sort of mimetic behavior see Franz Tinnefeld, "Zum profanen Mimos in Byzanz nach dem Verdikt des Trullanuoms (641)," *Byzantina* 6 (1974), 331.

Facsimiles, Copies, and Variations: The Relationship to the Model in Medieval and Renaissance European Illuminated Manuscripts

JONATHAN J. G. ALEXANDER
Institute of Fine Arts, New York University

MEDIEVAL ART LOOKED at from one point of view is very much concerned with models, with copying, and with patterns of expectation. Cennino Cennini in his late fourteenth-century treatise of instruction tells the aspiring artist that he must first learn to copy his master's style before he can hope to add anything of his own.[1] The apprentice system of the late Middle Ages institutionalized Cennino's advice, but even in the early Middle Ages, when many of the craftspersons, especially those involved with the manuscript book, were monks or nuns, the framework in which they lived, the Rule of Saint Benedict, prescribed absolute obedience to the abbot. The texts to be copied and the works of art to be made and used in the monastery must have been largely dictated by the abbot and the officials under him, the prior, sacrist, or librarian, for example.

In so far as most of the art made in the Middle Ages and the vast majority of medieval works of art now surviving have a Christian subject matter and were used in a Christian context, they depended on the text of the Christian revelation, the Old and New Testaments, and on the Apocryphal additions to those texts, as well as on the exegetical and devotional literature that developed around them. The images produced, therefore, related to common sources in many cases. They formed, in Saint Gregory's constantly repeated phrase, the Biblia Pauperum, the Bible of the Poor Illiterate. In theory at least they should have been understandable by those who could not read, and, therefore, it was important for them to be easily recognizable so that they could fulfill their didactic purpose or their function in encouraging devotion. Such central Christian subjects as the birth of Christ or the Crucifixion, even though episodes from a narrative context, thus presenting the artist with many different possibilities of representation, are nevertheless shown in such a way that essential clues to the subject matter are never lacking. It is hardly possible to show the cross of the Crucifixion other than centrally, for example. This also applied to devotional images. The icon, which is the most specialized type of devotional image and a sort of holy relic as well, must be copied as exactly as possible.

From another point of view, however, medieval art seems almost incapable of direct copying.[2] Variations of style and content are constantly introduced. In book illumination facsimile copies are so rare that in each case they require special explanations. The majority of images can be considered, therefore, to be both copies and variations.

It should be emphasized that attitudes toward originality and innovation and copying and variation are culturally produced. A twentieth-century discourse stresses the contrary pull between tradition and innovation. In this discourse politics, morality, and economics are all described and perceived as being concerned with the relations of an individual to a wider group but with that individual always somehow primary or inalienable. The individual is defined in terms of difference—difference of character—or, in artistic terms, difference of talent (the genius). The difference must be expressed in doing different or innovative things. Thus we have a medieval art history that has been very concerned precisely with the debts of artists to models on the one hand and with stressing change and innovation made by individuals on the other. For the former, the emphasis on tradition and copying, we think of Aby Warburg and Fritz Saxl and their studies of the transmission of images across cultures or of Erwin Panofsky and Adolf Katzenellenbogen stressing the debt of the image to the preexisting text through which it has to be understood or of Adolph Goldschmidt and Kurt Weitzmann stressing pictorial recensions in manuscripts, which have to be traced to a particular archetype. In contradiction to this work on the tradition there has also been the need to identify certain individual heroes. These are the medieval artists considered responsible for innovations that proved so influential that they were widely copied, such as the anonymous sculptor known as the Headmaster at Chartres west front, about 1145; the architects, both anonymous, responsible for Suger's new choir at Saint-Denis and for the rebuilt Cathedral of Chartres after the fire of 1194; Giotto; or Jean Pucelle, the Parisian book illuminator who died in 1338. Another type of artistic hero has also been singled out in medieval art-historical literature. This is the artist who seems to anticipate much later developments, for example in realism, such as the thirteenth-century Naumburg sculptor, or to have made iconographic innovations like the artist of the Saint Albans psalter, about 1120, who introduces the widely copied motif of the chalice into the scene of the Agony in the Garden.

For each, one could point to some problem. The Headmaster at Chartres works with at least two other masters (the Saint-Denis Master and the Etampes Master), and even if priority of certain inventions could be established between them, which is questionable, it is still important to stress the collaboration of these artists.[3] Similarly with the problems of attribution of the frescoes of the Upper Church at Assisi, Millard Meiss wrote: "Of one thing there can be no doubt whatever: if the Isaac Master is not Giotto then he and not Giotto is the founder of modern painting."[4] One might justifiably ask why Meiss should feel this desperate need to identify one single founder of modern painting.

The proposed dialectic between tradition and innovation in medieval art corresponds to a social conflict noted by Walter Ulmann between what he called the descending and ascending themes of government; that is, authority imposed and coming down from above and resistance or change welling up from below.[5] Change in art certainly took place whether we seek to explain it by economic, social, or artistic causes.

Whatever cause or causes are invoked, however, it seems clear that almost all medieval art worked within the parameters of established power relations rather than against them. Artists may be innovative and original, but they do not often seek to oppose or subvert the existing power relations. They are not revolutionary in social terms. They do not seek to "épater les bourgeois" as a nineteenth-century artist might have or subvert male dominance as a contemporary feminist might. In that sense newness is not a means to revolutionary social criticism.

Criticism, however, is present in medieval art and sometimes in surprising places, as in the margins of medieval service books or misericords in the choirs of cathedral or abbey churches.[6] Some of these representations are of interest as original images for which there appear to be no precedents. Even such obviously critical representations as those of the fox as priest preaching to the gullible geese or of emperors and popes being tortured by devils in Hell do not seek, however, to subvert the notion of a male priesthood supported financially by the hard labor of the peasantry or to destroy empire or papacy as institutions. They only criticize royal or priestly moral or financial corruption in a way any emperor, king, or bishop would have immediately assented to.

This observation extends even to medieval peasant risings in which a return to an experienced or mythical earlier arrangement of rights, rewards, and prices thought to be fairer in a still feudally organized society was at least the stated aim.[7] Michael M. Postan has also commented on the medieval economy where the objective was not unlimited growth aided by the investment of capital but rather a slow increase.[8] For example, on the estates of the bishops of Winchester when a bishop died, any excess stock or equipment beyond that which he had taken over on his appointment would be liquidated, with the effect that the estate capital equipment did not grow.

As for the marginal drolleries, although they may not directly relate to the texts they accompany, they still occur in expensive books made for powerful patrons, and their style is that of the scriptural scenes on the same pages. They can sometimes be literally repeated in different manuscripts and generally fall into certain genres.

Medieval artists, not surprisingly, were content to work within a tradition, therefore. Just as in political or religious writings change or innovation was overtly distrusted or disguised as a return to a better, ancestral way, so medieval writing about art did not praise the new for its own sake or condemn the copy.

Medieval writings on art are overwhelmingly concerned with two matters. The first is the value and qualities of the materials used in particular works of art. The second is the technical virtuosity and skill of the artist. Newness in the sense or originality is rarely mentioned. For example, in looking through the medieval texts on art collected by Otto Lehmann-Brockhaus, although there are numerous references to new work, mainly buildings, they are mostly neutral references to the replacement of something older. In two instances, concerning the building of Lincoln Cathedral and celebrations of the wedding of Henry III of England, the phrases *novitas moderna* (contemporary innovation) and *novitas mirabilis* (admirable innovation) are explicitly used as praise. They are balanced by another instance, concerning practices of worship, where the phrase is *novitas temeraria* (rash innovation).[9]

The artist's own contribution comes from his or her *ingenium* (genius) and at least some twelfth-century writers, Heraclius and the so-called Anonymous of Bern, for example, emphasized that artists must invent or add something to what they had learned from others.[10] For Hugh of Saint Victor, also of the twelfth century, *ingenium* is a force of nature, but he stresses that *exercitatio* (practice) and *disciplina* (discipline; learning) are necessary to enable the student to acquire *scientia* (knowledge) and the artist to make art.[11] In the Renaissance *ingenium* gradually comes to be stressed more and more at the expense of *exercitatio* and *disciplina*.

The emphasis on a contrast and even conflict between tradition and innovation is part of a twentieth-century discourse. It was not of concern to medieval artists or patrons. That there were overriding authorities was taken for granted just as there were traditional skills that should be practiced.

Medieval book illumination is distinguished from other forms of medieval art in its physical and thematic relationships to the text written in a certain way on certain materials for certain uses. These contextual relationships formed a set of constraints on the artist that dictated, for example, the physical surface on which he or she worked (normally parchment) and the space available for picture or decoration (normally left blank by the scribe, implying that someone other than the artist often made important preliminary decisions). The book normally was a codex but could sometimes be a roll or in different formats, for example, circular or heart-shaped as well as, if in the codex form, larger or smaller, squarer or more oblong. Ultimately its size was limited by the size of the animal skin available or by other considerations, such as portability.

Aside from materials and format, subject matter and decoration were linked to the text more or less closely. At all times the text was the major determinant. This also necessarily means that there was always an artistic problem in aesthetic terms of relating two different signifying systems, usually for a single viewer, but exceptionally, as in the case of certain books such as a choir book containing musical texts for singing the office, for a small group of viewers. The one signifying system is the conventional sign system of the script. The other is the iconic sign system of the picture and decoration that operated, admittedly to a greater or lesser degree at various periods, referentially (that is, with some representation of perceived objects in space), whereas the script is read two-dimensionally on the flat surface of the page.

In regard to copying, each text implies an exemplar, going back ultimately to the author's archetype. The task of the scribe was to copy accurately, and it was a task requiring thorough training and painstaking discipline and effort. Generalizations about processes taking place over such long periods for such different purposes and in such different social contexts are risky, but the relationship between the scribe and the illuminator remained a fundamental determinant in all book illumination. Sometimes scribe and artist were one and the same, sometimes the illuminator seems not to have been in any direct contact with the scribe and perhaps even to have been illiterate. Middlemen, the librarian entrepreneurs who bought and sold books, programmatic advisors, or patrons often intervened to express certain demands and perhaps, especially in the late Middle Ages, to dictate subject matter.

Where, as was often the case in the early Middle Ages, scribe and illuminator were one, however, such instruction was often unnecessary.[12] In such contexts a conception of the authority of the text often included the images accompanying it, which were taken over, even if modified, from the exemplar. How this happened in the early

Fig. 1. *Ezra*, c. 700, tempera on vellum. Biblioteca Laurenziana, Florence (Ms. Amiatinus 1, fol. V).

Middle Ages is indicated in an important paper by Hans Swarzenski, in which he speaks of these modifications as "creative copies."[13]

The closer the illustration related to the text, for example with scientific or mathematical diagrams or astronomical and astrological pictures, the more likely the image was to be taken over and accurately retained. There are also many texts in which certain forms of decoration or illustration were so conventional as to be almost invariably present. Examples are evangelist portraits, canon tables, and initials in Gospel books in the early Middle Ages and the cycles of Labors of the Months and zodiac scenes in calendars in later medieval Books of Hours or service books.

I would now like to discuss the terms I will use with relation to copies in manuscript illumination. When we speak of a copy as faithful or slavish, we judge it according to the context, praising it where we require accuracy but in other cases condemning it. The word *copy* is, therefore, relatively neutral.

The word *reproduction* seems to imply a greater intention to accuracy. There is also a sense of something admired or canonical in the object, which causes it to be copied. It would sound odd to speak of a slavish reproduction. We also commonly imply a more numerous or even serial production when we speak of reproduction. That is the sense in Walter Benjamin's well-known essay "The Work of Art in the Age of Mechanical Reproduction."[14] Benjamin argued that what is lacking in the mechanical reproduction is what he called the "aura" of the original work of art. A reproduction is inferior to the object reproduced, the original, therefore.

The term *replica* implies as great or even greater accuracy than a reproduction. For example, a replica is likely to be the same size as the object copied. Replicas are sometimes made in large numbers, in a commercial production. In some types of medieval art, for example thirteenth-century Limoges enamels or the Ubriachi ivories in Venice or fourteenth–fifteenth century Nottingham alabasters, a serial production of replicas was a practice that approaches mass production.[15] Replicas are also sometimes made by artists of their own works for different patrons, as opposed to fakes, which are unauthorized replicas.

Finally there is the word *facsimile*, which suggests a copy as accurate as possible, and the more accurate the more praiseworthy. Facsimiles can exist in great number, but that is not their most important feature, and in the Middle Ages facsimiles are unlikely to have been made in quantity. I use the term *facsimile* to describe historicist copies made of earlier works as opposed to replicas produced at the same time or after only a short interval.

The portrait of Ezra in the Codex Amiatinus, made about 700 at the twin monastery of Wearmouth/Jarrow in Northumberland under Abbot Ceolfrid, is generally accepted as an exact copy of a portrait of Ezra made to preface a Bible written in the Vivarium monastery in southern Italy for Cassiodorus, who died in 597 (fig. 1).[16] Although it has been argued that the Amiatinus portrait was the actual portrait from the Cassiodorus Bible, retained and inserted into the later manuscript, or that it was painted not by an Anglo-Saxon artist but by an Italian visitor to Northumbria, Rupert L. S. Bruce-Mitford's arguments to the contrary that the portrait is integral and Anglo-Saxon are convincing.[17] In that case we have something very unusual in medieval art, a facsimile copy made of an original, which was some 100 to 150 years earlier in date, and we need to ask how this was done

Fig. 2. *Saint Matthew*, c. 700, tempera on vellum. British Library, London (Cotton Nero DIV, fol. 25v).

and why.

Ceolfrid and his community evidently were quite conscious of what they were doing, and the fact that the Bible was made as a present to the Shrine of Saint Peter in Rome is explicable in the context of the struggle between the Roman and Celtic parties in the church in England after the Synod of Whitby in 664. The Celtic bishops had withdrawn, and the Roman party to which Benedict Biscop, founder of Wearmouth/Jarrow, belonged had triumphed at the synod. The imported Mediterranean style of the Ezra portrait corresponds to the imported Roman cult. The gift, which Bede informs us was one of three identical Bibles, two of which were retained but do not survive, affirmed the commitment to Rome and was perceived as being in a style acceptable there, a suitable gift.

The Lindisfarne Gospels, made at about the same time but in a monastery founded from the Irish Columban monastery of Iona in 635, contains a portrait of Saint Matthew (fig. 2) that depends on the same or a similar Cassiodoran model.[18] Here, however, the Mediterranean aesthetic is challenged, in that even if the authority of the model is to some extent accepted in pictorial form and content, its appearance nevertheless is transformed with an alternative space construction and color composition. The Lindisfarne artist, probably Eadfrith, bishop of Lindisfarne, operated by means that can be claimed as much more characteristic of medieval art; that is, he combined motifs from different sources, taking, for example, the trumpeting angel from an illustrated Apocalypse, so that he achieved a whole in which authority and variation are both present. Since the Lindisfarne style is the style encountered in other Irish and Anglo-Saxon artifacts of the period, we can see how the Ezra picture of the Amiatinus must be the result of self-conscious effort. The text and script of the Amiatinus similarly copy Italian models.

It is not certain whether the Codex Amiatinus sought to reproduce the Cassiodoran Bible as a whole in facsimile terms with regard to size or layout, but it is unlikely to have been a complete facsimile, since it has been argued that a second miniature prefacing the New Testament and showing the Majesty is not copied accurately from the earlier Bible but is a pastiche by the Anglo-Saxon artist.

In any medieval attempt at a facsimile copy the script was liable to present a problem, since it had to be legible, and writing styles changed. For example, in England at Canterbury in the early eleventh century the monks of Christ Church decided to make a copy of a Carolingian psalter made at Rheims about 820.[19] That psalter, now known from its present home as the Utrecht Psalter, had a text written in conscious antiquarianism in rustic capitals. When the Canterbury scriptorium copied the illustrations, which they did in part very faithfully, they nevertheless altered the textual recension of the Jerome Latin version of the psalter and the type of script. They wrote the text in a Caroline minuscule to which they were more accustomed. Even the illustrations, although faithful in content and style, introduce a particular modification, the use of colored inks rather than the bister of the model.

The second attempt at a facsimile to be discussed was made for the bishop of Padua, Pietro Donato, in 1436. While present at the Council of Constance he had managed to borrow an ancient manuscript from the Cathedral Chapter Library at Speyer. This contained a text on the military organization of the late Roman Empire, now known as the *Notitia Dignitatum*.[20] It was a compi-

Fig. 3. *Palestine*, 1436, tempera on vellum. Bodleian Library, Oxford (Ms. Canon. Misc. 378, fol. 128v).

Fig. 4. *Palestine*, 1427, tempera on vellum. Fitzwilliam Museum, Cambridge (Ms. 86.72, fol. 1).

lation probably made in the early fifth century and also illustrated then, but the Speyer manuscript, of which only a single unillustrated leaf now survives, was a Carolingian copy of the late ninth or early tenth century. The early fifth-century illustrations, therefore, had already gone through at least one process of being copied. The artist employed by Donato can be identified by style criticism as Peronet Lamy, a French illuminator whose documented works were made for Amadeus of Savoy. Lamy attempted to provide the bishop with a facsimile copy but distorted his copy by making involuntary errors where his own stylistic idiom took over or making his own insertions where his exemplar was damaged or defective. A page showing coins was probably damaged, so he inserted accurate representations of coins of Tiberius, Nero, and Domitian, which were no doubt provided for him from the bishop's collection, even though they are unsuited to the context. A slightly earlier copy of the *Notitia* of which only a fragment survives was probably made for Cardinal Giordano Orsini, who was papal legate in Germany in 1426. The fragment is dated 1427. Where comparisons can be made, the Orsini copy is less accurate, introducing such impossibilities as the arms of the Anjou of Naples into the miniature of Palestine (figs. 3–4).

The wider context into which both copies of the *Notitia* must be set is the antiquarian interests of humanist scholars. The *Notitia* was of importance not only for its text but because its illustrations provided evidence for the reconstruction of the classical past. Even so, it remained extremely difficult for the artist to provide an accurate facsimile copy, and it was not until the mid-sixteenth century that this was done using tracings of the Speyer manuscript (fig. 5). It is interesting that such historicizing facsimiles were not made apparently in the Gothic period. They are a feature of the classical revivals, the so-called Northumbrian and Carolingian Renaissances as well as of the Italian Renaissance.[21]

Fig. 5. *Palestine*, mid-sixteenth century, tempera on vellum. Bayerisches Nationalmuseum, Munich (Clm 10291, fol. 198v).

As it happens a second copy of the *Notitia* survives also made by Lamy and this, now in Paris, is no doubt a replica for a different patron. Other examples of replicas occur in the most numerous class of all fifteenth-century illuminated manuscripts, Books of Hours. An example is a pair of miniatures of the Virgin on the Crescent Moon (figs. 6–7) attributed to an artist from the northern Netherlands known as the Master of Nicolas Brouwer. The miniatures are found in two early fifteenth-century Books of Hours, one now in Liverpool, the other formerly at Upholland College, Lancashire.[22] Here and in many other examples, the miniatures are inserted on single leaves that are not integral to the structure of the book. A document of 1426 forbids the importation into Bruges of single-leaf miniatures, and no doubt these leaves are the sort that the Bruges Guild was trying to keep out in order to retain a monopoly for its members. James Douglas Farquhar has drawn attention to other guild regu-

Fig. 6. *Virgin on the Crescent Moon*, second quarter fifteenth century, tempera on vellum. Merseyside County Museum, Liverpool (Mayer 12009, p. 16).

Fig. 7. *Virgin on the Crescent Moon*, second quarter fifteenth century, tempera on vellum. Formerly Upholland College, Lancashire (fol. 20v).

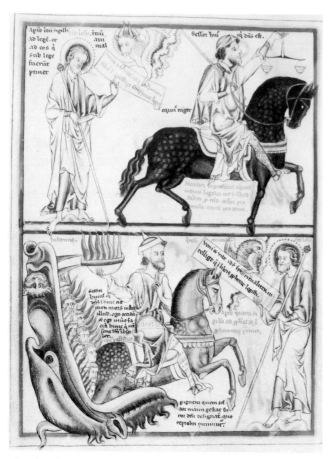

Fig. 8. *The Horses of the Apocalypse*, mid-thirteenth century, tempera on vellum. Bodleian Library, Oxford (Ms. Auct. D4.17, fol. 4v).

Fig. 9. *The Horses of the Apocalypse*, mid-thirteenth century, tempera on vellum. Pierpont Morgan Library, New York (M524, fol. 2v).

lations, which state that illuminators must stamp their products with a personal mark.[23] The implication is that only miniatures so stamped are legal. Farquhar has now discovered a number of such stamps not noticed before. In these two miniatures the stamps are visible in the right-hand border. Here then is a system of multiple copies for a mass market. They were easily transportable, and maybe the patron could go to a bookshop and actually choose from stock the miniatures that he or she would like inserted in a particular manuscript. The same kind of replication took place in Books of Hours made in the more prolific Paris workshops of the time, among them the shop of the Boucicaut Master.[24] This replication responds to an economic need for illuminated texts to be more quickly and cheaply produced, and this need led at about the same time to the replication of images by printing techniques, that is, by woodcuts and engravings.[25]

Another form of replica is of whole manuscripts. Sev-

eral thirteenth-century Apocalypses and Bestiaries made in England form pairs, for example, the Apocalypses in New York and Oxford (figs. 8–9).[26] These are texts that were quite likely to be owned by the laity, and it may be that patrons demanded a replica of a book that they had seen and admired. There are also a number of examples of particular texts being made in two or even multiple copies. Thus the abbey at Fulda in the ninth century, over a period of about thirty years, produced copies of the illustrated text, "de laude sanctae crucis," by its abbot Rhabanus Maurus that were then sent as presents to Alcuin at Tours and the pope in Rome, for example.[27] In the late Middle Ages such multiple illustrated copies were also quite frequently made. Examples are the texts urging a new crusade, written by Marino Sanudo and Paolino Veneto in the early fourteenth century and by Philippe de Mézières in the late fourteenth century.[28] These are not historicizing copies of earlier manuscripts, aiming to be facsimiles, but were produced serially at the same time.

In the late Middle Ages another type of copying is found, the copying of compositions or motifs that have been created by panel or mural painters. A well-known early example is the copying about 1325 by Pucelle in the Hours of Jeanne D'Evreux of compositions from the Maestà of Duccio painted about fifteen years earlier.[29] Pucelle must have visited Siena and have noted these compositions in a model book. Although he made certan alterations, these may be called reproductions, since they exemplify the sense of admiration referred to earlier. Many other examples could be noted in Italy and the Netherlands. Compositions by Jan van Eyck or Hugo van der Goes were reproduced in manuscripts, and David Alan Brown has drawn attention to a borrowing by the Milanese illuminator Antonio da Monza from the London version of Leonardo daVinci's *Virgin of the Rocks*.[30]

Even more widespread was the use of prints by illuminators for motifs or whole compositions. It is difficult to establish whether the illuminator made his copy as an openly acknowledged act of homage, one sanctioned or perhaps required by the patron, or whether the copy was a matter of using the print to enrich an illuminator's repertoire as the model book was used to do. I am uncertain whether the Dutch illuminator of very moderate talent who copied an Annunciation composition of Martin Schongauer (figs. 10–11) would have regarded himself as found out if challenged as to his source.[31] Albrecht Dürer's engravings at least must have been so well known that the very numerous copies of them both in northern European and in Italian manuscripts must always have been recognized as reproductions.

In conclusion I wish to discuss the problem of copies in which the designer selected only what was thought to have been the significant identifying feature of the orig-

Fig. 10. *The Annunciation*, late fifteenth century, tempera on vellum. Merseyside County Museum, Liverpool (Mayer 12023, p. 26).

Fig. 11. Martin Schongauer, *The Annunciation*, before 1484, engraving. National Gallery of Art, Washington, Rosenwald Collection (1952.8.294).

Fig. 13. *Saint Matthew*, mid-ninth century, tempera on vellum. Staatsbibliothek, Berlin (Ms. theol. lat. 20733, fol. 22v).

Fig. 12. *Saint Luke*, late ninth century, tempera on vellum. Walters Art Gallery, Baltimore (W1, fol. 77v).

inal. Very many medieval copies would seem to fall into this category. In attempting to determine what constitutes the similarity that is the significant identifying feature, we reach a very problematic area. An example is the portrait of Saint Luke from a late ninth-century Breton Gospel Book (fig. 12).[32] The image was derived directly or indirectly from a Carolingian evangelist portrait made at Tours some fifty years earlier, which must have looked something like the Saint Matthew in the Gospels now in Berlin (fig. 13). The seated pose with the pen held in the left hand and book held on the lap can be argued to be similar. But in comparing these two representations the degree to which they seem similar now or were thought similar by artist or patron in the ninth century becomes highly problematic.

The problems of describing similarity are forcefully stated by Nelson Goodman.[33] He points out that "similarity . . . tends to require for its explanation just what it purports to explain." The similarities we think we see and use as empirical evidence for classification may depend on previously established modes of classification. He gives as one of his examples baggage at an airport check-in station. "The spectator may notice shape, size, color, material and even make of luggage; the pilot is more concerned with weight, and the passenger with destination and ownership. Which pieces of luggage are more alike than others depends not only on what properties they share, but upon who makes the comparison, and when."

In the Breton Saint Luke one might argue that the

artist retained what was thought of as the essential feature of the Carolingian model, the outline of the figure, but through lack of skill was unable to copy the modeling and foreshortening of the classicizing exemplar. The Breton artist would have thought his copy adequate, as might a child, because it retained the essential components, albeit in a linear convention.

Alternatively the Breton artist may have been conscious not only of the similarities expressed in the outline but also of the differences expressed in the lack of modeling. It could be argued, therefore, that he wished consciously to signal his allegiance to his own native, Celtic aesthetic, which valued qualities of outline and pattern, and at the same time to emphasize his opposition to the Carolingian classicizing aesthetic as an alien import. The political situation of the period can be invoked in support of such an interpretation. Charles the Bald, the Frankish emperor, was attempting to establish political domination over Brittany. Salomon, the Breton ruler, was in turn trying to play his two, equally dangerous enemies, the Franks and the Vikings, off against each other, allying himself sometimes with one, sometimes with the other. There was also a parallel attempt at domination by the Frankish Church, since the archbishopric of Tours was trying to subjugate the Breton bishoprics to its control. The Breton evangelist seems a similar compromise, taking something from the Frankish model but also resisting it in aesthetic terms. This is an interpretation that rests on that additional historical evidence and not on any empirical measurement of similarity or dissimilarity of the Frankish and Breton miniatures.[34] The similarity described depends as Goodman states on "who makes the comparison, and when."[35]

NOTES

1. Cennino d'Andrea Cennini, *Il libro dell' arte: The Craftsman's Handbook*, ed. D. V. Thompson, 2 vols. (Oxford, 1932–1933). See also Bruce Cole, *The Renaissance Artist at Work: From Pisano to Titian* (New York, 1983), 30.
2. As Professor Carl Nordenfalk remarked in discussion after the session "Visual Innovation in Late Medieval Manuscript Illumination," Seventy-third College Art Association Meeting, Los Angeles, February 1985.
3. Willibald Sauerländer, *Gothic Sculpture in France, 1140–1270* (London, 1972), 383–386.
4. Millard Meiss, *Giotto and Assisi* (New York, 1960), 25.
5. Walter Ulmann, *The Individual and Society in the Middle Ages* (Baltimore, 1966; London, 1967).
6. Lilian M. C. Randall, *Images in the Margins of Gothic Manuscripts*, California Studies in the History of Art 4 (Berkeley and Los Angeles, 1966); G. L. Remnant, *A Catalogue of Misericords in Great Britain* (Oxford, 1969). An important paper by Michael Camille, "Labouring for the Lord: The Ploughman and the Social Order in the Luttrell Psalter," *Art History* 10 (1987), 423–454, discusses the ideological nature of the representations in the margins of the Luttrell Psalter.
7. Rodney Hilton, *Bond Men Made Free: Medieval Peasant Movements and the English Rising of 1381* (London and New York, 1975).
8. Michael M. Postan, *Medieval Economy and Society: Economic History of Britain, 1100–1500* (Harmondsworth, 1975).
9. Otto Lehmann-Brockhaus, *Lateinische Schriftquellen zur Kunst in England, Wales, und Schottland vom Jahre 901 bis zum Jahre 1307*, 5 vols. (Munich, 1955), 2: nos. 2367, 2693, and 3: no. 5421.
10. Edgar de Bruyne, *Etudes d'esthétique médiévale* (Bruges, 1946), 1:304–305. I wish to thank Donald Garfield for this reference.
11. De Bruyne 1946, 2:384–385 and 414 (Heraclius). For another useful collection of texts see Rosario Assunto, *Die Theorie des Schönen im Mittelalter* (Cologne, 1963). For Filippo Villani's writing on Giotto's *ingenium* see Julius von Schlosser, *Quellenbuch zur Kunstgeschichte des abendländischen Mittelalters* (1896; New York, 1976), 370–371. For the coupling of *ars* and *ingenium* in Villani and elsewhere see M. Baxandall, *Giotto and the Orators: Humanist Observers of Painting in Italy and the Discovery of Pictorial Composition, 1350–1450* (Oxford, 1971), 15–16, 74. See also Walter Cahn, *Masterpieces: Chapters on the History of an Idea* (Princeton, 1979); Charles R. Dodwell, *Anglo-Saxon Art: A New Perspective* (Manchester, 1982).
12. Jonathan J. G. Alexander, "Scribes as Artists," in *Medieval Scribes, Manuscripts, and Libraries: Essays Presented to N. R. Ker*, ed. Malcolm B. Parkes and Andrew G. Watson (London, 1978), 87–116.
13. Hans Swarzenski, "The Role of Copies in the Formation of the Styles of the Eleventh Century," in *Romanesque and Gothic Art: Studies in Western Art. Acts of the Twentieth International Congress of the History of Art*, ed. Millard Meiss et al. (Princeton, 1963), 1:7–18.
14. Walter Benjamin, "The Work of Art in the Age of Mechanical Reproduction (1936)," in *Illuminations*, trans. Harry Zohn, ed. Hannah Arendt (London, 1973).
15. Richard C. Trexler, "The Magi Enter Florence: The Ubriachi of Florence and Venice," *Studies in Medieval and Renaissance History* 1 (1978), 129–213.
16. Jonathan J. G. Alexander, *Insular Manuscripts, Sixth–Ninth Century* Survey of Manuscripts Illuminated in the British Isles 1 (London, 1978), no. 7.
17. Rupert L. S. Bruce-Mitford, "The Art of the *Codex Amiatinus*," *Journal of the Royal Archaeological Association* 32 (1969), 1–25. That the painting is, on the contrary, by a visiting foreign artist is argued by Per Jonas Nordhagen, "An Italo-Byzantine Painter at the Scriptorium of Coelfrith," in *Studia romana in honorem Petri Krarup septuagenarii* (Odense, 1976), 138–145. See also Per Jonas Nordhagen, *The Codex Amiatinus and the Byzantine Element in the Northumbrian Renaissance* (Jarrow Lecture), 1977.
18. Alexander 1978, n. 16, no. 9.
19. Elżbieta Temple, *Anglo-Saxon Manuscripts, 900–1066*, Survey of Manuscripts Illuminated in the British Isles 2 (London, 1976), no. 64, Janet M. Backhouse, "The Making of the Harley Psalter," *British Library Journal* 10 (1984), 97–113.
20. Jonathan J. G. Alexander, "The Illustrated Manuscripts of the *Notitia Dignitatum*," in *Aspects of the Notitia Dignitatum*, ed. Roger Goodburn and P. Bartholomew, British Archaeological Reports (Oxford, 1976), 11–25.
21. For Carolingian facsimiles see Charles R. Dodwell, *Painting in Europe, 800–1200* (Harmondsworth, 1971), 23.
22. Jonathan J. G. Alexander et al., *Medieval and Early Renaissance Treasures in the North-West* [exh. cat.], Whitworth Art Gallery] (Manchester, 1976), nos. 34–35. The Upholland Hours was sold at Christie's, London, *Early Printed Books and Manuscripts*, 2 December 1987, lot 36.
23. James Douglas Farquhar, "Identity in an Anonymous Age: Bruges Manuscript Illuminators and Their Signs," *Viator* 11 (1980): 371–384.

For another example see Sotheby's sale, *Western Manuscripts and Miniatures*, 23 June 1987, lot 121.

24.   Millard Meiss, with the assistance of Kathleen Morand and Edith W. Kirsch, *French Painting in the Time of Jean de Berry: The Boucicaut Master* (London, 1968).

25.   William M. Ivins, Jr., *Prints and Visual Communications* (London, 1953). Ivins perhaps overexaggerates the extent to which these printing techniques came as a sudden and revolutionary change.

26.   Nigel J. Morgan, *Early Gothic Manuscripts*, Survey of Manuscripts Illuminated in the British Isles 4, pt. 1 (London, 1982), nos. 17, 19 (Aberdeen and Ashmole Bestiaries), and pt. 2 (London, 1988), nos. 122, 131 (Morgan Library and Bodleian Apocalypses), and nos. 153–154 (Douce and Paris Apocalypses). For the Bestiaries see Xénia Muratova, "Bestiaires: An Aspect of Medieval Patronage," *Art and Patronage in English Romanesque*, Society of Antiquaries of London, Occasional Papers, n.s. 8, ed. Sarah Macready and F. Hugh Thompson (London, 1984), 118–144. Also Xénia Muratova, "Les manuscrits-frères: Un aspect particulier de la production des bestiaires enluminés en Angleterre à la fin du XIIᵉ siècle et au début du XIIIᵉ siècle," *Artistes, artisans, et production artistique au Moyen-Age. Colloque internationale, Rennes, 1983*, ed. Xavier Barral y Altet, vol. 3 (Paris, forthcoming).

27.   Hans-Georg Mueller, *Rhabanus Maurus: De Laudibus sanctae crucis*, Beiheft zum Mittellateinischen Jahrbuch (Düsseldorf, 1973).

28.   For Marino Sanudo and Paolino Veneto see Bernard Degenhart and Annegritt Schmitt, *Corpus der Italienischen Zeichnungen, 1300–1450, Part II, 1: Venedig* (Berlin, 1980), nos. 636–638. For Philippe de Mézières see Otto Pächt and Jonathan J. G. Alexander, *Illuminated Manuscripts in the Bodleian Library, Oxford, 1: German, Dutch, Flemish, French, and Spanish Schools* (Oxford, 1966), no. 613.

29.   Kathleen Morand, *Jean Pucelle* (Oxford, 1962), 6–8, 14.

30.   David Alan Brown, "The London *Madonna of the Rocks* in the Light of Two Milanese Adaptations," in *Collaboration in Italian Renaissance Art*, ed. Wendy S. Sheard and John T. Paoletti (New Haven and London, 1978), 167–177. See also Jonathan J. G. Alexander, "Constraints on Pictorial Invention in Renaissance Illumination: The Role of Copying North and South of the Alps in the Fifteenth and Early Sixteenth Centuries," *Miniatura* 1 (1988), 123–135.

31.   Alexander 1976, n. 22, no. 40.

32.   Francis Wormald, *An Early Breton Gospel Book*, ed. with "A Note on the Breton Gospel Books" by Jonathan J. G. Alexander (Roxburghe Club, 1977).

33.   Nelson Goodman, "Seven Strictures on Similarity," in *Problems and Projects* (Indianapolis, 1972), 437–446, reprinted in *Modernism, Criticism, Realism*, ed. Charles Harrison and Fred Orton (London and New York, 1984), 85–92.

34.   Jonathan J. G. Alexander, "La resistance à la domination culturelle Carolingienne dans l'art Breton du IXᵉ siècle. Témognage de l'enluminure des manuscrits," *Landévennec et le monachisme breton dans le Haut Moyen Age. Colloque scientifique du quinzième centenaire, 25–27 April 1985*, ed. Marc Simon (1986).

35.   This paper was submitted for publication in June 1985. Although I have added a few references to publications appearing since then, the paper has been left substantially in its original form.

Paradigmatic Social Function in Anglican Church Architecture of the Fifteen Colonies

ALAN GOWANS

THIS PAPER addresses itself to two different sorts of architectural copying and thereby, by extension, to the general problem of copying, influences, and originality in architecture. One initial observation: if by copying we mean something like exact replication, then copying in architecture is a priori impossible, since no two buildings can ever be exactly alike. To speak of architectural replication in the sense of photographic or print replication is by definition an exercise in futility—all buildings are originals and none is a copy. But there are other kinds of copying in architecture besides imitation of forms. There can be copyings of those architectural meanings whereby all architecture above the utilitarian level does something in and for the society that commissioned it and bore its expense—that is, copyings of social function. What follow are two examples of such copyings, in the first case to convey a general idea, in the second to convey a specific idea. (The first instance of copyings, from King Carter's Church in Lancaster County, Virginia, may well have involved a specific social function also, that is, copying of the social function of a family mausoleum/memorial, in addition to a general expression of the wealth and power to which a colonial family had risen; but that cannot be proved, as will be shown.)

By the 1770s, the decade of the American Revolution, three recognizably distinct subtypes of Anglican church architecture had developed in the colonies (fig. 1–3). There was the traditional and pan-European sort of parish church descending from Romanesque times, as much at home in Sweden or Germany or France as in England, represented by Saint Luke's in Smithfield, Virginia, about 1683, basically a rectangle with a frontal tower attached

Fig. 1. Saint Luke's, Smithfield, Virginia, c. 1683. Medieval survival.

Fig. 2. Saint Michael's, Charleston, South Carolina, 1752. The Saint Martin-in-the-Fields paradigm.

and perceptible as a separate element (a feature probably deriving from ancient traditions of a separate campanile), its ornament stylistically updated as decades went by but surviving into the 1770s with basic elements unchanged.[1] Second, there was a type recognizably derived from the Wren/Gibbs style of London parish churches, to be found in nearly all the colonial capitals. Its most distinctive features were incorporation of the tower within the body of the church to provide space for a columnar portico and interior galleries manifested on the exterior by two superimposed rows of windows. Third, there was a subtype represented epitomatically by Christ Church in Lancaster County, Virginia, whose arms were more or less equal so that the plan approximates a Greek cross (fig. 4); no towers or evidence of planning for towers can be detected; galleries are only at the ends of the arms or there are none; elaborate brick moldings appear around doors and windows. Its more common name is King Carter's Church, and with it we shall begin.

The date for completion of King Carter's Church is generally given as 1732, but it may have been as early as 1728 or 1722[2] or as late as 1735–1736.[3] It is also generally supposed that, aside from restoration of the churchyard wall and cleaning of interior walls in 1965–1966, which may have altered its appearance somewhat (fig. 5), King Carter's Church is in pristine condition,

Fig. 3. Christ Church (King Carter's Church), Lancaster County, Virginia, 1722–1736(?). The Virginia planters' church paradigm. Photo before restoration, 1963.

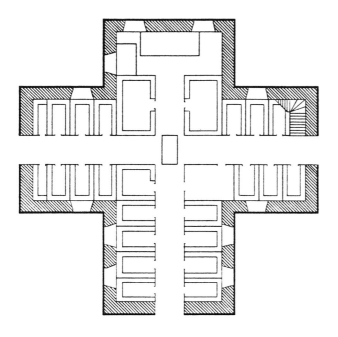

Fig. 4. Ground plan of King Carter's Church drawn by F. D. Nichols, F.A.I.A.

Below: Fig. 5. King Carter's Church after the 1960s restoration. Photo after restoration, 1983.

especially on the interior,[4] but this view too may need some modification (see further, below).

King Carter's Church is not the only church in this distinctive form. In the thirty years after its completion perhaps a dozen or more churches were built in recognizably similar forms throughout the Virginia plantation country. The most notable ones, perhaps, were (and one has to say "were," because so many now are ruinous or altered or gone) Saint Mary's Whitechapel,[5] Christ Church, Lancaster's sister parish; Vauter's and North Farnham, on opposite sides of the Rappahannock,[6] and Abingdon (figs. 6–10).[7] All are cruciform and towerless, with central groin vault simulating a dome, brickwork and proportions in descending degrees of excellence from Christ Church (figs. 11–14), they and some others[8] seem to constitute something like a "family," unique in North American architecture.

What is the family connection? Was it merely visual? Did eighteenth-century Anglican church builders in other parishes copy the forms of King Carter's Church solely for their aesthetic niceties and associations with aristocratic elegance—for the same sort of modern reasons, that is to say, that King Carter's Church was the model for the Methodist church built in nearby Kilmarnock in 1963 (fig. 15)?[9] (By "modern reasons," I mean, of course, modern popular/commercial, not avant-garde. Avant-

Above: Fig. 6. Saint Mary's, Whitechapel, Virginia, 1739–1741(?). Present south end; the once-elaborate brickwork of the door has been rebuilt in recent years. Photo, 1983.

Below: Fig. 7. Saint Mary's. Present east end; the patched-up brickwork indicates where the east wing with chancel once stood. Photo, 1983.

garde modernism by definition copies nothing, it only builds in the nature of the materials, expressing structure and so forth. Modern popular/commercial architecture carries on older traditions of unashamedly copying some form rendered desirable to copy by visual associations or appeal or symbolism.) If only aesthetics were involved, how does one account for the fact that this subtype appeared only in the Virginia plantation country? Did this form have some special significance for or associations with the great planter class, the landed gentry who dom-

inated the social and political scene in eighteenth-century Virginia?

In *King Carter's Church* I have argued that it did and presented in detail the case for King Carter's Church being not a parish church in the ordinary sense of the word but initially a memorial church/mausoleum to the Carter family generally and to King Carter in particular, which accounts for its distinctive form. Central-type churches or chapels functioning as memorials and mausolea for "great families," and especially "new great fam-

ilies," appeared in great numbers throughout Europe from the sixteenth century on,[10] but especially toward the end of the seventeenth and in the early eighteenth centuries, as a result of upheavals and realignments in social structure occasioned by the civil wars of religion that raged all over the Continent. Especially in England, two revolutions and a civil war raised many families from obscurity to prominence thanks to astute choosing of sides in perilous times.

Family memorial/mausolea church/chapels might be created in several ways during this period. One was to add a family chapel/mausoleum to an existing church so as to give that building an additional social function. Probably the most famous example is the chapel/mausoleum built for the "Catholic Kings" in the early sixteenth century adjacent to the Cathedral of Granada in Spain; others are the two Medici chapels attached to San Lorenzo in Florence and the Chapelle des Valois proposed for Saint-Denis.[11] Archetypal examples are the chapel/mausoleum built by and for Carl Gustav Wrangel at Skokloster in Uppland, on plans by Nicolas Tessin the Younger in the 1660s (Tessin also completed reworking

Fig. 9. North Farnham Church, Westmoreland County, Virginia. Present west front and south wing. Photo, 1964.

Fig. 10. Abingdon Church, near Ordinary, Virginia. West front and north wing. Photo, 1964.

plans for Wrangel's mansion originally drawn by Kaspar Vogel), and his father's Karlinska mausoleum/chapel attached to Stockholm's Riddarsholm Church in 1671.[12] Signal component elements here are a central-type configuration (usually a dome inside indicated by a cupola outside), an effigy of the deceased usually set on a sarcophagus, emblems of worldly (as distinct from saintly) success, and a vault with coffins below.

A second way was to make the family chapel/mausoleum an integral part of an existing church fabric. Such was the Henry VII chapel erected to commemorate the Tudor family's rise to royalty, at the east end of Westminster Abbey, intended in some sense (unsuccessfully) to make the abbey into a witness to Tudor legitimacy.[13] Only in a smaller church could such a method succeed—an outstanding example is the parish kirk of Durisdeer in Dumfriesshire, a traditional Scottish T-kirk made into a memorial/mausoleum to the Queensberry family by the addition of a north "aisle" in the 1710s.[14] The church remained a parish church, but everyone attending services was constantly aware of the Queensberry family and its preeminence in the community by a highly visible entrance to the mausoleum behind the minister's pulpit.

A third way was to create a family memorial chapel/mausoleum first and let parish church functions, if any, fit into it later. Here the preeminent example is the Fox family chapel/mausoleum at Farley in Wiltshire, built in the 1690s, the functions of a parish church being an obvious afterthought (apse and tower were added only about 1875) (fig. 16). A fourth alternative, the building of a mausoleum proper separate from any church al-

together, became common in the mid-eighteenth century and, therefore, too late for relevancy to our discussion here.[15]

King Carter's Church had a similar function to chapel/mausolea like Durisdeer and Farley because its social functions were similar: they were symbols of the success of new families. The Queensberry memorial wing con-

Fig. 11. King Carter's Church. West front. Photo, 1983.

Fig. 12. Vauter's Church. West front. Photo, 1983.

tract specifies that the bones of earlier generations of Douglases should be collected and put into that wing along with the sarcophagi of its builders, apexes of the family success.

Like Carter's, Farley was a family memorial church, with one wing set aside for family tombs—opposite the principal entrance, just as in Christ Church; and it too commemorates the founding of a new Family, for it was out of this Wiltshire obscurity that Stephen Fox rose to his high offices under successive rulers from Charles II to Anne, preparing the way for his son Henry's ministeries under George III, a peerage in 1762, and the even more notable career of his grandson Charles James Fox.[16]

(The parallel with subsequent generations of Carters is almost too obvious to mention.)

To the argument here it is irrelevant who, if anyone specific, was the architect;[17] the relevant question is, can the similarities of form between King Carter's Church and its "family" in the Virginia plantation country be explained in the same way as the similarities between King Carter's Church and family memorial/chapels/mausolea like Durisdeer and Farley? Did churches like Saint Mary's Whitechapel, Vauter's, North Farnham, Abingdon, and the rest derive their cruciform plans comparably from a specific social function—that is, were they too primarily built as family memorials/mausolea by the great plantation families in their respective parishes? Or

were they primarily parish churches, which took cruciform shape (instead of the more orthodox Latin cross or plain rectangular single nave) because the general associations of that shape with the rise of new landed families (established in Britain by families like Queensberry and Fox, transplanted to Virginia by Carter) made it attractive to other aspiring families (whether or not those families, like Carter, actually made substantial contributions to funding the church building or were just influential vestry members who decided on questions of plan and shape)?

Of some obvious, although not crucial, importance to this question is speculation as to whether the Carter sarcophagi might have been located within Christ Church, in which case this actually was a mausoleum in addition to being a family memorial and parish church. Was King Carter buried there, along with his wives? Carter's will in successive revisions[18] consistently spelled out that his bequest to build the church held only "provided always the chancel be preserved as a burial place for my family as the precent chancel is."[19] This has commonly been interpreted to mean that "Robert Carter offered to build the new church at his own expense if the identical site were retained and the graves of his family preserved at the chancel as in the earlier church."[20]

The graves of King Carter's father John and John's four wives were thus left undisturbed in the chancel of the new church, it being built around them, but the graves of King Carter and *his* two wives are located out-

side, under the sarcophagi imported from England to mark them, in their present position against the outer wall of the altar wing (fig. 17). How can such an interpretation be justified, contradictory as it is both to what the will specifies many times and also to contemporary usage, where chapels built by families with family funds as memorials always and invariably had the donors buried within? Myth has it that King Carter's Church was an absolutely pristine monument, without changes ever having been made in the interior arrangements (or anywhere else)—and in the present arrangement there is no space for the three sarcophagi. They *must*, therefore, have stood outside; but is that myth infallible?

Certainly the sarcophagi as they now stand are not in pristine condition. All have been smashed to pieces and reassembled at least once, perhaps several times. Bishop William Meade in 1837 noted that the wives' sarcophagi "appear to have been riven by lightning and are sepa-

Fig. 15. Methodist Church, Kilmarnock, Virginia, 1963. Photo, 1981.

Fig. 16. Fox Memorial Chapel and Farley Parish Church, Wiltshire, England, 1690s. North side; bricked-up window indicates the Fox burial wing. Photo, 1984.

rating and falling to pieces."[21] "Lightning" was "the belief and testimony of the neighbours"; but it seems odd that lightning should strike, not only twice in the same place but on the two lower slabs rather than the higher one, for the bishop assured his readers that "the tomb of the husband is entire" (it is to be assumed, therefore, that the extensive damage now evident must all have been suffered at some time later in the nineteenth century; William G. Stannard has suggested as much).[22] Further, when Bishop Meade wrote that "at the east end of the house [church], within a neat enclosure, recently put up, are to be seen the tombs," it has always been assumed that "recently" refers to the enclosure, not the tombs themselves. Yet I myself have been told, also by "neighbours," that the three sarcophagi were assembled in their present position only in the early 1920s.

Another scenario is at least possible in these circumstances. Recalling that revolutionaries characteristically smash symbols or visual emblems of the establishment being challenged—witness Cluny and Saint-Denis and Notre-Dame, Paris, in the French Revolution, witness Puritans smashing church windows, witness George III's statue on the battery in New York being demolished and so on and on; recalling that King Carter would have been, and we know was, envied and hated by many,[23] it is not beyond probability to suppose that the sarcophagi were originally smashed where they stood in the chancel, as an act of defiance; that the pieces were then dragged outdoors and flung about, like the royal sarcophagi in

Saint-Denis or Lord Botetourt's statue at Williamsburg; that they then lay about during the long decades when the church stood vacant and abandoned; that during the

Fig. 17. King Carter's Church. East wing, showing the Carter sarcophagi in their present location near the outer wall of the chancel.

first revival period, around 1830, the pieces were assembled outside the church, Carter's sarcophagi being neatly repaired, the others less so; and that they were put back together again after the depradations Stannard talks about? This is at least as plausible a hypothesis as the present one. What stands in its way is the present interior arrangement, which allows no place for the sarcophagi in the chancel. But have the pews and pulpit always stood exactly where they are now? That this furniture could be dismantled is known from its having been taken down and reassembled for termite proofing in the 1930s.[24] What happened to church interiors in the years between the Revolution and the revival of the 1830s is also known, in sad detail; for example, at North Farnham, when the church was

> said by the neighbours not to have been used for the last thirty or forty years. Thus deserted as a house of God, it became a prey to any and every spoiler. An extensive brick wall which surrounded the church and guarded the graves of the dead was torn down and used for hearths, chimneys, and other purposes, all the country round. The interior of the house soon sunk into decay and was carried piecemeal away.[25]

Why then should King Carter's Church, vacant and abandoned for the same period of time, have been preserved intact? Because, I propose, that some who cared about the church in general and church buildings in particular dismantled the interior to save it from the fate of other churches, storing it somewhere; that around 1830 it was put back, but not put back exactly the same way, by people who in the interval had forgotten the original arrangement or who did not care to reproduce it. As Rawlings wrote very neatly, "Christ Church has been repaired more than is readily apparent."[26]

The above digression provides a starting point for considering why King Carter's Church was so often imitated in the Virginia plantation country. It is at least possible to speculate that some if not all of that "family" similarly functioned as memorial churches, perhaps even mausolea, for prominent members of leading families. By no means were all burials made in plantation cemeteries; all these churches had churchyards around them. Did they have burials inside also? For example, when Saint Mary's Whitechapel was made into a cruciform shape by the additions of 1741 were those new wings intended in some sense, or entirely, as family memorials? It is known, for example, that "the existing gallery in the south end was built at private expense by members of the Ball family following their request for permission made in May 1741. Two other private galleries were built, one over the 'North door' and one in the west end."[27] Likewise, at Abingdon, the Thruston and Lewis families are said to have had the south gallery set aside for themselves, the Burwell and Page families the north.[28] Might such donors likewise have had burial places in the church? At the very least it is plain that leading families in these churches used the churchyard for burials rather than their own plantation cemeteries. To prove such a hypothesis is, however, quite beyond the realm of practicality. It demands evidence that has not been, and in the nature of things never can be, found. Revolution and Civil War have destroyed the bulk of documentation once available. One would have to excavate churchyards to ascertain whether graves lay beneath now demolished chancels and if they could be found, to whom they belonged. What records survive would need to be fine-tooth combed for chance references. This is out of the question.

The form of these churches can fortunately be explained without having to prove that burials took place within them. The cruciform shape may have been borrowed from memorial churches in Britain and simply used for its distinctiveness as a symbol of a successful

Fig. 18. Saint Martin-in-the-Fields, London, 1721–1726. Facade and south side (from Gibbs 1728).

Fig. 19. Saint Martin-in-the-Fields. Nave, looking to altar (from Gibbs 1728).

new family founding. That burials cannot be proved to have taken place in them does not necessitate any swing to an opposite extreme, which explains similarities among these churches as nothing more than products of aesthetic taste among some builders in that time and place. It is quite reasonable to suppose that these churches were seen as witnesses, if not memorials/mausolea, to the greatness, achievement, and aspiration of leading families; that King Carter's Church as built was understood as a visual metaphor of family success, at the very least; and that its cruciform, towerless distinctiveness was consciously understood as an image of the standards and values of the plantation society of eighteenth-century Virginia, a self-made class whose stability and perpetuation needed visual metaphorization all the more because of the demographic chaos that preceded it. Families like Carter and Ball, Page and Lewis, and the rest could not claim aristocratic status by ancestral descent, any more than could their Old World contemporaries like Queensberry of Drumlanrig, Fox of Farley, or Wrangel of Skokloster—all were survivors of social upheavals (in the one case by wars and revolutions, in the other by transatlantic migrations and unexpectedly novel conditions of life). They did indeed render themselves nobility in one traditional Western sense, by the establishment of a new landed family, whose interests were expected to continue over generations and centuries, but they were self-made rather than hereditary. It would be difficult to imagine

an architectural form better calculated to set forth an image of that kind of newly stable institution than the even-armed, central-type, solidly rooted, decidedly non-vertical paradigm of Anglican church developed in the Virginia plantation country during the years 1730 to 1760. The kind of family success therein imaged has, in fact, remained a measure for American civilization.[29]

In my second example of paradigmatic social function in eighteenth-century Anglican church architecture, those churches generally referred to as in the Wren/Gibbs style, it is much easier to demonstrate specifically what that body of architecture was intended to do in and for society. The structures were built not only in one relatively narrow area but all over the First British Empire and not only in the eighteenth century but well into the nineteenth as well. You could (and often still can) find them prominently at the center of almost every colonial capital, in India and what is now Canada and the West Indies as well as the original thirteen American colonies.

"Wren/Gibbs" is the common, although imprecise name for the churches. Almost all were manifest copies or variants of one particular church—Saint Martin-in-the-Fields, built to the designs of James Gibbs, following and modifying the tradition of Christopher Wren's city churches, in 1721–1726 (figs. 18–19).[30]

Saint Martin's owed its contemporary fame only in part to its success as a work of architectural art. Its great size and magnificence were real enough qualities,[31] but what made the building *the* great model of church architecture in colonial capitals was its significance as a symbol of imperial seapower.[32] Saint Martin-in-the-Fields was not just one of London's fifty new churches commissioned in Queen Anne's time, however grand, however artistically successful it may have been. Saint Martin's was the official church of the admiralty and the parish church of the sovereign. It was from Saint Martin's that the admiralty's white ensign flew on state occasions, as it still does, and had since 1544, when the second Saint Martin's was built for Henry VIII.[33] This alone would have given the church unique ideological importance in the eighteenth century, when the British were mightily expanding a colonial empire based on seapower. Saint Martin-in-the-Fields also had George I as its first churchwarden, the only instance of a reigning sovereign holding such an office.[34] It was consciously designed as a potent symbol to project an image of that Protestant establishment come to power in the Glorious Revolution of 1689 and consolidated by the Hanoverian succession of 1714. By "conscious" I mean that Gibbs knew he was designing something special; he knew at the time it was the most prestigious commission available,[35] that it would make his fame and fortune, which it did.[36] For Saint Martin's, Gibbs deliberately abandoned the Berninian baroque curves and papal Roman reminiscences of Saint Mary-le-Strand, a few years earlier, not for artistic reasons but because he had been dismissed from his post as surveyor to the New Churches in January 1716 because of Saint Mary's blatantly Catholic associations (although allowed to see his church through to completion).[37] For Saint Martin's, Gibbs deliberately composed a design that would be unique, combining a number of distinctive elements each with particular associations. This whole uncompromisingly set forth the values of the new Establishment that dominated the eighteenth century and created the first British Empire.

Setting Saint Martin's tower within the body of the church allowed for a classical portico in Pantheon form to encircle the front, plainly an allusion to the great empire to which some Britons began to connect themselves (although the full parallel would not be drawn until the times of Pax Britannia through Queen Victoria's late reign to George V's reign).[38] On such an inset base a heavy tower could be erected as a sequence of geometric forms with a prominent clock—since medieval times the mark of an establishment ordering the community's hours.[39] A roof-level balustrade and row of urns visually anchored the building firmly to the ground, making emphatic contrast with baroque verticality. This Protestant,

rational, Low Church stance was underscored by the double row of windows in the side walls, which proclaimed the galleries within that marked this as a preaching-oriented rather than a sacrament-oriented church.[40] It was, then, the church of sober William of Orange rather than fervent and feckless James II; of stoutly Protestant Queen Anne and of the stolid Hanoverians and those who put them on a constitutional throne. This was not a reworked medieval church nor a revised Roman one but something definitely new and appropriate to its function in and for the new Establishment.

Saint Martin's interior was equally distinctive, comparably symbolic. Its arcades, with giant columns to which the balconies are attached, and arcades springing from a detached piece of entablature above the capitals, would remind empire-building Englishmen not so much (if at all) of Filippo Brunelleschi the creative artist, as of the Medicis for whom Brunelleschi worked and for whose churches of San Lorenzo and Santo Spirito he perfected this motif.[41] For England's eighteenth-century Establishment, composed as it was not only of hereditary aristocrats but also of self-made merchant lords, the Medici were admired prototypes and models (as they have been for comparable classes ever since). They were rich, competent in business and finance, yet much more than mere money grubbers—civic leaders and great art patrons both, capable not only of amassing wealth but of creating a great state.[42]

Ostentatiously set in a flat east end—traditional in English churches of importance since the early Middle Ages—was the most prominent of all symbolic elements in this subtype: the Palladian, or what they would have called it in the eighteenth century, Venetian, window. Howard E. Stutchbury has admirably described how

> of greatest significance [for understanding the appeal of Andrea Palladio in the eighteenth century] was . . . admiration of Whig society for the Venetian constitution and its reflection in the way of life of an aristocracy similarly dependent upon sea-borne trade as much as upon inherited landed wealth. This admiration was to be most clearly expressed in the imitation of architectural forms, of which the full exposition was to be found in the plains of the Veneto. . . . The important points in the revival of Jones-Palladianism are, first that it accorded to the movement the respectability of native precedent, and second, that it provided a reflection in architectural enterprise of a recurrence of religious and political motives.[43]

By such a combination of key signal elements Saint Martin's in all respects became an especially compelling visual metaphor of the goals and justifications of the First British Empire as promoted by an oligarchy based on seapower and at every point interrelated with the interests and ambitions of a rising mercantile class. It more precisely perhaps was a visual metaphor of the basic values and justifications of that empire—a metaphor of British law and institutions and the religious verities that underlay them. To replicate such a metaphor in the capital city of every colony was as natural to the eighteenth-century British Empire as was replication of imperial images in the Roman Empire of antiquity.[44]

By replication or copying I mean not so much a literal reproduction of forms as a copy of meaning, a copy of metaphoric values—a copy, that is, in some such sense as defined by Owen Barfield in "Poetic Diction and Legal Fiction" or Richard Krautheimer in "Introduction to an Iconography of Medieval Architecture."[45] What Barfield wrote about the law exactly applies to buildings purporting to be visual metaphors of laws and institutions:

In fact it is the very essence of a law that it should apply to every case. . . . If there is a different law for every case that arises, then what is being administered is simply not law at all but the arbitrary (though not necessarily unjust) decisions of those who govern us [or, one might say, buildings functioning as visual metaphors of law must be perceived as notably similar to be effective]. But that is exactly what the word law *means*—something which is *not* such a series of arbitrary decisions or events, something which will be *the same* for the next case as it was for the last. This is where the difficulty arises; for it is the nature of life itself (certainly human life) never to repeat itself exactly. Phenomena exactly repeated are not life, they are mechanism. Life varies, law is of its nature unvarying [therefore, to condense a long following argument and apply it to architectural metaphor, a visual metaphor of law must have constant elements but will in the nature of life never be mechanically reproduced nor should the attempt be made].

Krautheimer's article was, of course, directly about the historical uses of replication in architecture. The medieval mind, he wrote, had quite a different approach from the modern mind to the whole question of copying: "In the Middle Ages, it would seem as though a given shape were imitated not so much for its own shape as for something else it implied." Noting that some "copies of the Holy Sepulchre" had, to our eyes, "nothing in common with the original but the name," he said:

The common element between a church which shared with its prototype only the name or the particular manner of its dedication, and an architectural copy proper, was evidently the fact that both were mementoes of a venerated site. The difference is rather between a more or less elaborate reproduction; and one might say that the more elaborate one only adds some visual elements to the "immaterial" features, that is to the name and dedication. Both immaterial and visual elements are intended to be an echo of the original capable of reminding the faithful of the venerated site, of evoking his devotion, and of giving him a share at least in the reflection of the blessings which he would have enjoyed had he been able to visit the Holy Site in reality.

Another way of putting this principle is to see it as a parallel process to the workings of abstract causality in science. In the world of time and history and mass no two events ever recur in exactly the same way. No terrestrial event, therefore, is ever, nor ever can be, compared with or seen as a repeat of another. To make sense of experience you must posit an abstract formula based on hypothetical uniform conditions. Having posited this formula, you then test it experimentally against the actual nonreplicable happenings of the material temporal world and "prove" the abstraction by showing that it can account for all happenings with minimum variation. What problems can arise if one attempts to equate replication with literal copying, and only literal copying, are neatly illustrated in an article by Charles E. Peterson on Christ Church, Philadelphia (figs. 20–21).[46]

The general resemblance of Christ Church, Philadelphia, to Saint Martin's has long been recognized. The key elements are almost all there: ordered sequence of tower stages quite like an alternate design in Gibbs' *Book of Architecture*; balustrade; urns; a Venetian window formed in brick on the east end and prominent on the interior as well, where can also be seen the giant columns with attached galleries; the arcade with detached entablature. It is not an exact copy; the front portico is missing, for instance, and no reference to Gibbs appears in the records, only to a Dr. John Kearsley who seems to have been in charge of the building program. This puzzles Peterson:

We must agree that the building of Christ Church was indeed a splendid accomplishment. Today it is often declared to be the finest American church. But how can the design be accounted for? While Dr. Kearsley's enthusiasm and persistence was obviously an essential factor, it has not been shown that during his lifetime

Fig. 20. Christ Church, Philadelphia. East end.
Photo, c. 1955.

he ever drew an architectural line. . . . Two authorities
on Stuart and Georgian church architecture, Marcus
Whiffen and Kerry Downs, have been consulted. They
write that while the various design motifs at Philadelphia are familiar to them, the church as a whole is not
a copy of anything known to have been built in England. Of the great Anglican churches erected on these
shores, Christ Church is the fourth, following St. Phil-
ips Charleston, begun 1711, Christ Church (Salem
Street, Boston, begun 1723) and Trinity (Newport,
begun 1725). The basic facts concerning the latter three
are just as mysterious as they are in Philadelphia. The
writer is forced to conclude that plans for Christ Church
were imported (like the great urns) by Dr. Kearsley.

There is no mystery. The three earlier churches are
copies, in the medieval sense, of Wren city types, sim-
plified. Christ Church is a copy, in the medieval or ab-
stract-causal-hypothesis sense, of Saint Martin's, where
Gibbs had created so much better a symbol. As for the
objection that Christ Church was begun before Gibbs'

Book of Architecture was published in 1728 and so made
details and alternates to Saint Martin's widely accessible,
that is no problem either; there are several eighteenth-
century examples of New World buildings derived from
Old World patterns not yet published but known from
loose plates or drawings. For example, Westover, the
Byrd seat in Virginia, whose doorways were taken from
William Salmon's *Palladio Londinensis*, seems to have been
in place almost a decade before the first edition of that
work appeared in 1734; or the Carlyle house in Alexandria, where a plaque on the east gate informs us that
the structure was built in 1752 by architect John Arriss
from plates in *Vitruvius Scotticus*, although *Vitruvius Scotticus* was not, in fact, published until 1823; or the several
instances cited by Terry Friedman of Gibbsian designs
being available or in circulation before their official publication.[47] The real block against understanding here is
the twentieth-century notion of architects as creative ge-
niuses, whose first and consuming interest is to create a
personal, inimitable style, which in the eighteenth century did not yet exist to any degree, certainly not in the
provinces. Certainly neither Kearsley nor Robert Smith
(who later collaborated on a Gibbsian church, Saint Pe-
ters, Philadelphia, of 1758) were considered in that sort
of creative genius category by themselves or anybody
else.[48] They were actually, in terms of social function,
much closer to the kind of modern architect-designers
who adapt to specific situations and climates standardized designs for fast-food outlets, cosmetic stores, and
shopping centers. In making such adaptations one or
two of the standardized elements could be varied or
eliminated without affecting the function of the design.
So in "copying" Saint Martin's in Philadelphia, the portico was not reproduced. At Saint Paul's in New York,
it was reproduced but on the "wrong end."

Saint Paul's was begun in the 1760s as a chapel-of-ease
for Trinity Parish, a few blocks further south on what
is now Broadway. By the Revolution the familiar Gibbsian rectangle had been completed under the direction
of an obscure Scot named Thomas McBean to whom the
design often is attributed ("to be Architecture, it must
have an Architect"). It had the Venetian window at the
east end, the giant columns, the detached entablature
carrying the arcade, and the attached galleries. Unlike
Virginia churches, Saint Paul's was not abandoned at the
Revolution but continued to function under patriot clergy;
George Washington attended services here before his
first inauguration. In the 1790s the building was "finished" with one James Crommelin Lawrence in charge.
"Finishing" meant adding the two most prominently

Fig. 21. Christ Church. Interior, looking to altar. Photo, 1984.

missing features of Saint Martin's: spire and portico.[49] The spire was duly built on the foundations within the west vestibule already provided, according to the Gibbsian formula; but the portico was added on the opposite, *east*, end, obscuring the Venetian window, because since the 1760s Broadway, which ran at the back of the church, had developed into a major thoroughfare and the portico would be seen to better advantage there! In other words, it did not matter exactly how the signal element was fitted in so long as it was fitted, eventually! To this day one enters Saint Paul's to find oneself at the altar end of the church; the proper, west-end, entrance still exists but is used only for access to the churchyard. Of course, in part, this misplacing (in terms of the paradigm) of the portico reflects a change in the ideological meaning of Saint Paul's. No longer a symbol of the British Empire, which had disappeared from most of North America (set against the Venetian window is an urn containing the ashes of General Richard Montgomery of this parish, killed while attacking Quebec in 1776), Saint Paul's and its prototype, Saint Martin's, now stood for "important denomination." Already, in 1775, it had been adapted as a sign of "leading denomination," for the First Baptist Meeting House of Providence, and in this reincarnation Saint Martin's had a long life still ahead in America.

A classic example of the two kinds of problems encountered when the social function and meaning of Saint Martin's are not taken into account, only similarities of form and detail, is presented in various writings about Saint Michael's, Charleston (see fig. 2): both the "great unknown creative genius" and the "not-an-exact-copy-

so-must-be-an-original-design." The counterpart to Kearsley and McBean is the "Mr. Gibson" referred to in the *South Carolina Gazette*'s account of the cornerstone laying in February 1752: "This church will be built on the Plan of one of Mr. Gibson's designs." "No one known to be named Gibson and living in the province at this time can be identified, either by age or vocation, as qualified to have designed this building," wrote Albert M. Simons.[50] "It has been suggested, with considerable plausibility, that the intent of the *Gazette* was Gibbs, that is, James Gibbs 1682–1754 . . . [but] . . . the resemblance of St. Michael's to St. Martin's is only of a very general nature, such as the prostyle portico and the base of the steeple being concealed within the building." To this day one can find Charlestonians still hoping for more evidence of a great unknown South Carolinian architect named Gibson, encouraged all the more by the fact that Saint Michael's does indeed differ considerably in detail from Saint Martin's (the differences accentuated by rebuilding of much of the church after the 1886 earthquake, a 1905 redecoration of the chancel by Tiffany, and a 1938 project stripping all paint off the interior woodwork to reveal "natural dark cedar"). Actually much of Saint Michael's seems to have been based on the Marylebone Chapel designs in Gibbs' *Book of Architecture*, used here and elsewhere in the colonies as a means of replicating the "meaning" of Saint Martin's at less expense.[51] Failing Gibson, the builder Samuel Cardy is often invoked as the "Architect" required by the formula for "Architecture."

Another example of this practice is King's College

Chapel in Boston, similarly based on Gibbsian detail, especially from the Marylebone Chapel, similarly intended to convey the general "feel" and idea of Saint Martin's.[52] In this case the point can be demonstrated by comparison with Touro Synagogue in Newport, Rhode Island, assembled from Gibbsian details—many of them the same ones—by the same designer, Peter Harrison, just five years later (King's College Chapel dates 1749 to 1754, Touro Synagogue 1759 to 1763). There is absolutely no resemblance to Saint Martin's, for in this case, the ideological reference would have been totally inappropriate. To make a synagogue look like an official symbol of the Establishment would have been absurd at this time and place.

It may be argued, as an excuse for the modern mind's frequent mystification at buildings functioning as visual metaphors of institutional values, and their "copyings" being understood in this light, that such practice has vanished from the modern world. We can only with the greatest difficulty—so it is claimed—think ourselves back into such an obsolete frame of mind. But this social function is not obsolete; it has never been more operational than now. Only we do not find it in avant-garde, self-consciously creative architecture. Consider the structures that line commercial strips leading into all towns and cities nowadays, and you will find examples aplenty—fast-food shops like McDonald's, Long John Silver, Taco Bell; motel chains like the Ramada Inn, gas-station chains—all are designed to manifest a recognizable family resemblance to each other, although none is absolutely identical to another. Or—more elegant examples—you find the same principle manifest in Georgette Klinger stores on Rodeo Drive in Beverly Hills, on Fifth Avenue, in Houston. Why are they replications? To proclaim uniformity—to tell you that if you stop there to eat, sleep, get gas or cosmetics, you will find uniform quality, you will know what to expect, no matter how many hundreds or thousands of miles away from each other individual instances of the general paradigm may be. Such popular/commercial architecture is *about* something, as architecture traditionally always has been; it is made, as architecture traditionally always was made, to *do* something in and for society. If it is trivial, that is not because the principle involved is trivial; it is because what this architecture is *about* is trivial. Or put it another way: everyone still understands perfectly well how buildings can function to transmit ideas; it is just that in high architecture nowadays one is not taught to look for that sort of thing. Once one grasps that principle, how high architecture historically functioned to create metaphors of

institutional values becomes entirely clear. Consider, for an exceptionally good case, what happened to the Saint Martin's paradigm after the American Revolution, when its original meaning had lost validity.

That the Saint Martin's paradigm should survive in the two American colonies that did not secede in 1776 is only to be expected, once the operative principle is grasped. So, in addition to the replication of Saint Martin's already standing in Nova Scotia since 1750—Saint Paul's Halifax[53]—a dozen tinier ones appeared after the Revolution, inspired mainly by Bishop Inglis. Fervent Loyalist, sometime rector at Saint Paul's, New York, whence he had to flee, Inglis knew perfectly well what symbolism the Saint Martin's paradigm carried.[54] So did Bishop Mountain in Quebec, who complained bitterly when Roman Catholic Bishop Briand was consecrated in France ("how can there be two bishops in the same city?") and petitioned King George III for "a proper Church" that would "give weight and consequence" to the Church of England in Quebec. His model? The royal parish church, as Saint Martin's had by this time become.[55] There is, of course, the usual confusion here about Trinity Cathedral in Quebec being designed by "the architect, Major William Robe"—no more an architect than Kearsley or McBean or Cardy—or, alternatively, by Edward Cannon, the mason, but again it is just a matter of understanding the principle of replicating a meaning, not exact specific forms.[56] Likewise, the first Christ Church in Montreal and the first Saint James in Toronto carried the meaning and message of "uniform laws and institutions supported by Anglican religion" as Saint Martin's replications had in the old capitals of provinces now revolted and gone.[57]

And what of the paradigm in them? Did it disappear? By no means; it just altered meaning. Already before the Revolution that process was underway at the First Baptist Meeting House in Providence, assembled, from Gibbsian designs, by Joseph Brown in 1775. Here the object was to proclaim "leading denomination," which the Baptists then were, rather than Establishment Church, which they were not. The design was appropriately altered. Now the tower base was put into a narthex/porch rather than inset in the body of the church, so restoring a more traditional church appearance (see fig. 1). At the same time the main door was on the south side, as in a meeting-house proper, so the design represented, ideologically and social functionally, the best of both worlds.[58]

By 1812, when Ithiel Town drew up plans for Center Church (First Congregational) in New Haven (following *A Book of Architecture*, via Asher Benjamin, some think), there was no compromise.[59] Center Church *was* Saint Martin's (and so, with variations, was North Church beside it). Why? Because the Congregationalists hoped to make themselves the established church of Connecticut at this period, to supersede the Anglican, draw tithes, and all other perquisites. Saint Martin's proclaimed their ambition as it did in other variants in many Congregational churches throughout New England at this time—rural Connecticut's "famous foursome" of Milford, Southington, Cheshire, and Litchfield in the 1820s; Lavius Fillmore's somewhat earlier Congregational churches at Middlebury and Bennington in Vermont (c. 1805–1807).[60]

And afterward? Would it be fanciful to suggest that one reason for Saint Martin's being the model for Arthur Gilman's Arlington Street Church in Boston as late as 1859 might have been to proclaim "leading denomination" in the face of the enormous Irish immigration sweeping into Boston since 1848, transforming the old Puritan/Congregationalist city? Could that have been a reason, maybe even a principal reason, for Southern Baptist churches being so consistently in Saint Martin's variant forms from at least the 1880s to the present? Could we see something of that same social function in the extraordinary proliferation of Saint Martinesque churches in the Nation's capital—lining Massachusetts Avenue and Sixteenth Street, one after another, proclaiming the importance of the denomination that built them in and for American life. Such speculation is to enter into realms of the subliminal, of mass psychology—whence, to be sure, all matters of architectural taste ultimately derive—but without the degree of documentary demonstration with which one can make the cases for paradigmatic social function in Anglican church architecture of the fifteen eighteenth-century colonies.

NOTES

Some parts of what follows have appeared before, in different focus, in Alan Gowans, *King Carter's Church*, Maltwood Museum Studies in Architectural History, no. 2 (Victoria, British Columbia, 1969); Alan Gowans, "Architectural Symbolism in the First and Second British Empires" (paper delivered at a colloquium sponsored by the Center for Advanced Study in the Visual Arts, 1981); Alan Gowans, review of *Return to Camelot*, by Mark Girouard, and *Indian Summer*, by Robert Grant Irving, *Architecture* 13 (1983), 80–83.

At the time of writing this paper I had seen only a draft of Dell Upton's *Holy Things and Profane: Parish Churches in Eighteenth-Century Virginia*, since (1986) published by the Architectural Foundation, New York. I wish to thank Professor Upton for his helpful suggestions to me in preparing, and later revising, this paper. (I am not expecting him to endorse all my conclusions, of course!)

1. A 1638 date was proposed for Saint Luke's, Smithfield (or, more precisely for seventeenth-century usage, Newport Parish, Isle of Wight County), in James Grote Vanderpool's article on the church in *Journal of the Society of Architectural Historians* 17 (1958), 12–18; but Upton (1986) argues that a date near the end of the seventeenth century is more accurate. Newport Parish Church was unlike many others in having its tower built about contemporaneously with the nave; in many, perhaps most, other cases the tower was added later, often much later. A good example is Immanuel Church in New Castle Delaware, begun in 1703, which did not receive its tower until 1820! Compare Alan Gowans, *Architectural, Social, and Theological History in Immanuel Church New Castle on Delaware* (New Castle, 1965).

2. The 1732 date comes from Bishop William Meade, *Old Churches, Ministers, and Families of Virginia* (Richmond, 1855; reprint, Baltimore, 1966), 120: "the present house was completed about the time of Mr. Carter's death—that is, about the year 1732." Carter's will of 26 August 1726, however, leaves only "£200 sterling money" for the church and mentions that "bricks that are now made & burnt shall be appropriated to the building of the said Brick church or as many thereof as will perfect the building" ("Carter Papers," *Virginia Magazine of History and Biography* 6, no. 1 [1898], 3), so presumably something was already underway. Louise Belote Dawe wrote that "It was perhaps with the church in mind that Carter, in the early months of 1722, wrote his London agent to send him 'a good carpenter capable of framing a large building.' . . . In December 1722 Carter wrote in his diary, 'I began digging brick of the church earth,' and a few years later he recorded that he was sending 'a qt of rum to the brickmaker he being moulding today' " (Louise Belote Dawe, "Christ Church Lancaster County," *Virginia Cavalcade* 23, no. 2 [1973], 26). A mysterious (at least to me) article, appearing in the *Philadelphia Times,* 9 January 1898, under the heading "Christ Church Lancaster Co. Va.," gives an interesting account of a visit there in the late 1890s and obviously draws on Meade for historical information but adds "Much of the same material which had done service in the first church was used in building the second," an inference that could be drawn from Carter's references in his will to bricks already on the site "and if my son John shall have occasion to make use of any of the said bricks, then he be obliged to make & burn as many more for the use aforesaid [that is, building the new church]."

3. Upton wrote, "Christ Church, Lancaster, was probably not finished until 1735. A letter of John Carter, in the MS. letterbook, notes that he hopes to have the building finished by Christmas of that year. For what it's worth, that's three years after Robert Carter's death; three years is the time allotted to most church buildings [from start to completion]" (Dell Upton, letter to author, 22 May 1985).

4. Again, the idea of pristine condition seems to come from Meade [1855] 1966 (for example, 120: "Very few, if any, repairs have been made upon it"). It is repeated in G. W. O. Addleshaw and Frederick Etchells, *The Architectural Setting of Anglican Worship from the Reformation to the Present Day* (London, 1948), 62. The 1965–1966 operations unfortunately removed all graffiti from the interior walls, without photographing them and so perhaps identifying some visitors there; the churchyard wall was rebuilt straight, although in the early 1960s brochure soliciting restoration funds a photograph is reproduced that shows "excavated foundation of original s-shaped wall" (like the walls around Thomas Jefferson's University of Virginia campus); the height of the wall, which also defined spatial relationships, seems to have been an educated guess. A visitors' reception center has been built nearby, very much changing the character of the place from the "lonely majesty" commented on through the nineteenth and early twentieth century to a bustling touristy air.

5. Saint Mary's Whitechapel is located in Lancaster County, three miles south of Lively on Virginia Route 3. The Historic American Buildings Survey (hereafter cited as HABS), *Virginia Catalog* (Charlottesville, 1976), 173, locates it under the heading "Mollusk Vicinity"

and states that it was "blt c. 1740; extensively altered mid-19th C.; renovated mid-20th C." According to Meade [1855] 1966, 2:125, "it appears from the vestry book that the first church was torn down" and "the present built in 1740." A pamphlet, *St. Mary's White Chapel*, published by and for the church in 1969, states that the "construction of a church building was started sometime prior to 1675 . . . in the Order book of 1675 an entry records that the church was 'nearing completion.' The building was originally rectangular but was made cruciform in 1741 by the addition of two wings." In any event, the cruciform structure dated from the 1740s; Upton wrote, "St. Mary's Whitechapel Church was built by James Jones 1739–41 (MS. vestry book). There is nothing in the record to suggest that it was an addition rather than an entirely new church" (letter to author, 22 May 1985). From 1802 to about 1830 the church was disused, and the east and west wings collapsed; the present rectangular structure was patched together in the 1830s.

6. Vauter's may have taken a distinctive cruciform shape in the same manner as Saint Mary's Whitechapel, by additions to an originally rectangular church, in the 1730s; to some, although not all, the state of the north wall brickwork suggests that a north wing disintegrated or was pulled down sometime in the nineteenth century. See further Robert A. Lancaster, Jr., *Historic Virginia Homes and Churches* (Philadelphia, 1915), 295, and the article by P. S. Hunter on Vauter's in *Colonial Churches in the Original Colony of Virginia* (Richmond, 1908), which dates the original rectangle to 1719. In HABS 1976 it is listed under the heading "Loretto Vicinity, Essex County" (154). The nearest big town is Tappahannock.

North Farnham, in Richmond County across the Rappahannock, was, according to Lancaster (1915), "originally a large cruciform building and one of the best parish churches in the country." Built in the 1730s (ordered to be built in 1733, according to Upton's researches into the *Executive Journals of the Council of Virginia*, 4:306), it burned in 1787, was "refitted" in Bishop Meade's time (Meade [1855] 1966, 2:177, records its reconsecration in 1837); burned again in 1888 and again refitted; it was gutted in 1920–1924 and rebuilt yet once more, awkwardly.

7. Abingdon is in Gloucester County, near Ordinary. In HABS 1976 it is located under White Marsh: "built mid-18th C.; altered mid-19th C." William Byrd Lee's article on Abingdon in *Colonial Churches in the Original Colony of Virginia* (1908), 177, gives a date of 1755 and names as the leading families of the parish, Thrustons, Lewises, Pages, and Landons.

8. In addition to works cited in notes 6–8 above a bibliography on Virginia churches should include George Carrington Mason, *Colonial Churches of Tidewater Virginia* (Richmond, 1945), and James Scott Rawlings, *Virginia's Colonial Churches: An Architectural Guide* (Richmond, 1963), as well, of course, as Upton 1986.

Because of the present ruinous (not to mention vanished) state of so many early Virginia churches, and the loss of so much documentation about them, it is not easy to identify with certainty which and how many others belonged to the King Carter's Church "family." The following list owes many emendations and additions to Upton's generously sharing his research with me (in letter to author, 22 May 1985): (1) Mattaponi Church in King and Queen County, originally the lower church of Saint Stephen's Parish (a cruciform structure, it seems, with glazed bricks built somewhere between 1735 and 1750—it has a signed brick, "David Minetree"—abandoned 1783, made into a Baptist church in 1824, and, although gutted by fire and rebuilt in the 1920s, still existing as Mattaponi Baptist Church); (2) Petsworth Church at Poplar Spring, near Rosewell, in Gloucester Parish, begun about 1720 by James Skelton, finished "magnificently" in the 1730s and 1740s, demolished in the time of Bishop Meade who lamented this desecration and quoted old-time parishioners on its former grandeur ([1855] 1966, 1:321–322)—Petsworth was the church of the Porteus family, whence came a bishop of London, and of Austine Warner, and of Colonel John

Washington and his son Warner; (3) the Lower Church of Lunenburg parish in Richmond County, of which Meade [1855] 1966, 2:178–180), quoted a description: "Like most of the old churches in Virginia it was built of brick . . . cruciform in shape . . . built in 1737 . . . remained until about 1813 when its walls were thrown down . . . principal families were the Tayloes [of Mount Airy], Carters [of Sabine Hall], Lees [Col. T. L. Lee of Manakin]."

Upton suggested adding to my list the following: (4) Pungoteague Church, Saint George's Parish, Accomack County, about 1738, Greek cross church with apse; (5) Elizabeth River Parish Church (Saint Paul's), Norfolk, dated 1739, signed "SB" in glazed brick: Latin cross, burned out in the Revolution and reconstructed inside in 1848 and again in 1913; (6) Suffolk Church of the Upper Parish Nansemond County, 1748–1752, by William Rand: brick cross-shaped church of unknown dimensions (MS. vestry book, 46–47); (7) Wicomico Parish Church, Northumberland County: a brick cruciform church explicitly modeled on King Carter's Church, ordered to be built 1753 by Mourning Richards, builder of Aquia Church, 1757; not done, reordered 1763, built 1763–1771 by John Wily and successors (MS. vestry book, f. 58, 60–61, 75, 86, 89); (8) Bruton Parish Church, Williamsburg, 1710–1715; (9) Third Lower Church at Hanovertown, Saint Paul's Parish, Hanover County, ordered 1774, to be built by Paul Thilman, possibly never built; to be of the same dimensions as Abingdon Church (details from vestry book); (10) Third Upper Chapel, Christ Church Parish, Middlesex County, advertised in the *Virginia Gazette* for 26 March 1772 as a brick cruciform church.

One might conjecture further that the visual impact of these cruciform churches, as distinct from their power as visual metaphors with institutional meaning, was strong enough to influence the use of a cruciform ground plan for such two-story and obviously congregational churches as Saint Paul's in King George County, about 1766, and Aquia Church in Stafford County, 1757.

9. The church was, in fact, built just about on the spot where the vestry wanted to build the new Christ Church in the 1720s, before Carter offered to finance the building if they would keep it in the old place.

10. The association of central-type and especially domical buildings with memorialization is, of course, ancient. Hundreds of examples crowd to mind: the mausoleum of Galla Placidia and the tomb of Theodoric; the tombs of Augustus and Hadrian; the Church of the Holy Sepulcher and its innumerable copies; not to mention the Ming tombs and the Taj Mahal (see E. Baldwin Smith, *The Dome* [Princeton, 1950]).

11. Illustrations in Erwin Panofsky, *Tomb Sculpture* (New York, 1964).

12. In it were interred kings Charles X, XI, and XII of Sweden; of special interest was the creation of giant monuments in thirteenth-century style for largely mythical medieval kings.

13. "Unsuccessful," because the vast building overwhelmed it. The Tudors understandably were very sensitive about legitimacy. They made plans, and even started some projects, designed to make Winchester the new capital of England and thus make a return to "English beginnings." Henry VII arranged for his queen to be confined at Winchester so that the crown prince would be born there; he was, of course, called Arthur. After Arthur died and was succeeded as crown prince by the future Henry VIII, the Winchester capital idea was abandoned.

14. See the illustrations, pls. VII–VIII, of Gowans 1969. Salient points are that the burial wing is roofed by a groin vault, perceptible as a dome and so maintaining the ancient symbolic shape, and that the sarcophagus is inside (with effigies of the duke and duchess resting upon it) with bodies in the vault below. The discussion is in Gowans 1969, 22–29.

15. Gowans 1969, 29: "The period between about 1685 and 1715 . . . was a moment of transition, when instead of family memorials being integral or attached parts of churches, churches—i.e., for congrega-

tional use not simply chapels—could be conceived as part of a family memorial. To this moment in time the Durisdeer kirk or Queensberry memorial—the designations are literally interchangeable—plainly belongs. Quite as plainly, King Carter's church belongs to the same moment." Documentary references are found here.

16. Gowans 1969, 27–28, 31.

17. In Gowans 1969, I began by searching for some "form giver" in the modern sense, first among the brick workers in Colchester; then among clergy, especially that John Bell who served as rector of King Carter's Church through the entire term of its construction and who probably came from the same part of Scotland where the Queensberry memorial is; then among philosophic artist-types like Spottswood or even Bishop Berkeley; until realization that what I was looking for was not an artistic creation but a building type that functioned as a traditional visual metaphor. That led to the Fox Memorial at Farley. It having been attributed to Wren, the idea of Wren's plans being behind King Carter's Church followed naturally. But, it seems, one no more goes about attributing buildings to Sir Christopher Wren than one goes about conferring sainthood without consulting the Vatican. And this question of attribution has distracted from the historical significance of the building, in which context its authorship is totally irrelevant. Once one thinks of a building as a work of art, attribution becomes all-important, for: What is architecture? Architecture is what great architects do. And who are great architects? They are people who do Great Architecture. Conversely, no great architect, no great architecture. But once one thinks of buildings as made to *do* something, in and for society, before they are anything else, authorship becomes a secondary and, as in this case, distracting consideration.

18. The will seems first to have been prepared in 1726 then revised almost yearly. It is printed in "Carter Papers" (1898) 3 (see note 3 above).

19. This critical section has been consistently reprinted in brochures distributed at the church by the Historic Christ Church Foundation.

20. Quoted from a brochure distributed at the church in the 1960s, written by Louise Belote Dawe.

21. This and other quotes in this paragraph are from Meade [1855] 1966, 2:118.

22. William G. Stannard, "Christ Church Lancaster County Virginia," *Colonial Churches in the Original Colony of Virginia* (Richmond, 1908), 240: "Since Bishop Meade wrote, the Civil War and the poverty and distress which followed it have come. The venerable old church has suffered further from vandalism . . . portions of the gallery and pulpit stair railing carried off by relic-hunters, most of the windows broken . . . the tombs in the yard broken into fragments (it is stated in the neighbourhood that a large piece of the tomb of Robert Carter, containing the coat of arms, was stolen and carried away not many years ago by a party who were on the Rappahannock in a yacht belonging to a well-known New York man), and even the baptismal font broken."

23. Dave 1973, 23, Cleveland Amory, *Who Killed Society?* (New York, 1959), 237, among other references.

24. Rawlings 1963, 124.

25. Meade [1855] 1966, 2:178.

26. Rawlings 1963, 127. Rawlings emphasizes, as no other writer has, that not only was Christ Church abandoned from about 1790 to about 1832 but again from 1852 to the early 1880s! Meade [1855] 1966, 2:118, also noted that "a considerable sum of money has been subscribed for repairing the roof [which was in fact done], . . . and for improving the interior of this remarkable building [about which we know nothing else]."

27. *St. Mary's White Chapel* (1969). Meade [1855] 1966, 2:125, wrote that in 1740 "Major James Ball and Mr. Joseph Ball are allowed to build a gallery in the church for their families, provided it be completed at the same time with the church, and finished in the same style with the west gallery." George Washington's mother was a member of the Ball family.

28. Byrd Lee, "Abingdon Church," *Colonial Churches in the Original Colony of Virginia* (1908), 183.

29. A good account of the medieval concept of the hereditary landed family is Régine Pernoud, *La lumière du Moyen Age* (Paris, 1944). On the actual state of demographic chaos in the South during the seventeenth century (as opposed to the myth of cavalier families), see Cary Carson et al., "Impermanent Architecture in the Southern American Colonies," *Winterthur Portfolio* 16, no. 2–3 (1981), 135–196. Carter's was the first generation to know any substantial stability. To reinforce it by deliberate imagery was not only natural but perhaps inevitable; comparable instances can be cited abundantly before and since. Richard Morris Hunt's Vanderbilt mansions in New York and North Carolina are only the most obvious examples.

30. I am fortunate to be able to benefit at this point from the publication by Terry Friedman, *James Gibbs* (New Haven, 1984), who discusses at decisive length the biographical and architectural aspects of Gibbs' work. He evidences little interest, however, in the social function of Gibbs' buildings, which is my primary concern here.

31. The church was originally projected to be 88 x 188 feet, which would have made it bigger than the Madeleine in Paris (Friedman 1984, 57), and London guidebooks immediately called it "the most magnificent parochial church in London . . . [the] Fabric is looked upon as a masterpiece" (Friedman 1984, 16). Not everyone agreed in admiring this or other works by Gibbs; Horace Walpole disliked it, for example, but then Walpole was already a proto-romantic, taking an antiestablishment stance.

32. F. R. Banks, *The Penguin Guide to London*, 7th ed. (Harmondsworth, 1977), 103–104. The architectural significance of this common knowledge—it is in every standard guide to London—has generally been overlooked. Yet it surely is no coincidence that the rebuilding of Saint Martin's was immediately projected after the Treaty of Utrecht in 1713 established Britain's preeminence at sea: "Before that war, England was one of the Sea powers. After it, she was *the* Sea power, without any second" (James A. Williamson, *A Short History of English Expansion: The Old Colonial Empire*, 3d ed. [New York, 1968], 337).

33. Banks 1977, 104. There was an earlier church on the site dating from at least 1222.

34. Banks 1977, 104. Banks also mentions that Saint Martin's Parish includes Buckingham Palace. This, however, was not acquired by the Crown until 1764 and so added at best minor ideological thrust to what the church already had.

35. Gibbs' appointment as architect for Saint Martin's was dated 24 November 1720, although originally recommended 14 September, and was "one of the most prestigious ecclesiastical commissions of the eighteenth century" (Friedman 1984, 13). This is about as explicit a statement as we can hope for in the pre-Modern (that is, prepsychoanalytical, artistically self-conscious) age.

36. "Other public work emerged as a consequence of the prestige attached to this commission. . . . In 1729 Gibbs was elected a Fellow of the Royal Society" (Friedman 1984, 13, 16).

37. Friedman 1984, 50. Friedman also notes that Gibbs' completion in 1719 of Wren's Saint Clement Danes showed "sympathetic use of elements from the London churches clearly intended to honor . . . Wren"—that is, to put it into my terms, Gibbs was working with a keen eye to the ideological currents of that moment. Wren was a British hero (as Stowe's monument would say), Gianlorenzo Bernini was not. Gibbs himself was a Catholic, only nominally turned Anglican (if that); his awareness of the Protestant Establishment could only have been heightened thereby.

In the late Middle Ages another type of copying is found, the copying of compositions or motifs that have been created by panel or mural painters. A well-known early example is the copying about 1325 by Pucelle in the Hours of Jeanne D'Evreux compositions from the Maestà of Duccio painted about fifteen years earlier.[29] Pucelle must have visited Siena and noted these compositions in a model book. Although he made certain alterations, these may be called reproductions, since they exemplify the sense of admiration referred to earlier. Many other examples could be noted in Italy and the Netherlands. Compositions by Jan van Eyck or Hugo van der Goes were reproduced in manuscripts, and David Alan Brown has drawn attention to a borrowing by the Milanese illuminator Antonio da Monza from the London version of Leonardo da Vinci's *Virgin of the Rocks*.[30]

Even more widespread was the use of prints by illuminators for motifs or whole compositions. It is difficult to establish whether the illuminator made his copy as an openly acknowledged act of homage, sanctioned or perhaps required by the patron, or whether the copy was a matter of using the print to enrich an illuminator's repertoire as the model book was used to do. I am uncertain whether the Dutch illuminator of very moderate talent who copied an Annunciation composition of Martin Schongauer would have regarded himself as found out if challenged as to his source.[31] Albrecht Dürer's engravings at least must have been so well known that the very numerous copies of them both in northern European and in Italian manuscripts must always have been recognized as reproductions.

38. A mine of useful references on this subject is contained in Robert Grant Irving, *Indian Summer: Lutyens, Baker, and Imperial Delhi* (New Haven, 1981).

39. One thinks of the clocks in medieval cathedrals; in Strasbourg, for example, "Steeples are of Gothick Extraction; but they have their Beauties, when their Parts are well dispos'd" (Gibbs, cited in Friedman 1984, 66). Friedman also found what he considered to be a model for Saint Martin's spire in the church of the Madonna di San Biago at Montepulciano by Giuliano di Baccio, which he dates 1518–1564 (1984, 65). This is out of keeping with the general excellence of his book, I think, for the campanile is not related to its church the way Saint Martin's is; its forms are only superficially similar; it is too obscure to carry any significant connotations to eighteenth-century designers; most important it involves an assumption that Gibbs was incapable of inventing a tower form for himself by suitable composition of classical motifs, which is quite at variance with what Friedman's text so admirably demonstrates.

40. Friedman derives these galleries from plate 40 in Claude Perrault's publication in 1684 of Marcus Vitruvius Pollio (*Basilica at Fano*, bk. 5). One could think of other examples of galleries closer to the sentiment demanded of these times. They were in fact a staple of Protestant church architecture since the Reformation (for example, Burntisland, Fife, 1580s, Saint Paul's Covent Garden, La Charenton, Paris) so that by the 1720s "galleries" spelled "Protestant" (see further K. E. O. Fritsch, *Der Kirchenbau des Protestantismus von der Reformation bis zur Gegenwart* [Berlin, 1893]).

41. In contrast to the situation in eighteenth-century France the great merchant classes of London, Bristol, and Dublin were fully constituent parts of the Establishment in eighteenth-century England. This, it has often been noted, was one reason why there was nothing comparable to the French Revolution in England; the upper bourgeoisie already had a share of power. They too took those grand tours by which young English rulers were educated—including routinely in their itinerary the sites of quattrocento Florence, such as the Medici churches. Friedman (1984, 272) observed that the giant columns and detached entablature were Saint Martin's most single attention-getting feature at the time. He noted, somewhat irrelevantly, that Wren had used giant inside pilasters at Saint Augustine, Watling Street, in 1680–1683 (68) and that a similar motif can be found in the early Christian church of Santa Costanze; but that Gibbs knew Santo Spirito in Florence (68).

42. Much sport has been made of people like Henry C. Frick surrounding themselves with Medicean quattrocento paintings, allegedly in an effort to obscure their humble origins; actually the Medici patronized art in the same way and for the same reasons. Using wealth to promote culture is contemptible only to those who believe great wealth is morally repugnant in the first place. Henry C. Huntington

is a spectacular example of using art—in his case eighteenth-century English portraiture—to create aristocratic associations; but then the original patrons of Joshua Reynolds and Thomas Gainsborough and George Romney did the same. The logical consequence of such an attitude is, of course, to promote modern art, which is what a huge proportion of the present-day rich in fact do. Both kinds of patronage are represented by Paul Mellon—principal benefactor of I. M. Pei's East Building of the National Gallery of Art and the Yale Center for the Study of British Art.

43. Howard E. Stutchbury, *The Architecture of Colen Campbell* (Manchester, 1967). More than two centuries later parallels between the seapower empires of Venice and Britain still haunted British minds: "More often than I like, I am saddened by a historical myth. . . . I can't help thinking of the Venetian Republic in their last half-century. Like us, they had once been fabulously lucky. They had become rich, as we did, by accident. They had acquired immense political skill, just as we have. . . . They knew, just as clearly as we know, that the current of history had begun to flow against them . . . to keep going . . . would have meant breaking the pattern into which they had crystallised. . . . They never found the will to break it" (C. P. Snow, *The Two Cultures and the Scientific Revolution* [New York, 1959], 42).

44. It was normal for any city of importance in the Roman Empire to display statues of the reigning emperor, and usually the imperial family as well, in some prominently central place (see Cornelius C. Vermeule, *Roman Imperial Art in Greece and Asia Minor* [Cambridge, Mass., 1968]). Major Roman cities generally also displayed replications of the Temple of Capitoline Jupiter as symbols of adherence to the empire. Professor Alfred Frazer, Columbia University, wrote, "The best citation is Michelangelo Cagiano de Azevedo, 'I "Capitolia" del' Impero Romano,' *Memorie della Pontificia Accademia Romana di Archeologia*, V (1940). There have been additional capitals discovered since then but his is still the standard study of the class" (letter to the author, 4 March 1986). Caeserea Marittima built in Judea by Herod the Great had another example.

45. Owen Barfield, "Poetic Diction and Legal Fiction," in *Essays Presented to Charles Williams* (London, 1947), reprinted in *The Importance of Language*, ed. Max Black (Ithaca, N.Y., 1962), 65–66; Richard Krautheimer, "Introduction to an Iconography of Medieval Architecture," *Journal of the Warburg and Courtauld Institutes* 5 (1942), 1–32. A useful complimentary discussion to Krautheimer's argument is found in Earl Rosenthal, "A Renaissance 'Copy' of the Holy Sepulchre," *Journal of the Society of Architectural Historians* 17, no. 1 (1958), 2–11.

46. Charles E. Peterson, "The Building of Christ Church, Philadelphia," in *Christ Church, Philadelphia: Arts, Architecture, Archives, 1981 Loan Exhibit, 1981 Antiques Show* (Philadelphia, 1981), 135–137.

47. Upton drew my attention to a master's thesis by Mark Wenger of the University of Virginia, arguing that Westover was built in the 1750s following a fire in 1748 that destroyed the earlier house. If true, this would reduce the number of examples but not invalidate the principle; it seems, however, that one of Wenger's arguments was the disparity in date between the appearance of Salmon's book and entrances derived from it appearing on Westover. Among the instances cited by Friedman (1984, 257–259, 269) are designs from *A Book of Architecture* (projected as early as 1713) being in circulation as early as 1716, when Gibbs asks a correspondent "to give to nobody the designs of the church in the Strand." Gibbs actually published his book in sheets, leaving the binding to individual subscribers, so that it was always "loose leaf."

48. How deep and instinctive is the modern attitude to "artistic genius" was brought home to me once when I was lecturing on Gibbs and put a slide of his Gothic chapel at Stowe on the screen. A mature student, not an art major, expressed indignation: "That man had no principles at all!" she exclaimed, very audibly. "How so?" I inquired. "Why because that's not his style. He just did that to please a patron, the nobleman who built Stowe!" The idea that an architect might

consider the wishes of a client, or actually design in some style desired by a client, was simply incomprehensible; still less, the idea that some different style might be suitable for a garden fancy from what might make an effective Establishment symbol.

49. See Perry E. Borchers, "Saint Paul's Chapel Recorded," *Journal of the Society of Architectural Historians* 19, no. 1 (1960), 32–34; and Betty J. Ezequelle, "James Crommelin Lawrence (c. 1768–1804), Architect of St. Paul's Steeple," *New York Historical Quarterly* 42, no. 3 (1958), 285–299. Friedman 1984, 279–280, has some good illustrations of Saint Paul's but does not refer to these articles, spelling the name "Laurence." No writers that I know mention the fact that the portico is "backward"; again, I suppose, because of the idea that if Saint Martin's is copied exactly, there can be no question of any of its elements being "wrong," only "original."

50. Albert M. Simons, *An Architectural Guide to Charleston, South Carolina, 1700–1900* (Charleston, n.d. [c. 1968]), building 18. For factual information on Saint Michael's see Harley J. McKee, "St. Michael's Church, Charleston, 1752–1762: Some Notes on Materials and Construction," *Journal of the Society of Architectural Historians*, 23, no. 2 (1964), 39–43.

51. Friedman (1984, 280) called Saint Michael's "an inordinately heroic version of St. Martin's" and said (96n) that "the interior was inspired by Hawksmore's St. Alphege, Greenwich," an attribution that apparently rests on a statement made by a Reverend Charles Woodmason in 1766, recorded by McKee (1984, 8n), whose comment, "This appears plausible, even though the two are very different in detail" is somewhat incomprehensible, since the detail is what is at issue.

52. How a socially functional intent can be misunderstood if purely or mainly stylistic criteria are used is demonstrated by my own discussion of Harrison as a *retardataire* designer in *Images of American Living* (Philadelphia, 1964), 204. Priscilla Metcalf was on the right track in her "Boston before Bulfinch: Harrison's King's Chapel," *Journal of the Society of Architectural Historians* 13, no. 1 (1954), 11–14. For illustrations see Carl Bridenbaugh, *Peter Harrison* (Chapel Hill, 1949).

53. The Halifax church was prefabricated in Boston and shipped over for erection on foundations prepared in the new town. Intended as a deliberate riposte to Louisbourg on Cape Breton, Halifax was, therefore, a town with great symbolic importance for the empire. This may account for its having two Venetian windows, one in the west wall as well; a portico was never projected. Gibbs' Marylebone Chapel designs are usually taken as the source because the first rector said they were; but Philip McAleer has made a good case for Saint Peter, Vere Street, being closer; his "St. Paul's Halifax and St. Peter's Vere Street London," *Journal of Canadian Art History* 7, no. 2 (1984), 113–137, will be, I think, the last word. It is always understood, of course, that the ultimate reference is to the archetypal symbol, Saint Martin's, however economically rendered.

54. Inglis kept the two great essentials: the tower set into the body of the church and the prominent Venetian window in a flat east end, even when frontier exigencies allowed little else. The three best examples are Saint Mary's Auburn, Saint Stephen's, Chester, and Saint John's, Cornwallis, near Williams. All were consecrated about 1790. Saint Stephens was demolished about 1840 but is known from a drawing by Woolford (see Alan Gowans, *Building Canada* [Toronto, 1966], pls. 94, 94a).

55. Friedman 1984, 281, following Harold Kalman, *Pioneer Churches* (Toronto, 1967).

56. Sir William Robe was a professional soldier who naturally understood empire symbolism. I found his biography, quite by accident, in "St. Peter's Church, Bermuda," *Bermuda Historical Quarterly* 11, no. 1 (1954), 36–37, "The Robe Tablet," which commemorates the death from yellow fever of Lieutenant Colonel Thomas Congreve Robe in 1853: "He was the third son of Col. Sir William Robe, K.C.B., K.T.S., K.C.H., of the Royal Horse Artillery (1765–1820), who was born in Woolwich." Trained at the Royal Military Academy, Sir William spent his entire life in imperial service, being badly wounded in the Peninsular War. He was posted to Quebec in 1799 and stayed until 1805, time enough to supervise erection of Trinity Cathedral and marry Sarah Watt, daughter of Captain Thomas Watt of Quebec. They had five sons and four daughters; all the sons also entered military life and died in service, one at Waterloo, one at Chittagong in the Burmese War, one at Saint John's Newfoundland and another in Bermuda. The daughters were all named after battles in the Napoleonic Wars (Vimiera, Roleia) and none married. His "architectural" career is a close parallel to Kearsley's.

57. The Gibbsian impress was fainter by this time and overlaid by fashionable classical revival tastes (see Eric Arthur, *No Mean City* [Toronto, 1964], 39; Jean-Claude Marsan, *Montreal in Evolution* [Montreal, 1978]). Both were replaced by ecclesiological Gothic when this became the style of the Second British Empire, in the 1850s.

58. It also had a Venetian window in the west end, whether or not inspired by Saint Paul's, Halifax, would be hard, and not particularly relevant, to say. It may be significant that from the first this building was associated with Brown University; it was specifically dedicated "for the Public Worship of Almighty God, and also for holding Commencement in"—that is, the building had a public social function besides religious services. Bibliography usefully summarized by Friedman 1984, 350 n. 98.

59. Elizabeth Mills Brown, *The United Church on the Green* (New Haven, 1965); *Center Church on the Green* (New Haven, 1976); E. S. Bartlett, "The First Church of Christ in New Haven," *Historical Sketches of New Haven* (New Haven, 1967).

60. Much has been written about these classic New England churches, ranging from the reverentially romantic to the precisely scholarly. Nowhere—at least nowhere that has come to my attention—is there serious discussion of the curious anomaly that the classic type of New England church in the early nineteenth century should so obviously derive from the classic type of Anglican establishment church, that is, from just the type that the original Puritan/Congregationalists abhorred.

Notes on Renaissance and Baroque Originals and Originality

RICHARD E. SPEAR
Oberlin College

These remarks were made by Richard Spear in his capacity as one of the moderators of the symposium "Retaining the Original: Multiple Originals, Copies, and Reproductions," sponsored by the Center for Advanced Study in the Visual Arts, Washington, and the Johns Hopkins University, Baltimore, 8–9 March 1985.

IF OUR MODERN emphasis on the importance of artistic originality or our sense of what defines the original work of art versus a copy differs from that held during the Renaissance and baroque periods, then we run a very large risk of imposing inappropriate values on many earlier artistic products. Style and iconography have typically received most attention in discussions and definitions of artistic periods at the expense of a consideration of how artists, patrons, and the public were or were not concerned with originality as an artistic criterion. Many of the visual changes that we formally analyze are inseparably linked to theoretical, conceptual issues that spring from shifting attitudes toward originality or invention.

Copies present complex problems, given that what we now call a copy is not necessarily what others did. Saint Augustine and Jonathan Richardson hardly would have seen similar worth in copies. During the Middle Ages the "problem" of copies as we tend to see it scarcely existed. When truth was wed to a lack of change in received imagery, variables were undesirable. Thus we have Epiphanius' letter written in the fourth century, in which he condemns artists who "lie by representing the appearance of saints in different forms according to their whims." For him, images simply were false when "set down through the stupidity of the painter . . . according to his own inclination." Compare that attitude with the statement made a millennium later (1411) by Manuel Chrysoloras: "In images we are admiring the beauty not of bodies, but of the maker's mind."

Such a contrast signals the emergence of a new attitude and makes one realize that for Epiphanius, a copy not only was as good as an original but was *the* desired product precisely because it did not contain the error of personal invention. Since I have been bold enough to cite authors at the beginning and close of the Middle Ages, skipping ten centuries of thought, perhaps it will be no less audacious to refer to Richardson, whose late eighteenth-century attitude seems so different from ours yet was expressed just when profound shifts were occurring in attitudes toward originality. Richardson said,

A copy of a very good picture is preferable to an indifferent original; for there the invention is seen almost entire, and a great deal of the expression and disposition and many times good hints of the colouring, drawing, and other qualities. An indifferent original hath nothing that is excellent, nothing that touches which such a copy I am speaking of hath.

Richardson's vocabulary should alert us to certain key

ideas and terms. He praises a copy because it conveys invention, which completely reverses the value system of Epiphanius, whose copies were true just because they did not have invention. Richardson also cares about matters we identify as artistic, such as coloring and drawing, and there lies beneath his judgment a clear sense of the individuality of the maker.

These issues are central to a consideration of originality during the Renaissance and the baroque and pertain not only to paintings and sculptures but to prints as well. As multiple originals, or multiple copies, they present particularly complex problems. A consideration of prints might begin with the awareness that they sprang from a context of what the Greeks called *techne*, the teachable, learned trades. Moreover, like sculptures, prints unquestionably were reliant on manual activity, but they could not have any claim to antique authority in the way sculptures might. The origins of prints were anything but favorable to their admission into the category of intellectual activities or the liberal arts; and thus they were anything but attractive to the artist aspiring to the poet's status. To my knowledge no early case ever was made for the idea of "ut graphis poesis." Moreover, unlike painting and sculpture and virtually all the decorative arts, prints had no material value whatsoever.

In considering issues of originality in the graphic (and other) arts, one needs to watch for the emergence of conditions that would place value not only on technical virtuosity or more narrowly on the mundane utility of prints as multiple images for pilgrims, New Year's cards, and the like. We want to know when and why prints—or paintings or sculptures or buildings—began to be seen as bearers of inventions worthy in their own right, and we wish to know when it started to matter whose invention it was, the printmaker's or someone else's. We should try to understand the connection between these issues on the one hand and attitudes toward drawings as worthwhile, collectible works of art on the other.

It is worth asking two other questions in this context. When and why were the first facsimiles of drawings made? How does one explain the apparent paradox that reproductive prints, which we now tend to dismiss as unoriginal works of art, emerged and flourished at the time when a heightened sense of originality—an interest in disseminating an individual artist's inventions—took hold in the earlier sixteenth century, in the circle of Raphael and Marcantonio?

Related problems arise in considering cinquecento workshop practices. Was Veronese's bottega operated in a distinctively Venetian manner or were its procedures as common in centers such as Florence and Rome? More germane to the subject of this symposium is asking if Veronese's clients would have formulated the issues the way we do, would they have seen the assistants and family members as continuing "to produce paintings at an alarming rate," as Beverly Brown suggests? If so, then a critical point was reached in the evolution of our modern sense of the original. A nicer distinction perhaps needs to be drawn between wanting "a Veronese" and "an original." Here one is reminded of John Sherman's study of Andrea del Sarto's shop organization and conclusion that *no* single, primary autographic version existed, but multiple "originals" were instead produced.

It is important to bear in mind as well, whether with regard to Veronese or others, that the contractual stipulation that a work be "by the hand" of an artist "fatto di sua mano" had nuances quite different from our own notion of personal touch. Were it otherwise, one would have to concede that, already in the trecento and quattrocento, there was an unusually developed sense of individual creativity. Charles Seymour has shown, however, that "di sua mano" bore legalistic meaning and was more of a guarantee of personal, moral responsibility than necessarily of physical involvement.

In 1610 Maffeo Barberini wrote to his brother, Carlo, reminding him of a promise to lend Caravaggio's *Sacrifice of Isaac* to the French ambassador, who wanted to have a copy made. Once the original was lent, how was a copy actually effected? How could artists copy or even make close variants if the originals were not available? Did they keep cartoons, and if so how could the colors be accurately repeated?

Discussion of originals, copies, and reproductions made during the Renaissance and baroque periods also means consideration of individuality and period styles, as Enea Vico's mid-sixteenth-century sense of connoisseurship suggests. Such matters go right back to Horace's topos of Aesop's crow, which foolishly donned peacock feathers thinking that it could be accepted by the finer birds that way. The magnificent birds instantly saw through the disguise and drove out the crow with scorn. The moral of the story was not to try to be someone else. Petrarch rephrased this idea in critical terms:

I much prefer that my style be my own, rude and undefined perhaps, but made to the measure of my mind . . . rather than to use someone else's style . . . an actor can wear any kind of garment, but a writer cannot adopt any kind of style. . . . Certainly each of us has something naturally individual.

Petrarch's views, like those of many artists, were ambivalent toward the value of ancient authority. Imitation as a *creative* technique wants close analysis. In Vincenzo Danti's view (1567), copying "is much easier that imitating . . . copying [*ritrare*] is as different from imitating as the writing of history is from the making of poetry." One wonders if Giulio Mancini's condemnation of copies really is rooted in Platonic notions of shadows of shadows, for example, in a judgment that a copy is inherently inferior on moral grounds, or if, instead, Mancini's attitudes were not influenced by a new sense of the creative individual: that is, if criteria had not significantly shifted toward the maker from the thing made.

A unifying theme of certain of these essays is the rising awareness throughout the Renaissance and the baroque of the "problem" of the proliferation of replicas. The replicas were obviously made to meet a demand, which makes the question of why replication arose all the more pressing. Is it because, during the cinquecento, perhaps for the first time since antiquity, thought or creative imagination began to compete with handling (to borrow Richardson's division)? If so, by the later seicento, at least if one takes Marco Boschini's Venetian ideas (1676) as indicative, stress on invention as the jewel of art led to a new appreciation of spontaneity as the natural product of the creative imagination, which hierarchy of values, at least in principle, was antithetical to the making of copies.

We should not forget that however much artists, collectors, and writers theorized on these issues, many works of art continued to serve traditional religious purposes, in which capacity discrimination between originals and copies often faded. A case in point is Pierre II Legros' argument with the Jesuits in support of replication in plaster of his own marble sculpture *Saint Stanislas Kostka* in Saint' Andrea al Quirinale (1703):

> The piety that the statue is said to stimulate in the little chapel will be equally stimulated by a similar statue of the same shape, since it is not the material that stimulates piety but rather what is represented . . . if one induces piety, more of it will be induced by two . . . the veneration given to God and the saints increases through the multiplicity of their images . . . in venerating them one does not think about whether they are originals or copies by the artist.

The Print in Thrall to Its Original: A Historiographic Perspective

CAROLINE KARPINSKI

IN THE PREFACE to his *Recueil d'estampes d'après les plus beaux tableaux et d'après les plus beaux desseins qui sont en France*,[1] Pierre Crozat suggests the issues to be discussed in this paper: the aesthetic ideals reproductive prints were supposed to convey; the relative ranking of reproductive prints, prints of invention, and drawings; and the relationship between reproductive prints and letterpress printing. Crozat was wittingly prophetic on the function of multiple impressions in immortalizing perishable paintings: two paintings reproduced in his *Recueil* are now untraced.[2] Intaglio prints were for Crozat familiar, ubiquitous, and quotidien, identical in function to letterpress printing, which assured perpetuity to a literary masterpiece such as Tasso's *Gerusalemme liberata*. Compared for verisimilitude to the reproductive prints of other authors, Crozat deemed his own superior, for his engravers worked directly from the canvas, whereas most engravers worked only from an intervening drawing.[3] Declaring that nothing was omitted and nothing changed, Crozat especially invited comparison of drawings' reproductions—in a period when the execution, collection, critical reception, and reproduction of drawings effloresced—with Renaissance artists' prints of invention, which were, in his view, nothing but drawings transcribed onto copper.[4] One third of the plates, or thirty-one drawings, published in the first volume of the *Recueil*, testify to the esteem that drawings commanded. Prints, it seems, were but a tool: drawings' reproductions seen to fulfill the role of prints of invention; and prints of reproduction endorsed for being self-effacing.

The first part of this paper will consider prints of interpretation, from their origin in the fifteenth century until the mid-sixteenth century, a period in which parity prevailed among reproductive prints, the drawings they reproduced, and prints of invention. This parity was riven in France in the 1600s. Part two of my paper deals with the seventeenth and eighteenth centuries, when prints were devoted overwhelmingly to informational and other reproductive uses. That, combined with the altered perception of drawings as creatively central, effected a hierarchy in the graphic arts. Here and there prints of invention, irrespective of subject, were well received, but they were swept from the mainstream by the quantity and cultural function of reproductive prints. These judgments were affirmed in the rest of western Europe, where French artistic standards dominated. The hierarchy is one that is with us yet, among English-speaking scholars, despite the periodic creative and critical recoveries of prints.

Vasari's account of prints in the *Tre arti del disegno*, which preceded the first edition of the *Vite*, initially appears eccentric. He confined himself to nielli and chiaroscuro woodcuts and derived the origin of printed engravings from the proofing on paper of as-yet-unnielloed plaques. He gave technical descriptions of nielli and of woodcuts printed from two or more blocks in colors, although about single block woodcuts he had nothing to say.

Two characteristics set apart nielli and chiaroscuro woodcuts from other techniques of the printing art. They are rarer and more precious and are independent of literal reproductive function. Notwithstanding Ugo da Carpi's initial appeal in Venice to those who cherish drawings,[5] Raphael's *Death of Ananias* was printed in Rome during the painter's lifetime in greens and blues or in ochers and blues (impressions in Weimar and at the Bibliothèque Nationale, respectively)—colors that are without parallel in Raphael's drawings. Hence, it may be that in 1550 Vasari gave short shrift to engravings and ignored single-block woodcuts entirely because they were for him scarcely an art form but merely a tool of reproduction, comparable to commonplace letterpress printing. Although by 1564 he had become sensitive to the artistry of engraving, Vasari continued to regard the reproductive print as but a drawing in multiple originals.

Francesco Negri Arnoldi recently called attention to the importance of drawing in Leon Battista Alberti's mathematically rationalized reality that coincided with the introduction of engraving, and he proposed that engraving contributed to the generation of drawing.[6] Be that as it may, some time in the late 1480s Mantegna was the first eminent painter to perceive the value of engraving his drawings and of having them engraved by others. He assiduously maintained quality control, actually assaulting unauthorized reproducers.

When we consult the formal critical literature of the sixteenth and seventeenth centuries, as well as informal references, it becomes obvious that prints of invention and prints of translation were both regarded as expressions integral with an artist's drawings. That parity was assumed between prints by the artist and prints after his designs is evident by the way the two forms were interspersed and commingled without distinction detrimental to the reproductive print. When Anton Francesco Doni wrote Enea Vico in 1549 asking Vico to secure prints for his collection, Doni in two instances named the engravers as the authors of the prints he wanted: Marcantonio rather than Raphael, Caraglio rather than Rosso or Perino del Vaga—although in a third case, he named Bandinelli in preference to Marcantonio or Marco Dente.[7] Moreover, Malvasia and Baldinucci, both of whom were great collectors of drawings, imply not hierarchy but parity among the three forms of graphic art.

Baldinucci wrote eighteen "*vite*" in *Cominciamento e progresso dell'arte dell'intagliare in rame colle vite di molti de' più eccellenti maestri della stessa professione* (Florence, 1686). Eight of these lives were, exclusively or almost exclusively, about printmakers of invention, while ten were primarily about reproductive engravers. He arranged the lot chronologically. In the first category are Dürer, Lucas van Leyden, Aldegrever, Antonio Tempesta, Callot, Stefano della Bella, Rembrandt, and Pietro Testa. In the second category are Marcantonio, Hubert and Hendrik Goltzius, three of the Sadelers—Jan, Raphael, and Aegidus—Jan Sandredam, Cornelis Bloemaert, Robert Nanteuil, and François Spierre. Baldinucci's viewpoint may be summarized by the following characterization of Pietro Aquila paraphrased from the introduction: Aquila made prints after the works of Annibale Carracci in Palazzo Farnese, after Giovanni Lanfranco's works "negli Orti Borghese," and after Pietro da Cortona's "ne' Palazzi di casa Sacchetti"; he also made etchings after Ciro Ferri's inventions, after Carlo Maratta's, and after his own.[8] Had Baldinucci wished to distinguish qualitatively between Aquila's prints of reproduction and of invention, he undoubtedly would have expressed himself differently.[9]

Malvasia, in his *Felsina Pittrice* (Bologna, 1678), discusses the same issue more intricately. He devotes a section to twenty-two artists who, either as engravers or as designers, lavished a major portion of their talent on prints.[10] Malvasia opens with Marcantonio and Giulio Bonasone and moves on to Primaticcio whose incomparable draftsmanship, he asserts, was a natural gift for the medium. He lists the prints for which Primaticcio made drawings—the familiar etchings from the school of Fontainebleau and the less-familiar engravings by Giorgio Ghisi. But Malvasia does not confine himself to reproductive prints contemporary with Primaticcio; in fact, he first lists the prints of 1653 by Theodor van Thulden—the set of fifty-eight after the Gallery of Ulysses.[11] Obviously, the reproductive styles of the sixteenth and seventeenth centuries are distinct, yet Malvasia appears to have factored in the period style and to have seen Primaticcio as well served by both.

Malvasia then alternates designers and executors: Pellegrino Tibaldi, designer; Domenico Tibaldi, etcher; Giulio Cesare Procaccini, designer; Camillo, etcher; Lodovico Carracci, prints by and after; Agostino Carracci, prints of his own invention, by him after designs of others, and by others after his prints and drawings. Without examining each artist individually, we may summarize

Malvasia's four categories of artists as follows: the first consists of mainly reproductive engravers, such as Marcantonio and Bonasone; the second of designers for prints, such as Primaticcio, who possibly executed a print himself; the third of artists like Guido Reni and Lodovico Carracci, who executed prints after their own design and whose works were subjects of reproduction; and the fourth of artists such as Agostino Carracci, who made prints after their own inventions, who reproduced the designs of others, and after whom prints were made. As in Baldinucci, so in Malvasia, all four aspects of designing and engraving are mingled without discrimination.

Caveats need to be considered when faced with this overall confidence in the reproductive print. Vasari had reservations about the prints after Frans Floris, saying, in essence, that the artist's greatness could not be fully appreciated in his prints because the engraver, even if the best of craftsmen, is always far from achieving the effect, design, and style of the designer.[12] This disapprobation must be weighed against the praise Vasari heaped on Marcantonio, Vico, Lambert Zutman, and others.

A search for the correlative *stati* of prints of invention, prints of interpretation, and drawings may be aided by considering references to prints and references to prints in tandem with drawings found in literary sources, inventories of collections, and other casual records. Our knowledge and understanding of Italian sixteenth- and seventeenth-century graphic arts collections reside first in Paola Barocchi, then in two complementary studies, one by Michael Bury on Italian collections and the other by William W. Robinson on northern European collections.[13] Both Bury and Robinson isolated one specific organizational mode—that of gathering prints and drawings conjointly, as is illustrated modestly in Felice Feliciano's bequest in 1466 of "drawings and pictures on paper by many excellent masters of design"[14] and conspicuously in the Uffizi graphic arts collection. The nucleus of the latter collection was assembled by Grand Duke Leopoldo (1617–1675)[15] for whom Baldinucci, as custodian, drew up a list of the artists represented.[16] Malvasia, as a collector and dealer, presumably organized his holdings according to the disposition of the *Felsina Pittrice*.[17]

Another mode, adopted less frequently in northern Europe than in Italy, was to assemble prints and drawings together in albums or rolls. This is illustrated in the notation of Marcantonio Michiel in 1530 on the Foscari collection: "El libro de disegni a stampa e de man."[18] Similarly, an inventory of 1554 lists "uno fasso de desegni fra a pena et a stampa."[19] Then, the Gabriele Vendramin (d. 1552) inventory of 1567 and 1568 has "un libro grande con 25 carte in stampa de rame con 16 carte disegnate a man."[20] Further, Daniele Nis housed the two together in about 1615 in "un Archivio d'ebeno ... dentro si conservano ... intagli di Bullino, e tutti li Disegni di Alberto Durero, e Luca d'Olanda, e gran numero fatti a mano de' piu celebri maestri."[21]

Does the citation of prints and drawings together, in one breath as it were, tell us anything about the standing of these objects in respect to one another? Observers from Cennini onward were mindful of the differences between the two graphic techniques,[22] and although *disegno* in mannerist formulations is ambiguous, it would be perverse to assume that "design" was meant each time and not "drawing." While parity is unproven between the two kinds of "drawings" in print and by hand in passages such as "disegni a stampa e de man," two instances cited by Michael Bury disclose that the same level of technical achievement was perceived as characterizing both. In the first case, Bury reasoned that the recurrent presence in the collections of those virtuosi who produced pictorially and technically consummate engravings—Dürer, Lucas, Marcantonio, Caraglio, Vico—indicates the value that collectors placed on the prints' high finish.[23] He compared this to the similarly high finish that collectors desired in drawings, as evidenced by Georg Hoefnagel's recommendation to Niccolò Gaddi (1579) of northern drawings that were not only important but "finished" and by Gabriele Chiabrera's description of Cesare Corte's drawing in his collection (1594) as "finito-finito."[24] In the second case Bury argued for parity on the basis of a passage in Cellini's "Discorso sopra l'arte del disegno," which states that engravings are made to multiply the kind of pen drawings that are most difficult to execute, where the whites of the paper serve as lights.[25] Cellini is thoroughly confident that a drawing's *invenzione* and *disegno* in the senses of manner, design, and drawing can be transcribed into engraving. A passage in Giulio Mancini's *Considerazioni sulla pittura*, written in 1614–1621, may serve as a third avowal of parity.[26] In his discourse on outline, which he calls the first category of drawing, Mancini illustrates the category with examples from three different kinds of graphic art—woodcuts, drawings on paper, and engravings—choosing Dürer's woodcut illustrations to the *Four Books on Human Proportion*, Jacopo Ripanda's drawings of the Column of Trajan, and Mantegna's engravings as equally valid examples of drawings in outline.

When we turn to the theoretical definitions of drawings, and without rehearsing what Vasari, Federico Zuccaro, and all the rest had to say, we may agree that there is nothing in the critical definitions of the sixteenth and seventeenth centuries—whether *disegno* is defined at its most intellectually abstract or as impressionistic and useful—that precludes the integral reproduction or translation of a drawing into a print. Whether the *disegno* is preordained in the "divine mind" and transmitted to the artist or is a swift, momentary record "que le peintre jette sur le papier,"[27] it is not, in itself, thought to possess spiritual qualities that cannot be transferred into painting or engraving. The notion of the possession of the paper only developed in the work of eighteenth-century critics such as the just-quoted Antoine Dezallier d'Argenville.

I would now like to address Agostino Carracci's aggrandizement, which was both conceptual and expressive, of the mandate of the reproductive print. Agostino's aesthetic convictions were founded on principles in nature and sensory impressions melded to perfections he perceived in other masters. These convictions compelled him to enhance the models on which he executed reproductive prints, as we have learned from Malvasia and more recently from Argan, Ostrow, and DeGrazia.[28] Agostino was heir to a great vocabulary of engraving artfulness that developed in Italy and in northern Europe during the course of the sixteenth century. Inspired by Venetian painting, he espoused hereditary graphic terms as equivalents for Venetian colors, textures, values, luminosity, and crepuscular darkness. Because of the authority later wielded by his reproductive prints, we regret the lack of a comprehensive view of the changes Agostino wrought on his sources in light of his aesthetic principles. And it is chiefly because of his reputed coloristic innovation in reproductive prints that we wish to know to what extent Agostino succeeded in capturing the flush and depth of Venetian colorism.

Throughout the entire sixteenth century, reproductive printmakers altered their models according to their own aesthetic biases, without that aesthetic necessarily having been articulated. It is amusing to see Ugo da Carpi, who was of the same generation as Marcantonio and exposed first to the same Emilian late quattrocento classical ideal and later to high Roman classicism, equilibrate Parmigianino's *Apollo* figure, which sways backward off the perpendicular.[29] So too Marcantonio, when steeped in the experience of classical sculpture in Rome, as well as in Raphael's grave presences, altered the insubstantial figures in Giovanni Francesco Penni's *modello* in his engraving *The Vintage*.[30] These two examples of

changes are symptomatic of the engravers' profound convictions, which are deployed across the whole body of their mature work.

Glenn Gould said that everything there is to know about playing the piano can be taught in half an hour. In that sense, the same is true of the classic printmaking techniques. Of course, manual exercise remains important, as was affirmed by writers from Cennini onward. References are numerous to prints requiring skill and talent equal to that necessary for drawing or painting. In his *Aretino* Dolce remarked: "Drawing is a useful expressive tool as manifested in engraving and other arts and crafts"; the critic and print dealer Joullain noted in 1786 that "the engraver must comprehend drawing equally to the painter"; and a century later Emeric-David stated that "engraving depends foremost on drawing skill."[31]

Examples are legion among sixteenth-century engravings of the prodigious skill expended in the service of a complex pictorialism incorporating atmospheric, chiaroscurial, and textural effects. It is impossible to assess here all the technical features that facilitated Agostino's fusion of tone, color, and drawing into a mode that left the graphic arts equation intact. Agostino made scores of prints after drawings, whereas he made no more than twenty after paintings. It may be ventured that the same ratio pertains to other Italian printmakers circa 1600. Thereafter in France and elsewhere the balance shifted to painting as the preponderant model for engraving, which it steadfastly remained for the next two centuries, at the same time drawings came to be vested with creative quintessence.

Throughout the seventeenth and eighteenth centuries, reproductive prints were valued chiefly for their subjects rather than for their technique or style. How profound the reliance was on such prints may be seen in Roland Fréart de Chambray's disputation of 1662 when he argued almost wholly on the basis of prints in favor of Raphael's perfect *disegno* versus Michelangelo's anticlassicism.[32] This thrall of the print of reproduction to its original model was at intervals interrupted by an eloquent avowal of the autonomy, even primacy, of prints of invention. Nonetheless, the parity among the three forms of graphic art—drawings, original prints, and prints of reproduction—was at an end.

We may now turn to the destiny of prints in seventeenth-century France and eighteenth-century Europe, a destiny determined by the overwhelming number of prints that functioned as conveyors of pictorial, cultural, scientific, and technical information. In a period that sought comprehensive knowledge of the fitting and beautiful art of the past—with J. B. Colbert dictating "Faites faire aux peintres les copies de tout ce qu'il y a de beau à Rome"[33]—and when contemporary painting was official and respected, reproductive prints of great technical brilliance, executed by such artists as the Drevets (father and son) and Gérard Edelinck, carried on their traditional role as interpreters of paintings. Moreover, engravings of official events and historical subjects were legion, produced both as reproductions as by Sébastian Le Clerc after Charles Le Brun and as originals as by Callot. Poetical subjects—the other, besides history, of André Félibien's two highest categories of subject matter[34]—were reproduced in great number as, for instance, by Pierre Brebiette. What was lacking, however, was an intense printmaking activity on the part of painters. Theoretically, the seventeenth-century French emphasis on outline and the dominance of drawing over color would seem to favor prints. Practically, Abraham Bosse required beautiful contours, a fine execution, and invention, which he allowed even to an "eau forte croquée."[35] With neither theory nor practice precluding the execution of original prints, the onus falls on French painters for having renounced technical opportunities and starting prints of invention on a long decline. The dominance of French artistic standards in western Europe—whatever the degree and extent may have been[36]—ultimately resulted in the neglect of printmaking by painters with the exception of certain forays into historical subjects. Notwithstanding the philosophical complexion of Pietro Testa's etched inventions, appropriately critiqued by Passeri on the level of paintings,[37] the tide running in favor of prints of reproduction, as well as of drawings, could not be stemmed.

Thus, especially in France during the seventeenth century, painters' prints of poetic invention were neither nurtured in practice nor in theory, whereas drawings were praised in theory and executed as a matter of course and prints of reproduction were made in multitude. The intellectual spirit of the age encouraged cultivation of the practice begun in the sixteenth century of sorting prints into categories of knowledge for reference purposes.[38] Such a division by subject did not preclude monographic organization within a collection, either by inventor or by reproductive printmaker, with the purpose of illustrating the history of printmaking or painting or the aesthetic range of individual artists. Then as now, some collectors eschewed connoisseurship while others cultivated their eye. Collecting virtuoso fabrications in various materials required an acute connoisseur who sometimes placed among his other objects an engraving in an exquisite impression.[39]

The most important print collections assembled in the seventeenth century were the two of Michel de Marolles. Their classification and contents are known to us in detail from his catalogues: the first collection, organized half by subject, half by artist, and the second collection, organized one-third by subject, leave no doubt that Marolles viewed fine arts as but one aspect of culture.[40] The earlier of the two collections, now in the Bibliothèque Nationale, consisted of nearly a quarter of a million prints by six thousand masters in four hundred folios, plus eighty albums of smaller format. In the catalogue published in 1666, Marolles spelled out his dedication to assembling productions of human genius in art or science, as well as figurations of divinity and history, transmitted by or represented in prints.[41] His introduction sets forth some of the subjects comprehended in his collection: ceremonies, entries, devices, emblems, buildings, antique and modern sculptures, medals, tournaments, machines of war, the mechanical arts, sea and land battles, animals and plants, portraits, costumes, and maps. He further summarized the contents of individual volumes: the Raphael volume, for example, had 740 prints; volume 52 was devoted entirely to the ruins of Rome; volume 149 to images of the Virgin; volume 172 to gardens and fountains; and volumes 181 and 182 to city views.

The civilizing qualities of these prints harmonized with the interests of Colbert who furthermore looked to prints as vehicles for broadcasting current courtly glories. As the patron of some eleven publications of prints, illustrating, for instance, the Great Tournament at Versailles in 1662, he perceived, as had the Medici before him, the propagandistic value of conveying to the world, in ambitious and beautiful sets of engravings, the extravagant events at court.[42]

Given the view that prints constituted a historical record and didactic tool as well as ornaments of great libraries, as Marolles had it, it was inevitable when Colbert acquired the Marolles collection in 1667 that he placed it not in the museum of paintings at the Louvre but with printed texts of reference in the Bibliothèque Royale.[43] Four years after this acquisition Colbert purchased the Jabach collection of more than five thousand drawings and placed those not with the prints in the Bibliothèque Royale but with the objects of fine art in the Louvre.[44]

Of course, this bifurcation of the graphic arts rests on a theoretical basis, as relevant in France as in Italy. Of the six principal merits of prints noted by Roger de Piles in his *Abrégé de la vie des peintres* of 1699, three transmit the seventeenth-century values of cultural and intellectual instruction: prints as aide-mémoire, as precepts more forceful than words, and as representations of secluded objects or persons. The other three uphold sixteenth-century functions: prints as means of comparing different artists, as forming taste, and as giving pleasure by imitation.[45] In the usage of Roger de Piles, imitation had to be strictly faithful to the prototype, whose knowledge was the goal. One had recourse to a translation, as Watelet observed in Diderot's *Encyclopédie* six decades later, not for itself but solely to know the original.[46] Limited as de Piles was in his perspective, as Teyssèdre wrote, he was not restricted in his taste: prints in their own register were, for de Piles, susceptible to all parts of painting except color and in their function as surrogate paintings, could be perfect.[47] Jonathan Richardson senior, de Piles' somewhat younger contemporary, demurred on the point that all aspects of pictorialism but one were capable of expression. He maintained, as did those sixteenth-century artists and critics who gave tacit or overt agreement to changes in *disegno*, which de Piles, Pierre Crozat, and Watelet did not, that prints of reproduction can never have the "freedom and spirit" of the original and that only the invention can be conveyed.[48] The reproductive printmaker's impediments are insuperable: "It is impossible for anyone to transform himself and become another man; a hand that has always been moving in a certain manner cannot at once or by a few occasional essays get into a different kind of motion. . . . Every man will naturally and unavoidably mix something of himself in all he does."[49]

This allegiance to the supremacy of the invention and the cataloguing of reproductive prints according to painters, as in the eighteenth-century Dresden collection,[50] had two positive, albeit diametrically opposite, effects. The first was to impel Francesco Milizia and Giuseppe Longhi to elevate the rank of prints of translation.[51] Both attributed to printmakers the greatest technical versatility and artistic experience. Writing in 1797 and 1830, respectively, Milizia and Longhi regarded prints of translation as fruits of the archetypal *disegno* and classified them among the major arts.[52] They distinguished reproductive prints from the major arts only in what the prints imitated: whereas the major arts imitated nature, prints of translation imitated other arts.[53]

The second effect was to incite Bartsch to mount his heroic challenge and rise to the defense of original prints. Two of Bartsch's predecessors—one the senior Richardson, who looked with favor on original prints; the other Dezallier d'Argenville, who at least did not look askance—

were ironically principally champions of drawing, which, in the preceding century, had begun to advance to the pinnacle of creativity.

In 1637 Franciscus Junius, who was, as André Fontaine put it, absorbed by a love of drawing wherein laws of perfect proportion may be expressed without the interference of color, published his *De pictura veterum*.[54] Charles-Alphonse Du Fresnoy, writing in *De arte graphica* between 1641 and 1665, claimed dominance of drawing over color and prescribed a smooth, continuous contour line "in waves ressembling flames or the gliding of a snake."[55] Similarly, in the *Entretiens* Félibien affirmed drawing to be the very foundation of art: without a knowledge of drawing, all other aspects of art were unsecured.[56] Committed as Roger de Piles was to reproductive prints, he attributed greater potency to drawings. As for Félibien, so for de Piles, drawing was the foundation of painting, the light of understanding, the instrument of pictorializing man's deepest sentiments. Drawing disarmed the painter and laid bare the quality or absence of his talent.[57]

In 1719 Richardson turned away from Du Fresnoy's contour line "without either eminences or cavities" and advocated the vivid, spirited, and animated line, which he found not only in the drawings of Parmigianino, Annibale Carracci, and Guido Reni but also in their prints.[58] For a brief moment parity between prints of invention and drawings was restored. Original prints, Richardson said, if designed in the plate, are another kind of drawing, to be judged even as paintings by standards of invention, greatness, and grace, provided the beauty of the plate was undiminished.[59] Once the plate began to wear, the status of the print as drawing in multiple originals abated.

Ultimately for Richardson drawings were ascendant over prints and paintings because their excellence was sustained and concentrated. Only in drawings do materials and processes not intervene between creative thought and pictorial execution. The interruptive techniques of printmaking and painting remove the final products from the creative crucible and reduce all to little more than copies of the veritable original, which is the drawing itself.[60]

Broad syntheses are absent from the writings of Dezallier d'Argenville and Pierre-Jean Mariette, who vested their acute connoisseurship of drawings in analyses of individual works.[61] Mariette's collection of drawings surpassed all others: some eight thousand drawings, including those he had acquired from Crozat, were catalogued by François Basan for the posthumous sale in 1775.[62] D'Argenville's smaller-scaled authority, manifested in his *Abrégé de la vie des plus fameux peintres*, first published in 1750, resides in his celebration of the drawing as fire in the artist's imagination, its furious grip unrestrained by reason, its touch spiritual.[63] While characterizing painters' drawings as full of nobility and lofty sentiments, he was content to list what he considered infinitely inferior prints. Ultimately, prints also took second place in Mariette's esteem. Adam Bartsch owed much to Mariette's print connoisseurship, but he challenged Mariette's hierarchical values in which the draftsman stood foremost and the engraver nethermost.

In spite of Bartsch's panegyric to prints of invention, in disregard of a critical history of confidence in the reproductive print, in the face of an efflorescence of printmaking in the present day, notwithstanding scholarly publications engaging prints at the highest critical levels, and despite ardent support of prints by a few museums, prints of invention and certainly prints of reproduction remain among English-speaking scholars to this day in a hierarchy subordinate to drawings. These decisive works await restoration to the mainstream of art-historical discussion.

NOTES

1. Pierre Crozat, *Recueil d'estampes d'après les plus beaux tableaux et d'après les plus beaux desseins qui sont en France dans le Cabinet du Roy, dans celui de Monseigneur le Duc d'Orléans & dans d'autres Cabinets* (Paris, 1729), preface, 1:i–ii.
2. On the disposition of the collection, see Margaret Stuffmann, "Les tableaux de Pierre Crozat: Historique et destinée d'un ensemble célèbre, établis en partant d'un inventaire d'après décès inédit (1740)," *Gazette des Beaux Arts* 72 (July–September 1968), 11–143. The untraced paintings are no. 82, *La Pentecôte*, engraved by Frederic Hortemels as after Gaudenzio Ferrari; and no. 84, *S. Jerosme*, engraved by Nicolas Château, retouched by Louis Surugue, as after Balthazar de Siene. On Stuffmann's list they appear as no. 58, *Pentecost*, by Federico Zuccaro, and no. 27 bis [Saint Luke], by Giovanni Battista Mola.
3. See Crozat's letter to Francesco Gabburri, 29 May 1724, published in Giovanni Gaetano Bottari and Stefano Ticozzi, eds., *Raccolta di lettere sulla pittura, scultura, ed architettura scritte da' più celebri personaggi dei secoli XV, XVI, e XVII*, 8 vols. (Milan, 1822), 2:144, no. 62.
4. Crozat 1729, preface, 1:ii–iv.
5. Ugo's da Carpi's petition to the Venetian Senate of 1516 for a privilege on the printing of chiaroscuro woodcuts was first published in Michelangelo Gualandi, *Memorie originale italiane risguardanti le belle arti* (Bologna, 1841), 54.
6. Francesco Negri Arnoldi, "Technica e scienza," in *Storia dell'arte italiana*, pt. 1, *Materiali e problemi*, vol. 4. *Richerche spaziali e technologie* (Turin, 1980), 184.
7. Anton Francesco Doni, *Disegno* (Venice, 1549), leaf 52 r and v, cited by Evelina Borea, "Stampa figurativa e pubblico dalle origini all'affermazione nel cinquecento," in *Storia dell'arte italiana*, pt. 1, *Materiali e problemi*, vol. 2, *L'artista e il pubblico* (Turin, 1979), 383–384.
8. Filippo Baldinucci, *Cominciamento, e progresso dell'arte dell'intagliare in rame colle vite di molti de' più eccellenti maestri della stessa professione* (Florence, 1686), vi.
9. Baldinucci's reference to reproductive prints as excellent "imitations" (1686, i) may be understood in the same sense as his reference to Caraglio as Marcantonio's "imitator" (1686, iv). Compare Ettore Spalletti, "La documentazione figurativa dell'opera d'arte, la critica, e l'editoria nell'epoca moderna (1750–1930)," in *Storia dell'arte italiana*, pt. 1, *Materiali e problemi*, vol. 2, *L'artista e il pubblico* (Turin, 1979), 425.
10. Carlo Cesare Malvasia, *Felsina Pittrice: Vite de' pittori bolognese*, ed. G. Zanotti (Bologna, 1841), 1:57–106.
11. George Kaspar Nagler, *Neues allgemeines Künstler-Lexikon* (Munich, 1848), 18:449, no. 6.
12. Giorgio Vasari, *Le vite de' più eccellenti pittori, scultori, ed architettori* (1568), 9 vols., ed. Gaetano Milanesi (Florence, 1906), 7:585.
13. Paola Barocchi, "Storiografia e collezionismo dal Vasari al Lanzi," in *Storia dell'arte italiana*, pt. 1, *Materiali e problemi*, vol. 2, *L'artista e il pubblico* (Turin, 1979), 5–81; Michael Bury, "The Taste for Prints in Italy to c. 1600," *Print Quarterly* 2, no. 1 (March 1985), 12–26; William W. Robinson, "'This Passion for Prints': Collecting and Connoisseurship in Northern Europe during the Seventeenth Century," in Clifford S. Ackley, *Printmaking in the Age of Rembrandt* (Boston, 1981), xxvii–xlviii.
14. Charles Mitchell, "Felice Feliciano Antiquarius," *Proceedings of the British Academy* 47 (1961), 199–200.
15. Frits Lugt, *Les marques de collections de dessins & d'estampes* (Amsterdam, 1921), nos. 929–930. Upon the death of Leopold, an inventory mentioned prints in seven folio volumes and others in smaller format, but the actual prints owned by Leopold may be only tentatively identified: courteous communication from Annamaria Petrioli Tofani. See Giovanna Gaeta Bertelà, "Testimonianze documentarie sul fondo dei disegni di Galleria," in *Gli Uffizi: Quattro secoli di una galleria. Convegno internazionale di studi. Fonti e Documenti*. Florence, 20–24 September 1982 (Florence, 1982), 110–111.
16. Printed 8 September 1673. Julius Schlosser, *La letteratura artistica: Manuale delle Fonti della storia dell'arte moderna* (Florence, 1935), 413; Barocchi 1979, 61.
17. Barocchi 1979, 54.
18. Marcantonio Michiel, *Der Anonimo Morelliano (Marcantonio Michiel's notizie d'opere del disegno)*, trans. and ed. Theodor Frimmel, in *Quellenschriften für Kunstgeschichte und Kunsttecknik des Mittelalters und der Neuzeit*, n.s. 1 (1888), 22–23.
19. Inventory of the widow of a Venetian book dealer, Domenico di Soresini. Gustav Ludwigs, "Antonello da Messina und deutsche und niederlandische Künstler in Venedig. II. Zustand des Buchgewerbes in der zweiten Hälfte des XVI Jahrhunderts," *Jahrbuch der Königlichen Preussischen Kunstsammlungen* 23 (1902), supp., 46–51.
20. A. Rava, "Il 'Camerino delle Antigaglie' di Gabriele Vendramin," *Nuovo Archivio Veneto* 39, n.s. 22 (1920), 171, 174 (cited in Bury 1985, 21 nn. 62, 64).
21. Vincenzo Scamozzi, *L'idea della architettura universale* (Venice, 1615), pt. 1, bk. 3, chap. 19, 306 (cited in Bury 1985, 17 n. 34).
22. I am grateful to Terisio Pignatti for directing me to the significance of this point.
23. Bury 1985, 21–22.
24. Bottari and Ticozzi 1822, 3:324, quoted in Julius Held, "The Early Appreciation of Drawings," in *Latin American Art and the Baroque Period in Europe: Studies in Western Art*, Acts of the Twentieth International Congress in the History of Art (Princeton, N.J., 1963), 3:79, 83 (cited in Bury 1985, 21 n. 66); and a drawing of *Medea Killing Her Sons*, letter of 20 November 1594, in *Lettere di Gabriel Chiabrera a Bernardo Castello* (Genoa, 1838), 116 (cited in Bury 1985, 22.)
25. Benvenuto Cellini, "Discorso sopra l'arte del disegno," in *Scritti d'arte del cinquecento: Disegno*, ed. Paola Barocchi (Turin, 1979), 8:1929 (cited in Bury 1985, 23).
26. Giulio Mancini, *Considerazioni sulla pittura* (1614–1621), ed. Adriana Marucchi, with preface by Lionello Venturi and commentary by

Luigi Salerno, 2 vols., Accademia Nazionale dei Lincei, Fonti e Documenti inediti per la storia dell'arte (Rome, 1956), 1:15.

27. Antoine Joseph Dezallier d'Argenville, *Abrégé de la vie des fameux peintres, avec leurs portraits gravés en taille-douce, les indications de leurs principaux ouvrages, quelques réflexions sur leurs caractères, et la manière de connoître les desseins et les tableaux des grands maîtres*, 4 vols., new ed. (Paris, 1762), 1:xxxv.

28. Giulio Carlo Argan, "Il valore critico della 'stampa di traduzione,'" in *Essays in the History of Art Presented to Rudolf Wittkower* (London, 1967), 2:179–181; Stephen Edward Ostrow, "Agostino Carracci" (Ph.D. diss., Institute of Fine Arts, New York University, 1966); Diane DeGrazia Bohlin, *Prints and Related Drawings by the Carracci Family: A Catalogue Raisonné* (Washington, 1979); and Diane DeGrazia Bohlin, *Le stampe dei Carracci con i disegni, le incisioni, le copie, e i dipinti connessi: Catalogo critico*, ed. A. Boschetto (Bologna, 1984).

29. B. XII, 123, no. 24 [2]; collection Pierpont Morgan Library: A. E. Popham, *Catalogue of the Drawings of Parmigianino*, the Franklin Jasper Wall Lectures, 1969, at the Pierpont Morgan Library (New Haven and London, 1971), no. 390, pl. 130.

30. B. XIV, 231–232, no. 306; collection Leo Steinberg: Innis H. Shoemaker and Elizabeth Broun, *The Engravings of Marcantonio Raimondi* [exh. cat., Spencer Museum of Art, Ackland Art Museum] (Lawrence, Kans., 1981), 133–135, no. 38a, illustrated.

31. Mark W. Roskill, *Dolce's "Aretino" and Venetian Art Theory of the Cinquecento*, monograph 15, Monographs on Archaeology and the Fine Arts sponsored by the Archaeological Institute of America and the College Art Association of America (New York, 1968), 114–115; C. F. Joullain, *Réflexions sur la peinture et la gravure* (Metz, 1786), 29; and Toussaint Bernard Emeric-David, *Histoire de la gravure* (Paris, 1852), 178–179.

32. Roland Fréart de Chambray, *Idée de la perfection de la peinture* (Le Mans, 1662; reprint, Farnsborough, Hants, 1968).

33. Letter of 23 July 1672, *Lettres, instructions, et mémoires de Colbert* (Paris, 1861–1873), 5:331, quoted in H. Lemonnier, *L'art français au temps de Louis XVI (1661–1690)* (Paris, 1911), 113.

34. André Félibien, *Entretiens sur les vies et sur les ouvrages des plus excellens peintres anciens et modernes* (Trévoux, 1725), 5:310–311. See also André Fontaine, *Les doctrines d'art en France: Peintres, amateurs, critiques, de Poussin à Diderot* (Paris, 1909), 56.

35. Abraham Bosse, *Traicté des manieres de graver en taille-douce sur l'airin par le moyen des eaux fortes, & des vernix durs & mols* (Paris, 1645), folio A ii r.

36. Nikolaus Pevsner, *Academies of Art Past and Present* (Cambridge, 1940), 102, 110–111; and Anthony Blunt, *Art and Architecture in France, 1500 to 1700* (Melbourne, London, Baltimore, 1953), 229–230.

37. Giovanni Battista Passeri, *Vite de' pittori, scultori, ed architetti che anno lavorato in Roma morti dal 1641 fino al 1673* (Rome, 1772), 181–184, to which subject Elizabeth Cropper, *Ideal of Painting: Pietro Testa's Düsseldorf Notebook* (Princeton, 1984), especially 42–95, has given a distinguished exposition.

38. Seventeenth-century Italian and northern European collections that maintained these systematic divisions according to fields of learning are discussed in Bury 1985 and Robinson 1981.

39. Bernardo Vecchietti was such a collector of rare and precious objects, including prints. His palace is described by Raffaello Borghini, *Il riposo* (Florence, 1584), 13–14 (cited in Barocchi 1979, 26; and Bury 1985, 18 and n. 36).

40. Michel de Marolles, *Catalogue de livres d'estampes et de figures en taille-douce* (Paris, 1666); and Michel de Marolles, *Catalogue de livres d'estampes et de figures en taille-douce . . . fait à Paris en l'année 1672* (Paris, 1672). See also *Le Livre des peintres et graveurs par Michel de Marolles*, ed. Georges Duplessis, 2d ed. (Paris, 1872); and L. Bosseboeuf, *Un précurseur: Michel de Marolles: Abbé de Villeloin: Sa vie et son oeuvre* (Tours, 1911), 105, 256–266.

41. Marolles 1666, 9.

42. Antoine Jules Dumesnil, *Histoire des plus célèbres amateurs français et de leurs relations avec les artistes faisant suite à celle des plus célèbres amateurs italiens. 2. Jean-Baptiste Colbert surintendant des bâtiments du roi, 1625–1683* (Paris, 1857), 251–253.

43. Marolles 1666, 6; and Lugt 1921, nos. 244–246, 248–253.

44. For a history of the transaction see Dumesnil 1857, 227–234. According to Hugues-Adrien Joly, in 1775 custodian of the Cabinet des planches gravées et estampes of the Bibliothèque Royale, Colbert severed the drawings from the prints only to enhance the dominion of his son, the Marquis de Seignelay, in the Département des bâtiments. This interpretation may be self-serving, however, as Joly was eager to acquire the late Pierre-Jean Mariette's drawings as well as prints for the Bibliothèque Royale. He failed. See Antoine Jules Dumesnil, *Histoire des plus célèbres amateurs français et leurs relation avec les artistes faisant suite à celle des plus célèbres amateurs italiens. 1. Pierre-Jean Mariette, 1694–1774* (Paris, 1858), 385–387; Lugt 1921, nos. 1886, 2959; and Rosalie Bacou, *I grandi disegni italiani della collezione Mariette al Louvre di Parigi* (Milan, 1982), 60–62.

45. Roger de Piles, *Abrégé de la vie des peintres avec des réflexions sur leur ouvrages et un traité du peintre parfait, de la connoissance des desseins, & de l'utilité des estampes* (Paris, 1699), 84–86; Bernard Teyssèdre, *Histoire de l'art vue du grand siècle* (Paris, 1964), 31.

46. Claude Henri Watelet, "Graveur," in *Encyclopédie ou dictionnaire raisonné des sciences, des arts, et des métiers*, 3d ed. (Livorno, 1773), 7:865 (quoted in Spalletti 1979, 417).

47. Teyssèdre 1964, 245–246 n. 9; de Piles 1699, 73–74, as quoted in Teyssèdre 1964, 30.

48. Jonathan Richardson [senior], *Two Discourses. I. An Essay on the Whole Art of Criticism as it relates to painting shewing how to judge I. Of the Goodness of a Picture; II. Of the Hand of the Master; and III. Whether 'tis an Original or a Copy. II. An Argument in Behalf of the Science of a Connoisseur* (London, 1719), 178.

49. Richardson 1719, 186.

50. Karl Heinrich von Heinecken, *Idée générale d'une collection complette d'estampes: Avec une dissertation sur l'origine de la gravure & sur les premiers livres d'images* (Leipzig and Vienna, 1771), 1: "L'objet principal ayant toujours été étude des peintres, on a réuni par preference en corps d'ouvrages les estampes gravés d'après leur production."

51. Spalletti 1979, 417–418, 421.

52. Francesco Milizia, *Dizionario delle belle arti del disegno: Edizione corretta ed arricchita di moltissimi vocaboli* (Bologna, 1827–1828), 2:106, 112; Giuseppi Longhi, *La calcografia propriamente detta ossia l'arte d'incidere in rame coll'acqua—forte, col bulino, e colla punta* (Milan, 1830), 8–9.

53. On nineteenth-century critics, chiefly Ruskin, who were disgruntled with reproductive prints see the preface by Christopher Lloyd, *Art and Its Images: An Exhibition of Printed Books Containing Engraved Illustrations after Italian Painting* [exh. cat., Bodleian Library] (Oxford, 1975), 3–23.

54. Fontaine 1909, 22–33.

55. Charles-Alphonse Du Fresnoy, *De arte graphica: The Art of Painting* (London, 1695), 16.

56. Félibien 1725, 1:94–96, first published between 1666 and 1688.

57. Roger de Piles, *Cours de peinture par principes* (Paris, 1708), 126; de Piles 1699, 66–74.

58. Du Fresnoy 1695, 16; and Richardson 1719, 198.

59. Richardson 1719, 198. Even without the full context of English aesthetic judgments, it is worth citing one instance of comparable values assigned to master prints and drawings early in the eighteenth century. Writing in 1762, the younger Richardson recorded that the grandfather of the then duke of Devonshire, who at a time when he was purchasing only prints, had acquired a framed lot from an English collection. The prints were found to have behind them drawings by

Raphael, Parmigianino, Polidoro, and Giulio Romano. These were album leaves with prints and drawings mounted together as in the Arundel collection. See F. J. B. Watson, "On the Early History of Collecting in England," *Burlington Magazine* 85, no. 498 (1944), 223–224. I owe this reference to Noel Annesley.

60.   Richardson 1719, 50–51.

61.   On Mariette see *Dessins français du XVIIIᵉ siècle: Amis et contemporains de P.-J. Mariette,* introduction by Rosalie Bacou [exh. cat., Musée du Louvre, Cabinet des Dessins] (Paris, 1967), 7–9.

62.   François Basan, *Catalogue raisonné des differens objets de curiosités dans les sciences et arts qui composient le Cabinet de feu Mr Mariette* (Paris, 1775), nos. 113–1448. D'Argenville's collection was sold three years later: see Pierre Remy, *Catalogue d'une collection de dessins choisis des maîtres célèbres . . . et d'un recueil d'estampes de feu M. d'Argenville* (Paris, 1778).

63.   Dezallier d'Argenville 1762, 1:xxiv, xxxii–xxxiii, xlvii.

Replication and the Art of Veronese

BEVERLY LOUISE BROWN
National Gallery of Art, Washington

WHEN IN THE mid-sixteenth century Giorgio Vasari first met Paolo Caliari, better known as Veronese, he thought the young artist was not yet thirty.[1] Despite Veronese's age, Vasari felt that he had already perfected his craft, and he praised his painting in terms still used by modern critics. Paolo's skill lay in his power of inventiveness when composing and staging groups of figures and in his ability to manipulate color and light so that the exquisite beauty of brocaded fabric was stimulated in pigment. His public and private commissions were often carried out on a vast scale, for example, *The Triumph of Venice* from the Sala del Maggior Consiglio in the Palazzo Ducale in Venice or the *Mars and Venus* now in Edinburg but once part of a series of profane subjects painted for the Emperor Rudolf II.[2] These large works provide a delicious feast for the eyes, evoking a Venetian life that is stately, luxurious, and ripe with opulent beauty. They speak of the perennial pleasures associated with Venice's Golden Age, and it is not surprising that this vision of a city's self-glorification was also eagerly sought by patrons of lesser means on a smaller scale.

Small-scale works or cabinet pictures had been collected in Venice since the days of Giorgione, and by midcentury patrician and middle-class homes were filled with them. They became the stock-in-trade of a new breed of freelance art dealers, yet not even a prolific artist like Veronese could satisfy the demand of private patrons and the open market at the same time. He increasingly relied on the assistance of his large and well-organized family workshop: Benedetto, the faithful brother, Gabriele and Carletto, the proficient but uninspired sons, Alvise Benfatto del Friso, his nephew, and a non-Caliari, Montemezzano.[3] The bottega produced a recognizable "Veronese" style, the cinquecento equivalent of a brand name. Paolo's signature, especially during his later career, guaranteed quality control but not personal execution. Even after his death in 1588 the bottega continued to sign paintings with his name or sometimes more accurately "Haeredes Pauli."[4] Both *The Adoration of the Shepherds* now in the Gallerie dell'Accademia in Venice and *The Annunciation* in the Museo Civico of Reggio Emilia are signed "Haeredes Pauli" on the bases of columns in their backgrounds.[5] A small plaque, quietly floating among the reeds and rushes of the Jordan, similarly proclaims that *The Baptism of Christ* now in Saint John the Divine in New York was painted by Paolo's heirs.[6] Any one of these paintings might be loosely termed a Veronese pastiche. They all rely on stock compositions and figural types culled from Paolo's work, but the signature "Haeredes Pauli" was meant to legitimize them.

Fig. 1. Veronese, *The Martyrdom and Last Communion of Saint Lucy*, oil on canvas. National Gallery of Art, Washington, Gift of the Morris and Gwendolyn Cafritz Foundation and Ailsa Mellon Bruce Fund.

It was a reassurance to the buying public that despite Veronese's death the workshop still manufactured the genuine article.

The workshop aided Paolo in two important ways. First, they collaborated on his larger commissions, and second, they replicated his work for the mass market. A series of paintings illustrating the same subject would be repeated line for line, fold for fold, or in more freely adapted variations. *The Finding of Moses* from the National Gallery of Art in Washington (see fig. 15), for example, is a workshop replica of an autograph painting in the Prado (see fig. 16). There are, however, at least ten other versions of this composition that may be attributed to the bottega.[7]

In many respects the organization of the Caliari bottega was no different from that of the traditional Venetian workshop, where painting was practiced as a family endeavor. From Vivarini and Bellini in the late fifteenth century to Bassano, Tintoretto, and even Titian in the sixteenth, knowledge, technique, and responsibility were passed from father to son. According to age, skill, and propinquity, varying tasks would be assigned to individual members of the shop, generally with the unstated assumption that the most gifted would play the leading role.

The cooperative effort in a sixteenth-century workshop would begin with an idea generated by the principal artist, who would oversee the entire production. He might start by making a sketch for the painting or perhaps preparing a fully developed *modello*. In many cases, however, he would block out the subject on a freshly primed canvas, without making a preliminary study. Once the initial composition was determined, the canvas would be turned over to an assistant. The assistant would lay in broad areas of color, slowly begin to build up layers of transparent glaze, and perhaps even bring to completion certain subsidiary passages. During the final stage work would be resumed by the master, who would complete the most delicate and important areas of the painting:

Fig. 2. X-radiograph of *The Martyrdom and Last Communion of Saint Lucy* (detail).

Fig. 3. X-radiograph of *The Martyrdom and Last Communion of Saint Lucy* (detail).

hands, faces, principal figures, ravishing passages of drapery. He would adjust, correct, and modify any errors made by the assistant and through his own recognizable touch give the collaborative venture his unique signature.[8]

What was unusual about the bottega was the division of labor and its ability to create "Veroneses" without Paolo's personal intervention. An undated letter from Benedetto Caliari to Giacomo Contarini describes in specific terms how the collaboration among family members creating a single painting occurred.[9] After the patron had chosen his subject (in this case a complex allegory involving Hercules and San Jacomo), Benedetto would make sketches for the painting, presumably on paper. Carletto would transfer these ideas to the canvas, and Gabriele would complete the painting. Payments and other letters from Paolo substantiate that Benedetto and Paolo frequently collaborated.[10] Although such works, for example, *The Martyrdom of Saint Giustina* (see fig. 14) done for the church of the same name in Padua, were

released under Paolo's signature, it was clear to everyone, or at least those who held the purse strings, that Paolo's brother, Benedetto, was equally responsible for the painting's existence.[11]

The seventeenth-century historian and critic Carlo Ridolfi realized that Benedetto had often collaborated with Paolo.[12] He suggested that Benedetto had specialized in the architecture, preparing the elaborate scenographic milieu against which Paolo's dramatic narratives were unfolded. Modern advances in scientific technology have made the precise scrutiny of Veronese's oeuvre possible. X-radiographs of *The Martyrdom and Last Communion of Saint Lucy* from the National Gallery of Art in Washington (figs. 1–3) reveal that in fact the architecture was laid in independently of and subsequent to the completion of the principal figures. The difference in the coloration of the underpaint plus the sharp contrast between the silhouettes of the actors and architecture of the panoramic backdrop make it certain that the figures

Fig. 4. X-radiograph of *The Martyrdom and Last Communion of Saint Lucy* (detail).

were not painted over the previously sketched-in outlines of a setting. There is no overlap between these areas. The architecture and secondary figures were slipped in behind and between the crevices left by the main protagonists, and then the contours of these figures were lightly reinforced. Just as in the principal figures, where alterations in the position of the heads and hands are found,[13] there are a number of pentimenti in the background. A seated figure has been added to the group that watches a team of oxen futilely attempt to drag Saint Lucy off (fig. 4), and the composition of the buildings has been reorganized. These changes are wholly independent of those in the main figures. None of this confirms or denies Benedetto's authorship of the architectural passages, but it does suggest that if one member of the Veronese team executed the entire canvas, he did so in a manner consistent with the general working procedures of the bottega.

So harmonious is the image presented in *The Martyrdom and Last Communion of Saint Lucy* that no disjunction mars the fluid relationship between the figures and their setting. They are held in a delicate equilibrium of colored opulence and somber tonal gradation. The surging rip-

ple of rose-tinted drapery, the deep pathos of inescapable death, and the ghostlike apparition of the distant narrative are all reminiscent of Titian's late style. So too is the vigorous brushwork, which retains its spontaneity throughout and belies any calculated effect. If indeed a different hand added the architecture, it must have been a hand equally ignited by the fire of Titian's late style. Of course it is almost impossible to imagine that this was the case, if for no other reason than the undeniable quality of the overall painting. We need only to compare *Saint Lucy* with a Veronese with a marked discrepancy between the handling of the various passages to understand why the Washington picture is considered one of the masterpieces of the 1580s.

In the mid-1580s Paolo undertook a project to paint ten monumental scenes from the Old and New Testaments. These scenes included *Hagar in the Desert, Esther and Ahasuerus, Susanna and the Elders, The Flight of Lot, Rebecca at the Well, Christ and the Samaritan Woman at the Well, Christ and the Adulteress, The Centurion before Christ, The Adoration of the Shepherds,* and *Christ Washing the Feet of the Disciples.* Today the canvases are scattered among museums in Prague, Vienna, and Washington,[14] but it is still possible to imagine how impressive the ensemble of ten scenes, each a little under five feet high by ten feet long, would have appeared. Obviously such a series was not produced by the workshop for the mass market, but as of yet no likely patron has emerged. The series is first mentioned in a 1613 inventory made of a château at Beaumont belonging to Charles de Croy, duke of Arschot.[15] The duke visited Venice in 1595,[16] and it is probable that he acquired the series at this time from Paolo's heirs. I emphasize this because connoisseurs have long noted that the quality varies not only from scene to scene, but from passage to passage within a single painting. They have taken those paintings at the bottom end of the scale and given them solely to the "Haeredes," hypothesizing that they were completed after Paolo's death.[17] It could be that two or three of the more competent canvases were started or even finished before 1588 and that to satisfy the foreign visitor, members of the bottega simply manufactured more Veroneses that matched them. Most of the ten paintings are variations on themes and compositions repeatedly used by Paolo and the workshop.

Stylistically the paintings may be divided into three approximate, but not wholly distinct groups, all of which show some degree of workshop participation.[18] The poetic vision of an angel appearing to Hagar and Ishmael in the soft twilight (fig. 5) possesses a superiority of spirit

Fig. 5. Veronese and workshop, *Hagar in the Desert*, oil on canvas. Kunsthistorisches Museum, Gëmaldegalerie, Vienna.

Fig. 6. Veronese and workshop, *Christ and the Samaritan Woman at the Well*, oil on canvas. Kunsthistorisches Museum, Gëmaldegalerie, Vienna.

as well as a technical bravura. The gesturing angel, aglow with radiant light, hovers above the pair of weary travelers. Between them a diagonal swath of desert landscape is charged with an electrical tension seemingly generated by the shimmering satin of the angel's robe. The sym-

metrical balance controlling the composition of *Hagar in the Desert* is repeated in *Christ and the Samaritan Woman at the Well* (fig. 6), but it seems less sophisticated and more forced. The handling of the surface, however, has that special fluidity and lightness characteristic of Ver-

onese's best work. The highlights define form and dazzle the eye. By comparison *Susanna and the Elders* (fig. 7) lacks conviction in both its stiffly presented narrative and dark, brooding tonality, which swallows up the very life of any surface vitality. Hands and feet are awkwardly drawn, highlights gratuitously placed, and the architectural monstrosity in the background is sadly out of proportion. The painting is obviously less accomplished. When any one of the paintings from the series is compared to a substantially autograph painting from the 1580s, such as *The Martyrdom and Last Communion of Saint Lucy* (see fig. 1) or *The Agony in the Garden* (fig. 8) from the Pinacoteca di Brera, the perfunctory work of the bottega stands in sharp relief against the controlled touch of Paolo.

Rebecca at the Well (fig. 9) falls somewhere between the extremes of quality found in the series as a whole. The painting's asymmetrical composition, with its sharply receding landscape and protagonists pushed forward toward the picture plane, follows a formula often em-

Above: Fig. 7. Veronese and workshop, *Susanna and the Elders*, oil on canvas. Kunsthistorisches Museum, Gëmaldegalerie, Vienna.

Left: Fig. 8. Veronese, *The Agony in the Garden*, oil on canvas. Pinacoteca di Brera, Milan.

Opposite page, top: Fig. 9. Veronese and workshop, *Rebecca at the Well*, oil on canvas. National Gallery of Art, Washington, Samuel H. Kress Collection.

ployed by Veronese in his late works. The tragic lyricism of the painting *The Agony in the Garden* is heightened by just such a dichotomy of space, a dichotomy reinforced by a strong contrast between warm and cool colors. The sanguine robe of Christ pulsates against the glacial blue green of the background. Likewise in *Saint Lucy* Veronese set the violent pink of the martyr's robe and swirling banner against a high-keyed sky of aquamarine. The principal figures are framed on one side by a kneeling acolyte dressed in a muted version of the color of the sky and on the other by Saint Lucy's mother, who is wrapped from head to toe in an even deeper shade of blackish green. *Rebecca at the Well* does not share this refined sense of color. Although there has been some attempt to set the more brilliant passages of drapery against a dark ground, the definition of form is not made by a harmonious juxtaposition of warm and cool tones. The painting's tonality is dominated by the brownish vegetation and the matted coats of the numerous camels, who provide an unexpected architonic frame similar to the one in *Saint Lucy*. Isolated against this drab and murky setting are the gleaming copper pails, lush coral skirt of Rebecca's dress, and sun-drenched yellow of the servants' robes. These passages are colored by the same fluid strokes that characterize the robes in *Saint Lucy*. The nuances of touch were meant to impress, and it is apparent that they were laid down after the rest by the master himself. Paolo must also have completed the lightly blushed flesh of Rebecca's cheeks and her delicately poised hand, which fingers a golden bracelet.

The difference in technique as well as feeling in these passages is visible to the unaided eye, but if we look at the X-radiograph of Rebecca's two sleeves, we are struck by just how wide the gulf between the hands at work really is (fig. 10). Both sleeves were painted with short overlapping strokes defining the shape but not the essence of the garment. The surface texture is dull and mushy, the color dingy. Over this indifferent painting, on the left-hand sleeve only, a few strokes of dazzling white pigment have been rapidly laid in. Paolo's final

Fig. 10. X-radiograph of *Rebecca at the Well* (detail).

Fig. 11. Veronese and workshop, *Rebecca at the Well*, oil on canvas. Collection of the Earl of Yarborough.

Below: Fig. 12. Workshop of Veronese, *Rebecca at the Well*. Los Angeles County Museum of Art, The Mr. and Mrs. Allan C. Balch Fund.

Opposite page, bottom left: Fig. 13. Veronese, *Studies of a Pair of Hands, Camels, and Servants*. Private collection.

Opposite page, top right: Fig. 14. Veronese and workshop, *The Martyrdom of Saint Giustina*, oil of canvas. Saint Giustina, Padua.

editing—his last few adjustments to the chromatic intensity, selective manipulation of the highlights, and strengthening of the contours—breathes life into an otherwise limp composition. They supply, no matter how superficially, the spontaneity needed to rescue *Rebecca at the Well* from tedium.

X-radiographs of *Rebecca at the Well* conclusively show that the laying in of the underdrawing was not spontaneous. Unlike the *Saint Lucy*, where the numerous pentimenti bear witness to the composition's evolution and attest to Veronese's creative involvement, there are no changes in the underdrawing here. One is reminded of Benedetto's letter and the factorylike division of labor in Veronese's workshop. The person who transferred the composition to the canvas was not expected to alter the design. The poses of the principal figures in all ten scenes had been established years before the series was conceived or executed. They were blandly introduced from Paolo's repertoire of stock solutions. *Rebecca at the Well* had been preceded by other versions of the same subject.[19] Although I am not convinced that the painting of *Rebecca at the Well* in the Earl of Yarborough's collection (fig. 11) is wholly autograph,[20] it is clear that the figure of Rebecca has been reversed for the second composition. A chiaroscuro drawing, now in the Los Angeles County Museum of Art (fig. 12), repeats the same figure, but does not appear to have been the *modello* for either painting.[21] It is more likely to have been a workshop record of a painting, kept on hand by the bottega for future reference. Its stiff and overly precise delineation lacks the directness that characterizes a study for a pair of hands, camels, and servants, now in an English private collection, which may be linked with *Rebecca* paintings (fig. 13).[22] The affable camels and kneeling servant offer solutions to figural types required by the narrative. Nearly fifteen hundred drawings are listed in the 1682 inventory of the Caliari family's property.[23] The existence of so many drawings underlines the extent to which Veronese and the bottega depended on them during the preparatory stages of painting.[24] These drawings were the bread and butter of a workshop that continued to produce paintings at an alarming rate even after Paolo's death. Their ready-made formulas assured that the paintings would have at least the look of a Veronese. For this reason it is perfectly possible that Charles de Croy commissioned the majority of the Old and New Testament scenes from the shop as late as 1595.

Veronese's autograph drawings provide a link between his own practice and that of the workshop. Unlike earlier Venetian figure studies, many of Paolo's drawings depict jumbled sets of single figures and small groups rhythmically scattered across the same page. Delicately sketched images in pen and wash suggest multiple possibilities but do not impose final solutions. They are neither pictorial *modelli* for nor *ricordi* of Veronese's oeuvre. Challenged by a new commission, Paolo was apt to rely on his abundant accumulation of drawings, recasting old stars in new

productions. The *Saint Lucy* illustrates just how deftly he could recycle an old idea. Saint Lucy's combined martyrdom and last communion rarely occurs in her written or visual hagiography before the end of the sixteenth century.[25] Tradition has it that she met her death as a sword was plunged into her neck. Veronese's emphasis on the host must surely be an affirmation of Tridentine reforms if not a literal depiction of Lorenzo Surio's *De probatis Sanctorum historiis*, which was published in Venice in 1575.[26] Surio poignantly describes the last minutes of Saint Lucy's life: a priest offered her the Eucharist just after the executioner stabbed her in the abdomen. Since Veronese had no prototype for this scene, he invented one by transforming Saint Giustina (fig. 14). Stabbed in the breast, fallen to her knees, and gazing upward toward heaven, Saint Giustina became Saint Lucy.[27] Similarly, members of the bottega freely combined, isolated, or reversed individual poses and passages from Paolo's drawings and paintings to create new "Veroneses." They utilized the same inventive method that Paolo did when organizing a new composition, and consequently it is not always easy to separate their "Veroneses" from Paolo's Veroneses.

I have spoken at some length about the structure of the Caliari workshop, the sharing of responsibility among several individuals, and the collaborative process through which an original Veronese was created. The manner in which the workshop replicated Paolo's work for the mass market was based on techniques learned while assisting him on his larger commissions. Toward the end of Veronese's life the bottega began to reproduce paintings *seriatim*, an assembly-line production where sons and assistants duplicated compositions literally. Such a practice had been common in the Bassano workshop since 1567, and Carletto's training there may have encouraged the Caliaris' adoption of the practice once he returned to the family fold.[28]

Our initial impression that *The Finding of Moses* from the National Gallery of Art in Washington (fig. 15) and the autograph painting in the Prado (fig. 16) might well be twins is not a trick of the photographer. The paintings are in fact nearly identical in dimension, composition, and color.[29] Both possess an element of the exquisite and jewellike presence for which Veronese is so noted. Vibrant touches of rich ocher, soft red, and brick yellow flicker against a cool background of silvered brilliance. The rhythmically articulated group of figures is punctuated by the emphatic placement of feathery trees and a distant bridge. Veronese has transformed the entourage into an iridescent reflection of contemporary Venetian life. On close observation, however, we find that the copyist has introduced certain changes into the Washington composition. These changes are primarily of costume: the bodice, hemline, and fabric of the daughter's dress, her crown of pearls, and the striped overgarment of her right-hand companion. The foliage too has been altered in its density and color. The verdant hills of the Prado version have disappeared altogether, and the particulars of the cityscape have been adjusted to cover the now barren slopes. These changes appear to have been quite deliberately introduced into the Washington composition. The gown of the pharaoh's daughter was originally modeled on the one in the Madrid painting. The outlines of a square-necked bodice are still visible in the pentimenti. They become even clearer in the X-radio-

Fig. 15. Workshop of Veronese, *The Finding of Moses*, oil on canvas. National Gallery of Art, Washington, Andrew W. Mellon Collection.

graph (fig. 17), where it is also possible to discern the dropped waist, small gathers, and pleated folds falling exactly as they do in the Prado picture.

The Washington *Finding of Moses* is sometimes called "an autograph replica," in which case we must suppose that Veronese introduced the changes himself.[30] Richard Cocke has recently suggested that Paolo worked simultaneously on these two paintings as well as on the versions of the scene now in Liverpool, Turin, Dijon, Dresden, and Lyons.[31] One envisions a Chaplinesque workroom filled with nothing but canvases of *The Finding of Moses* and Paolo, like Chaplin's little tramp, rushing from one to the next. As much as I fancy this vision, I must doubt its validity, primarily because the Washington painting is simply not good enough to be called an autograph Veronese. The quality of the modeling, articulation of the poses, and attention to detail lack a sensitive touch. The graceful tilt of the daughter's head and faint smile on her lips are coarsened. Other passages are mindlessly painted to the point of being meaningless. A finger in the hand of the companion to the daughter of the phar-

Fig. 16. Veronese, *The Finding of Moses*, oil on canvas. Museo del Prado, Madrid.

probability made to be kept in the bottega as a *modello*. Other copies of the composition, for example, one from the estate of Robert Haagens and another last noted on the art market in 1945 (fig. 18), seem to be derived from it.[34] They repeat the costumes as well as the misunderstandings of the Washington version. The composition could also be reversed and enlarged as in the Dijon or Dresden variants (fig. 19).[35] The *modello* in painting was used by the workshop with the same inventive freedom that the drawings were and ultimately sold if a buyer could be found.

It is the wont of modern critics to give inferior works to minor hands, followers, and imitators. The genuine article, "the original," is always highly esteemed. This is, no doubt, of some comfort to a twentieth-century artist like Picasso, who is reputed to have remarked that art historians would do the weeding out for him by attributing his lesser works to others. Such a marked prejudice did not exist during the sixteenth century. The contracts for Veronese's work do not stipulate "di sua mano," by the hand of the master, as do so many fourteenth- and fifteenth-century documents.[36] Buying a Veronese meant buying a recognizable trademark: inspired and even

aoh becomes a fold of drapery, and the thumb of the lady in blue disappears altogether. The maid who adjusts her sandal while steadying herself against a tree has lost her tree and gestures futilely into space.[32] Such mistakes or misunderstandings are the hallmarks of a copy, not an original or even an autograph replica.

Why was such a copy made in the first place? Did Paolo want a *ricordo*, a keepsake of his own invention? Did the workshop need a replica as a guide for future work or had some patron become so enamored of the composition that he requested one just like it? I have no concrete evidence that such a discerning patron existed, but I can imagine that he might have. Throughout the sixteenth century collectors increasingly demanded paintings by particular artists, although not necessarily of certain subjects.[33] These were not always purchased directly from the master's studio but often through an agent who kept a handy supply in his back room. It was largely to stock these freelance dealers that workshops such as those of Bassano, Tintoretto, and Veronese replicated proven successes. The Washington *Finding of Moses* was in all

Fig. 17. X-radiograph of Washington *The Finding of Moses* (detail).

Fig. 18. Workshop of Veronese, *The Finding of Moses*, oil on canvas; noted on the art market in 1945.

Below: Fig. 19. Veronese and workshop, *The Finding of Moses*, oil on canvas. Staatliche Kunstsammlungen Dresden.

quality-controlled by Paolo but not necessarily "di sua mano." The smooth functioning of the workshop assured its ability to turn out paintings in the official style. One segment of the public demanded nothing else. There were, however, more discriminating eyes as well. The seventeenth-century critic Marco Boschini offered sage advice on how to judge a Veronese: "He never glazed drapery, so that if you ever see a glazed drapery in a painting attributed to Veronese, think twice so as not to be deceived. And if the touch in the flesh areas does not have that special vitality and animation it is clear that the work in question is more likely by the brother, Benedetto, or by Carletto, the son."[37] For Boschini as for the twentieth-century critic the difference between an authentic Veronese and a workshop replica was not one of method, subject, or even style but ultimately one of quality. The incarnation of Venetian life is there but less candescent: the brocades are duller, the silvery tones tarnished. The splendor of sheer visual substance laid on by Paolo's delicate touch is diminished by a faithful eye, but one working with an unfeeling hand. Exact replication was therefore impossible. Neither Paolo nor his heirs, whatever their intentions, could suppress the fact that some Veroneses were more original than others.

NOTES

I wish to thank Elizabeth Cropper and Sydney J. Freedberg for reading an early draft of this essay and offering sage advice. Michael Swicklik and Jia-sun Tsang of the Conservation Department of the National Gallery of Art, Washington, carried out the technical examination on some of the paintings discussed here and provided the X-radiographs. Their careful analysis was invaluable in helping to determine the ways in which Veronese's workshop functioned.

1. Giorgio Vasari, *Le vite de' più eccellenti pittori, scultori, ed architettori* (1568), 9 vols., ed. Gaetano Milanesi (Florence, 1906), 6:369–374. Vasari's arithmetic is faulty. Veronese, who was born in 1528, was thirty-eight when Vasari visited Venice in 1566 to collect material for the revised edition of his 1550 book. Veronese had not been mentioned in that earlier edition. We might surmise that Veronese simply looked young to Vasari or that Vasari had appropriated, as a firsthand observation, the fact that Veronese had begun to work for Venetian patrons while still in his early twenties.

2. The major source on Veronese's life and work is Terisio Pignatti, *Veronese*, 2 vols. (Venice, 1976). It contains an extensive bibliography and catalogue of 764 works by or attributed to Veronese. Recent publications by Richard Cocke, *Veronese* (London, 1980); Richard Cocke, *Veronese's Drawings* (New York, 1984); and Rodolfo Pallucchini, *Veronese* (Milan, 1984), offer some revisions in Pignatti's catalogue but do not supersede it. For color reproductions of *The Triumph of Venice* and *Mars and Venus* see Pallucchini 1984, 135 and 123, respectively.

3. The literature on Veronese's workshop and its individual members is small and largely negative. That is to say, it tries to establish Veronese's autograph work while disparaging everything "non-Veronese." The best discussions are found in Pietro Caliari, *Paolo Veronese: Sua vita e sue opere* (Rome, 1888), 177–186; Hans Tietze and E. Tietze-Conrat, *The Drawings of the Venetian Painters in the Fifteenth and Sixteenth Centuries* (New York, 1944), 165–166, 191, 352–354; Luciana Crosato-Larcher, "Per Gabriele Caliari," *Arte Veneta* 18 (1964), 174–175; Luciana Crosato-Larcher, "Per Carletto Caliari," *Arte Veneta* 21 (1967), 108–124; Luciana Crosato-Larcher, "Note su Benedetto Caliari," *Arte Veneta* 23 (1969), 115–130; David Rosand, *Veronese and His Studio in North American Collections* [exh. cat., Birmingham Museum of Art and Montgomery Museum of Fine Arts] (Birmingham, Ala., 1972); Rodolfo Pallucchini, *La pittura veneziana del seicento*, 2 vols. (Milan, 1981), 2:21–23; Kurt Badt, *Paolo Veronese* (Cologne, 1981), 37–49.

4. No catalogue of works signed in this way exists. In addition to the works mentioned below one can add *Saint Andrew* from a private collection in Madrid, reproduced in Richard Cocke, "Observations on Some Drawings by Paolo Veronese," *Master Drawings* 11 (1973), 144, fig. 7.

5. Illustrated in Crosato-Larcher 1964, 112, fig. 125, and 117, fig. 132.

6. Illustrated in Rosand 1972, 31.

7. See the discussion below and in Ralph Fastnedge, "Two Italian Pictures Recently Restored at Liverpool," *The Liverpool Libraries, Museums, and Arts Committee Bulletin* 3 (1953), 15–28. Versions exist in Dresden: Pignatti 1976, 1:147, no. 242; Dijon: Pignatti 1976, 1:178, no. A63; Dublin: Pignatti 1976, 1:179, no. A75; Liverpool: Pignatti 1976, 1:189, no. A151; Naples: Pignatti 1976, 1:198, no. A217; Turin: Pignatti 1976, 1:210, no. 312; Lyons: Pignatti 1976, 1:189, no. A150; Oxford: Christopher Lloyd, *A Catalogue of the Earlier Italian Paintings in the Ashmolean Museum* (Oxford, 1977), 191, no. A143; estate of Robert Haagens: Pignatti 1976, 1:147, under no. 241; and a painting last seen in Switzerland on the art market in 1945 reproduced here in fig. 18.

8. Rosand 1972, 6–7; Joy Thornton, *Renaissance Color Theory and Some Paintings by Veronese* (Ph.D. diss., University of Pittsburgh, 1979), 192–278; and W. R. Rearick, "Jacopo Bassano's Later Genre Paintings," *Burlington Magazine* 110, no. 782 (May 1968), 245.

9. Giovanni Gaye, *Carteggio inedito d' artisti dei secoli XIV, XV, XVI*, 3 vols. (Florence, 1840), 3:551, doc. 444 (also reprinted in Caliari 1888, 177–178 n. 2). Rosand 1972, 6, presumed that this letter was written after Paolo's death. Even if this were the case, we may assume that the working procedures in the bottega before and after Paolo's death remained constant. It would, of course, be a mistake to believe that every painting produced by the workshop was done in precisely the same manner. It is only my intention to sketch general working procedures, not establish absolute rules that hold true in every case.

10. Crosato-Larcher 1969, 115–130, discusses this collaboration but does not publish the documentation. For the documents see Pignatti 1976, 1:249–260, especially, docs. 51 and 59.

11. The painting was commissioned from Paolo in 1575 and is still in the church of Santa Giustina in Padua (Pignatti 1976, 1:137, no. 182). For the payments see Pignatti 1976, 1:256, docs. 42–43.

12. Carlo Ridolfi, *Le maraviglie dell'arte*, ed. D. von Hadeln, 2 vols. (Berlin, 1914), 1:358–360.

13. This is especially evident in Saint Lucy's head and in the hands of the acolyte.

14. *The Adoration of the Shepherds* and *Christ Washing the Feet of the Disciples* are in the Národní Galerie, Prague; *Rebecca at the Well* is in the National Gallery of Art, Washington. The remaining seven paintings belong to the Kunsthistorisches Museum, Gemäldegalerie, Vienna. All ten are illustrated and discussed in Pignatti 1976, 1:159–161, nos. 301–307, and 1:220–221, nos. A383–A384, A388; 2: figs. 659–661, 663–666, 1048–1049, 1054.

15. Charles de Croy died on 13 January 1612. The inventory of his château at Beaumont is dated 24 April 1613. It was at this time that the contents of his household were sent to his executors in Brussels. Reprinted in A. Pinchart, "La Collection de Charles de Croy, duc d'Arschot, dans son Château de Beaumont," *Archives des arts, sciences, et lettres* 1 (1860), 158–173. Only nine of Veronese's biblical scenes appear in the inventory, 163–164, nos. 44–45, 48–54. *Christ Washing the Feet of the Disciples* is not listed, but two other paintings by Veronese are included: *Anointing of David*, no. 46, and *Flight into Egypt*, no. 47. Measurements are given for all eleven paintings, and each was framed by "sa molure d' escrignerie, peincte de noir, e dore politement." All ten biblical scenes were listed at York House, London, in a 1635 inventory of the estate of George Villiers, the first duke of Buckingham, who had been assassinated in 1628 (Randall Davies, "An Inventory of 1635," *Burlington Magazine* 10 [October 1906–March 1907], 375–382). In 1648 they and *Anointing of David*, which had not appeared in the 1635 inventory, were sold in Antwerp by the second duke of Buckingham to Archduke Leopold Wilhelm (B. Fairfax, *A Catalogue of the Curious Collection of Pictures of George Villiers, Duke of Buckingham* [London, 1758], 6–7, nos. 2–12). Loren Campbell, "Notes on Netherlandish Pictures in the Veneto in the Fifteenth and Sixteenth Centuries," *Burlington Magazine* 123, no. 941 (August 1981), 473 n. 56, is mistaken about the appearance of *Anointing of David* in the 1635 inventory but is probably correct in stating that *Flight into Egypt* of the 1613 inventory can no longer be identified with certainty.

16. F. de Reiffenberg, *Une existence de grand seigneur au XVI* siècle (Brussels, 1845), 15.

17. There is no scholarly consensus as to which paintings in the series are autograph and in which members of the bottega may have played a significant role. They are all dated after 1585. G. Fiocco, *Paolo Veronese, 1528–1588* (Bologna, 1928), 97–98, suggested that Montemezzano collaborated with Paolo but saw *Hagar* and *Susanna* as primarily autograph works. Alessandro Ballarin, "Osservazioni sui dipinti veneziani del Cinquecento nella Galleria del Castello di Praga," *Arte Veneta* 19 (1965), 71–82, sees all ten as substantially autograph with only marginal assistance. Jaromir Neumann, *The Picture Gallery of Prague Castle* (Prague, 1967), 290–300, divides the works into three groups. The first group, where a larger participation of Paolo Veronese may be detected, includes *Hagar, Christ and the Samaritan Woman, Rebecca,* and *Christ Washing the Feet*. Only *Hagar*, however, is seen as wholly

autograph. The second group includes *Adulteress, Centurion,* and *Lot,* which show the hand of Benedetto. Group three includes *Esther, Susanna,* and *Adoration of the Shepherds,* which show the hand of Carletto. Pignatti 1976, 1:159–161, nos. 301–307, and 1:220–221, nos. 383–384, 388, accepts seven of the paintings as autograph and three, *Centurion, Adulteress,* and *Esther,* as workshop pieces with the possible participation of Benedetto and Montemezzano. Pallucchini 1984, 155–162 and 187–188, sees Benedetto's participation in *Adulteress, Centurion,* and *Esther.* Cocke 1980, 108, and Cocke 1984, 281, basically follow Neumann's division between autograph and workshop paintings but sees no participation of the bottega in the first group. The author further points out that the differences in viewpoint in the paintings suggests a change in plan after Veronese's death. He feels that the four autograph paintings and *Adoration of the Shepherds* were intended for a conventional height, but the remaining five were meant to be hung higher. Cecil Gould, "Observations on the Role of Decoration in the Formation of Veronese's Art," in *Essays in the History of Art Presented to Rudolf Wittkower,* ed. D. Fraser, Howard Hibbard and Milton Lewine (London, 1967), 125, also hypothesized that the paintings were meant to be hung in tiers.

18. I am roughly in agreement with Neumann's division; see note 17 above. Only *Hagar* can be considered substantially autograph.

19. He also used similar compositions in paintings of Jacob and Rachel at the well. The two subjects are often confused, and it is not all together clear when one or the other subject was meant. The following is a list of examples variously identified as one or the other or both of these subjects: Musée de Versailles: Pignatti 1976, 1:219, no. A379, and 2: fig. 1045; collection earl of Yarborough: Pignatti 1976, 1:185, no. 122, illustrated here fig. 11; collection marquess of Exeter, Burghley House: Pignatti 1976, 1:208, no. A292; private collection, London: Pignatti 1976, 1:161, no. 309, and 2: fig. 669, see also Theodore Crombie, "*Jacob and Rachel at the Well* by Veronese: A Newly Discovered Painting," *Apollo* 96 (August 1972), 111–115, and Cocke 1984, 291, where it is recorded as having been sold at Sotheby, London, 12 December 1973; Cahors, Musée Municipal: Pignatti 1976, 1:161, under no. 309, and 2: fig. 671; former collection Constance Askew: sold at Christie's, New York, 14 March 1985, no. 37, now at Piero Corsini, New York.

20. Luisa Vertova, "Some Late Works by Veronese," *Burlington Magazine* 102, no. 683 (February 1960), 68–71, believed that "everything speaks clearly of Paolo Veronese's hand." Pignatti 1976, 1:185, no. A122, rejected the attribution to Paolo. The painting is characterized by a rigidity of pose and awkwardness in modeling that belie Veronese's authorship.

21. Ebria Feinblatt, "A Drawing by Paolo Veronese," *Los Angeles County Museum of Art Bulletin* 14 (1962), 11–21, comes to a different conclusion. Cocke 1984, does not mention the sheet.

22. Cocke 1984, 238–239.

23. Gregorio Gattinoni, *Inventario di una casa veneziana del secolo XVII* (Mestre, 1914).

24. See the recent discussion of the use of drawings in Veronese's shop by Howard Coutts, "Veronese's Paintings for Carlo Emanuele I of Savoy," *Burlington Magazine* 127 (1985), 330–302.

25. A. Niero et al., *Culto dei Santi nella terraferma veneziana* (Venice, 1967), 61–63; G. Taibbi, *Martirio di Santa Lucia, Vita di Santa Marina* (Palermo, 1959) and J. Bridge, "Lucy," in *The Catholic Encyclopedia,* 24 vols. (New York, 1913), 9:414–415. For a complete discussion see Beverly Louise Brown, "Paolo Veronese's *The Martyrdom and Last Communion of Saint Lucy,*" *Venezia Arti* 2 (1988), 61–68.

26. Lorenzo Surio, *De probatis Sanctorum historiis* (Venice, 1575), 7:247–249. Reprinted in Taibbi 1959, 15–17. Paolo's painting would appear to be the first instance of this theme in the visual arts. It enjoyed particular popularity in Venice, where, perhaps following Veronese's lead, Giovanni Battista Tiepolo and Sebastiano Ricci painted it. See Antonio Morassi, *A Complete Catalogue of the Paintings of G. B. Tiepolo*

(Greenwich, 1962), 24, 55; and Jeffrey Daniels, *Sebastiano Ricci* (Hove, 1976), 90.

27. The similarity between the two female saints is underscored by the fact that during the nineteenth century *The Martyrdom and Last Communion of Saint Lucy* was identified as *The Martyrdom of Saint Giustina* (Pignatti 1976, 1:155, no. 279). The pose appears to have been a stock one in Veronese's repertoire. He also used it for Saints Afra, Christina, and George.

28. W. R. Rearick, "Jacopo Bassano, 1568–1569," *Burlington Magazine* 104 (1962), 524–533; and Rearick 1968, 241–249.

29. The Prado version measures 57.0 x 43.5 cm (22½ x 17⅛ in.) and the Washington version, 58.0 x 44.5 cm (22⅞ x 17½ in.) (Pignatti 1976, 1:146–147, nos. 240–241). The measurements for the Prado painting have been widely mispublished. X-radiographs of the Washington version reveal that a border of approximately 1.5 cm (½ in.) has been added to all four edges.

30. For example, Pignatti 1976, 1:146–147, no. 241; Pallucchini 1984, 138; and Cocke 1984, 242.

31. Cocke believed that the Dijon canvas, which is generally considered a workshop piece, was the prime version and that it was rapidly followed by the others (Cocke 1980, 100; Cocke 1984, 241; and Jane Martineau and Charles Hope, eds., *The Genius of Venice, 1500–1600* [exh. cat., Royal Academy of Arts, London] [London, 1983], 299). The painting is illustrated in Fastnedge 1953, 18, fig. 3.

32. The hand of the woman furthest to the right, who bends over the dwarf, is in a different position in the two paintings. Technical examination of the Prado painting, however, reveals that the area around this hand has been overpainted (possibly in the eighteenth century) and that it originally was in the same position as the hand in the Washington painting. I would like to thank Maria del Carmen Garrido and Manuela Mena for allowing me to study the Prado painting under ultraviolet light and to consult the X-radiographs of the painting.

33. This was certainly true of Isabella d'Este and her brother Alfonso, who both tried to assemble works by all the principal living artists of their day.

34. Pignatti 1976, 1:147, under no. 241, and 2: fig. 563.

35. I do not, as Cocke does, think that the Dijon picture is the prime version (see note 31 above). It combines, for example, many elements found in either the Prado or Washington pictures but not found in both. This is especially true of the costumes and greatly expanded background. A greater claim may be made for Veronese's intervention in the Dresden canvas, but it is difficult to say if it was the prime version. The two pages with studies for the finding of Moses both show the main group of figures facing in the opposite direction of the Dijon and Dresden pictures. See Cocke 1984, 241, fig. 102: *Study for Finding of Moses* (Fitzwilliam Museum, Cambridge, no. PD 21 1977), and 243, fig. 103: *Studies for a Finding of Moses* (Pierpont Morgan Library, New York, no. IV 81).

36. Hannelore Glasser, *Artists' Contracts of the Early Renaissance* (Ph.D. diss., Columbia University), 1965, 72–78; and James Lawson, "New Documents on Donatello," *Mitteilungen des Kunsthistorischen Institutes in Florenz* 28 (1974), 359 n. 18.

37. Marco Boschini, *La carta del navegar pittoresco,* ed. Anna Pallucchini (Venice, 1966), 733–734.

"The most exact representation of the Original":[1] Remarks on Portraits of George Washington by Gilbert Stuart and Rembrandt Peale

EGON VERHEYEN
George Mason University

Fig. 1. Rembrandt Peale, *Portrait of George Washington* (So-called Porthole Portrait), 1824–1825, oil on canvas. U.S. Capitol, Old Senate Chamber, Washington, D.C.

I asked him to cover the titles at the bottom of the portraits and to make character sketches of the subjects from their appearance. This would be delightful if it were done by the Marquis. We would then compare these moral sketches with the true-life history of the men and determine to what extent facial features tell the truth or lie.[2]

IN JANUARY AND FEBRUARY 1832, during the centennial year of Washington's birth, the Senate voted to approve the purchase from Rembrandt Peale[3] of a Washington portrait for the Senate Chamber (figs. 1–2). At the same time members of the House of Representatives on recommendation of Leonard Jarvis, chairman of the Committee on Public Buildings, commissioned from Vanderlyn a full-length portrait of Washington (fig. 3) as pendant to Ary Scheffer's *Lafayette* (fig. 4) and a "pedestrian statue" of Washington from Horatio Greenough.[4] The House and Senate were competing with each

To the memory of Fordyce Mitchel

Fig. 2. Interior of Old Senate Chamber with Rembrandt Peale's *Portrait of George Washington* (from *Ballou's Drawing Room Companion* 1852, 2:168).

other, and each had to fend off the activities of the newly founded Washington Memorial Society, which strove to fulfill the promise made by the Continental Congress in 1783 to erect a Washington monument.[5] Each of the commissions left "the accessories to the judgment of the artist" but prescribed the source for the head. Vanderlyn was told that "the head [was] to be a copy of Stuart's Washington" (fig. 5);[6] Greenough had to follow Houdon's model.[7] The final vote was preceded by a debate that concentrated on the choice of Vanderlyn as painter.[8] A much more important question, however, was raised by Representative Mercer, who questioned the wisdom of the stipulation that Vanderlyn "adopt the head by Stuart as his model." Mercer maintained that

> Stuart's head of Washington, though a fine painting, was not the best likeness which had been taken. That painted by Mr. [Rembrandt] Peale bore a much closer resemblance especially about the eyes. This had been the opinion of the late Judge Washington, and, if he was not mistaken, it was also that of Judge Marshall. He should be sorry if the artist were compelled to adhere closely to Stuart's portrait.

Mercer's argument was countered by Representative Taylor, who reminded his colleagues in the House of Representatives that in January 1826, acting on a resolution introduced by General Van Rensselaer, "the House

had expressed its opinion that Stuart's portrait was the standard likeness of Washington."[9] Representative Taylor may have been stretching the evidence, but he was justified in pointing out that Stuart's portrait was indeed considered the best likeness.

The resolution to which Representative Taylor referred poses an interesting question. How does one, in the absence of photographic records—the earliest known presidential photograph is of John Quincy Adams—determine a quarter century after a person's death which of the many portraits is the "correct" one and most importantly, how does one determine "correctness"? An artist may claim that he can produce the true likeness of a person, and the number of replicas and copies may be used as a means to measure success. But if a political body votes on the "standard" likeness or is understood to have done so, preferring Stuart's portrait of Washington (fig. 5) to Rembrandt Peale's (see fig. 1), then this act is not primarily an aesthetic decision but a political one: it is a decision in favor of one "image" of Washington over another. The differences may be subtle, but they exist and are acknowledged through the action taken.

The claim to possess the true likeness needed authentication, especially after Washington had died and Stuart's portrait had assumed the role of a substitute. Rembrandt Peale could not place his portrait next to a living Washington but had to place it next to Stuart's painting. With-

out certification of authenticity, without someone in authority saying "Yes, this was the way he looked," no new image could even hope to be accepted. This was, in a nutshell, Rembrandt Peale's problem. To solve this problem Peale solicited opinions from those who had known Washington, and he printed these opinions together with his own history of Washington portraits. All Peale could hope for was a statement saying that his portrait confirmed the writer's recollections. Peale's portrait might agree with what Chief Justice Marshall remembered, but this did not have to mean that Peale had captured Washington as he was. Nevertheless, the publication of these letters assured perpetuation of these opinions. Accepting Peale's portrait meant questioning the value of Stuart's, which so far had been the norm. Any deviation from that norm amounted to a reevaluation of the original and thus constituted a potential threat to an accepted image. It is not coincidental that Rembrandt Peale's efforts to establish his, and by implication his family's, portraits of Washington as the only correct ones takes place at a time when a change in the perception of Washington can be observed. It might have been prompted by the approaching centennial of Washington's birth, and it might have been the desire of a new generation to take a less-partisan look at the events of the Revolution and the first years of the Republic. In 1835, Edward Everett, a member of the House of Representatives, delivered an oration "before the citizens of Beverly, without distinction of party" on the "Youth of George Washing-

Above: Fig. 3. John Vanderlyn, *Portrait of George Washington*, 1832, oil on canvas. U.S. Capitol, House of Representatives, Washington, D.C.

Fig. 4. Interior of Old House of Representatives Chamber (now Statuary Hall) with Ary Scheffer's *Portrait of Lafayette*, after a sketch by E. T. Coke.

Fig. 5. Gilbert Stuart, *Portrait of George Washington* (Vaughan-Sinclair portrait), 1795, oil on canvas. National Gallery of Art, Washington, Andrew W. Mellon Collection.

poraries, whose personal knowledge and convictions lend additional value, as by those of a later day, whose careful study and critical analysis render their testimony of equal weight and importance. These tributes, scattered throughout many publications, have been brought together, so that all may become familiar with the details of a character, which, in its gradual development, reached the highest degree of excellence humanity can attain. . . . The character of Washington is a national possession. To its courage and perserverance we owe the successful issue of our war for independence; to its integrity and judgment, the permanence of our constitutional experiment; and, to its firmness and patriotism, our position as a nation. All Americans should study and venerate it. At all times and places, in peace and in war, in tumult and in quiet, its contemplation will be a benefit, its example an influence, and its imitation an assistance. "God be praised, that character is ours forever!"

The question of Peale or Stuart had lost all its urgency. While Stuart's portrait of Washington had maintained

ton," maintaining that "the present generation is better able to do justice to his character, than that in which he lived."[10] The search for the real Washington brought forth the first publication of his letters but also a legion of new fiction and new images, of which Currier and Ives' *Washington's Dream*, 1857, and Carl Schmolze's *Washington Sitting for His Portrait to Gilbert Stuart*, 1858 (fig. 6), may serve as examples.[11] What had begun in the 1820s and 1830s culminated in 1889, on the occasion of the centennial of Washington's election as the first president of the United States. Exhibitions were arranged and books were published eulogizing the man and stirring pride and patriotism. One of these efforts was W. S. Baker's *Character Portraits of Washington*, which abounds with descriptions of the president's character stemming from the pens of "historians, orators, and divines."[12] It is, Baker wrote,

> the purpose of these pages to exhibit the character of Washington as understood and portrayed by some of the best writers and thinkers; as well as by contem-

Fig. 6. Carl Hermann Schmolze, *Washington Sitting for His Portrait to Gilbert Stuart*, 1858, oil on canvas. The Pennsylvania Academy of the Fine Arts, Philadelphia, John Frederick Lewis Memorial Collection.

its leading role, other portraits could be used, and were used, as the occasion demanded.[13]

Apart from monetary interests, the Peales and Stuart were aiming at creating a national icon.[14] Portraits were believed to have the power to bring the dead back to life, make the absent present, and preserve the portrayed's features for posterity.[15] This challenge to the artist coupled with the artist's fear that he or she might not be able completely to render a sitter's beauty, a beauty that was understood as a reflection of his or her soul, or beyond this, the disclaimer of any ability to encompass in a painting or print what makes out the *persona* of the depicted. Ghirlandajo's portrait of a Tornabuoni lady, Dürer's unsuccessful efforts with the features of Erasmus, and Cranach's struggle with the face of Luther may serve as reminder of what must have seemed to be insurmountable artistic difficulties.[16] Physiognomic studies were conducted in an effort to understand the assumed relation between a person's appearance and his or her character. A man's aquiline nose was believed to reveal his noble character; in contrast, a man's sheepish face would indicate that he possessed a sheepish character.[17] By the end of the eighteenth century Johan Caspar Lavater's *Essays on Physiognomy designed to promote the knowledge and the love of mankind* reflected the new belief in the ability to read a person's character from the face.[18] The portrait was the ideal means to record a person's character in a few lines.[19] Lavater asks:

> What is portrait painting? It is the communication, the preservation of the image of some individual, or of some part of the body of an individual: the art of suddenly depicting all that can be depicted of that half of man which is rendered apparent, and which never can be conveyed in words.[20]

Nowhere perhaps is the influence of this scientific interpretation of a person's countenance, combined with the mechanical device of the physiognotrace (fig. 7), more obvious than in the large number of silhouette portraits or strict profile views.[21] They must have seemed ideal means not only for recording but also for presenting a person's character. Looking at two such profiles of Washington done by Simitière, 1780–1781 (fig. 8),[22] and Wright, about 1790 (fig. 9),[23] one becomes aware of differences that cannot be explained only by the passage of time between these renditions. Each seems to project a different Washington. The same observation applies also to portraits in three-quarter view.[24] The situation is not different if one consults contemporary descriptions of Washington's appearance.

In 1778 James Thacher saw "a fine symmetry in the features of his face, indicative of a benign and dignified spirit. His nose is straight, and his eyes inclined to the blue."[25] Writing in the same year, John Bell considered "his features manly and bold, his eyes of a bluish cast and very lively; his hair a deep brown, his face rather long and marked with the small pox; his complexion sun-burnt and without much color, and his countenance sensible, composed, and thoughtful."[26] Without going into detail, Claude C. Robin, in 1781, spoke of Washington's features as "a fine, cheerful, open countenance, a simple and modest carriage."[27] One year later, in 1782, the Prince de Broglie mentioned only the eyes, which he considered "more attentive than sparkling."[28] Joseph Mandrillon, writing in 1784, spoke of the common inclination to see the powerful and famous as endowed with a body corresponding to this view even if nature has done otherwise. In the case of Washington, however, "the features bear the image of that genius which distinguishes him above his fellow men. . . . Imposing in size, noble and well proportioned, a countenance open,

Fig. 7. *A Sure and Convenient Machine for Drawing Silhouettes*, engraving (from Lavater 1789–1798, vol. 2, pt. 1, facing p. 179).

Fig. 8. Benoit Louis Prevost, *Portrait of George Washington*, engraving, after a drawing by Pierre du Simetière, 1780–1781. National Portrait Gallery, Smithsonian Institution, Washington, D.C.

Fig. 9. Unidentified artist, *Portrait of George Washington*, c. 1810, engraving, after a drawing by Joseph Wright, c. 1790. National Portrait Gallery, Smithsonian Institution, Washington, D.C.

calm and sedate, but without any one striking feature, and when you depart from him, the remembrance only of a fine man will remain, a fine figure, and exterior plane and modest, a pleasing address."[29] The Marquis de Chastellux considered the strongest characteristic of this respectable man "the union which reigns between the physical and moral qualities which compose the individual."[30] Later on, the marquis spoke of Washington's face: "His stature is noble and lofty, he is well made, and exactly proportioned; his physiognomy mild and agreeable, but such as to render it impossible to speak particularly of any of his features, so that in quitting him, you have only the recollection of a fine face."[31] Another Frenchman, Brissot de Warville, explicitly referred to Chastellux's characterization of the general.

> You have often heard me blame M. Chastellux for putting too much sprightliness in the character he has drawn of this general. To give pretensions to the portrait of a man who has none is truly absurd. The General's goodness appears in his looks. They have nothing of that brilliancy which his officers found in them

when he was at the head of his army; but in conversation they become animated. He has no characteristic traits in his figure, and this has rendered it always so difficult to describe it: there are few portraits which resemble him.[32]

Much of what we know about Stuart's portrait of Washington derives from a report written by the artist's daughter, Jane, at the time of the centennial celebrations in 1876.[34] Her immediate concern was to answer the many questions regarding the authenticity of Stuart's portraits. The main issue, however, was the daughter's effort to establish her father's portrait as the only truthful likeness of Washington, a task provoked by the challenge that something was wrong, that Stuart did not know Washington well enough to transmit his features with unquestionable accuracy. With this purpose in mind she first tries to establish her father's claim and then attacks the detractors. Being confronted with a painting allegedly by her father, she emphatically states that "my father, knowing how much he was impressed with the grandeur, dignity and self-possession of the face of Washington, and how well he succeeded in portraying it," could never have painted that painting. To strengthen this point she refers to her father's initial agonies only to emphasize his final triumph. "Toward the Spring of 1795, Stuart painted his first portrait of Washington, with which he was very much dissatisfied. His admiration and respect were so great, that he could not feel at ease in his presence, and he ultimately erased this picture."[35] Nevertheless, Jane Stuart assures us that others found this unsuccessful beginning not such a failure and commissioned another portrait from Stuart, the Landsdown portrait. This in turn lead to further commissions, among them one instigated by Martha Washington herself, the Athenaeum portraits, which Stuart painted in Germantown. "Having by this time become better acquainted with the great man, Stuart gained his entire self-possession; and the general could not fail to be interested in the accomplished artist. . . . The enthusiasm this portrait occasioned during the life of Washington, is another proof of his truthfulness." Finally, Jane Stuart assures her readers that Washington "promised [Stuart] that if he should sit again for his picture, it would be to him."[36]

The most observant comment on Washington's appearance is contained in Isaac Weld's report of 1796 which also alludes to observations by Stuart.

His [Washington's] head is small, in which respect he resembles the make of a great number of his countrymen. His eyes are of a light grey colour; and in proportion to the length of his face, his nose is long. Mr. Stewart, the eminent portrait painter, told me, that there are features in his face totally different from what he ever observed in that of any other human being; the sockets for the eyes, for instance, are larger than what he ever met with before, and the upper part of the nose broader. All his features, he observed, were indicative of the strongest and most ungovernable passions, and had he been born in the forest, it was his opinion that he would have been the fiercest man among the savage tribes. In this Mr. Stewart has given proof of his great discernment and intimate knowledge of the human countenance; for although General Washington has been extolled for his great moderation and calmness, during the very trying situations in which he has so often been placed, yet those who have been acquainted with him the longest and most intimately say, that he is by nature a man of a fierce and irritable disposition, but that, like Socrates, his judgment and great self-command have always made him appear a man of a different cast in the eyes of the world. He speaks with great diffidence, and sometimes hesitates

for a word; but it is always to find one particularly well adapted to his meaning.[33]

The variety of physiognomic expressions recorded in descriptions and depictions is astonishing and leaves only the conclusion that no effort was undertaken to establish one portrait as official or most reliable. At a time when the verification of the features of a sitter was next to impossible for anyone who could not instantly compare the portrait with the sitter, the claim that a portrait was done from life could serve as an incentive for a buyer and potentially result in a lucrative business for the painter. A skilled artist could establish a monopoly on a given portrait. By the mid-1790s the Peale family had for all practical purposes obtained such a position. Any painter who intended to challenge them had to produce a portrait that was not only better and different but was better in terms of rendering Washington's feature and character. The showdown between the Peales and Stuart occurred in September 1795.

In retrospect, and with due filial attachment, Stuart's success must have seemed like the end of a long period of struggle with the general's likeness. In fact, if one compares the early descriptions and contemporary depictions, one cannot escape the conclusion that Stuart's portrait is an attempt to create a new Washington image that would far transcend the efforts of artists like Peale, Dunlap, Sharples, and Wright (fig. 9). Despite obvious differences, their paintings concentrate on details and the not-always-flattering features of Washington's face. One has only to recall descriptions that spoke of the impression the presence of Washington made on the visitor: they all asserted that there were no outstanding, striking features. As long as the painting contained other elements, like horses, battles, or subsidiary figures, attention was not primarily focused on the face. Once the face alone became the focus, the lack of striking features had either to be accepted or transformed, that is, ennobled. What distinguishes Stuart's portrait (see fig. 5) from previously painted ones is his ability to give the figure a more commanding physical presence. This trait was achieved by the adaptation of Renaissance compositional devices embodied in Raphael's *Castiglione*. Choosing a three-quarter view, yet fixing the eyes on the viewer, ignoring the hands and thus implying an above-average-size man, places the spectator at the same time at a distance from, but also in direct contact with, the person represented. Since there is nothing to detract one's attention, the interaction is complete. Some of the effect was achieved by softening the features, that is, by leaving in a "painterly" state what in the past had been so carefully and meticulously rendered. Stuart, whose London experience gave him an advantage over the Peales, had claimed that he could render the sitter's character and not only his or her countenance. Comparing Stuart's portrait to those of other painters, the viewer must have been struck by the implications of the artistic differences. Did Stuart reveal character traits that had eluded other painters? Was Washington's character different from what had been assumed? By the mid-1790s sympathies for and admiration of Washington were waning. There were attacks on the president's character. The unlimited veneration of the general underwent scrutiny and was no longer the cohesive force in American life. Washington ceased to be a demigod. Newspaper writers called him a "tyrant" and "dictator," an "imposter who should be hurled from his throne." The Philadelphia *Aurora* declared: "If ever a nation was debauched by a man, the American nation was debauched by Washington."[37] Slander or at least misleading statements on one side were answered by hero worship on the other; hero worship that is best exemplified by Weems' *Life of Washington* and the multivolume set written by Marshall, a work which John Adams once called a big mausoleum.[38] Could it have been that in such a situation Washington would have welcomed the opportunity to be painted by an artist who claimed that he could portray the character and not just the appearance of a person? Only in the hands of an artist like Stuart could Washington hope for a change of his image. A portrait could, of course, never change an adversary's mind, but it could propagate a new image of the president.

Years later, Rembrandt Peale asserted that Martha Washington regretted after her husband's death that no portrait of the "real" Washington existed. Rembrandt Peale began work on the still-lacking true portrait of the general. If he wanted to be successful and restore the Peale's family reputation enjoyed before the appearance of Stuart, he had to prove that Stuart's portrait was not reliable. Shortly before Washington's death, Rembrandt Peale completed a portrait with which he was not totally satisfied and which he reworked, until, in 1824–1825, he had completed a portrait that he considered the best ever painted (see fig. 1). To promote it he published a booklet in which he described the various efforts made by painters and sculptors to capture Washington's likeness.[39] Of his father's portrait he said that it "had ever since been disadvantageously seen in his Gallery of Distinguished Characters at Philadelphia. The features being very indefinitely marked and difficult to imitate, but few

copies have been made of it. It is esteemed for the expression of the eyes and the characteristic turn of the head."[40] Of his own portrait of Washington he remarked that it remained with him and "has chiefly served in producing those repeated attempts at a correct likeness." Of Stuart's portraits he said that the first one was called by Stuart himself "a complete failure," and that the second one, unfinished, was only painted after Mrs. Washington's intervention.[41] After speaking of some copies after Stuart's portrait, Peale singles himself out for what is a very interesting argument:

> At the death of Washington, in December, 1799, his family and friends grieved that there was no Portrait of him which conveyed an accurate idea of his mild, thoughtful, and dignified, yet firm and penetrating countenance. The same judgment which was pronounced by the whole body of Artists in Philadelphia in the year 1795, when the last portraits were painted, continued to be their opinion; and no artist was more sensible of this deficiency than Rembrandt Peale, the author of one of these last portraits. The youngest of those whom Washington honored with the opportunity of studying his features from the life, his enthusiasm was perhaps greater and the impression he received were more sacredly treasured up. Neither satisfied with his own, his father's, nor Stuart's, he made repeated attempts to improve his Portrait, and to fix on canvas the image which was so strong in his mind. These attempts were not satisfactory, and from time to time, while he resided in Philadelphia, and on every return to it, he continued his exhortations, until his last and successful attempt. These attempts could only be made in Philadelphia, because it was there alone the Artist could profit by the study of his father's paintings, in conjunction with his own, under the rigid observance of men who were capable of criticizing a work which had no chance of succeeding with them, unless it should accomplish what seemed next to impossible; and, that too, when time had almost consecrated the very faults of Stuart's Portrait.

The final qualification Rembrandt Peale claimed in his favor was that "he, born on Washington's birthday, was annually, from infancy, excited to greater admiration of his character."[42]

Rembrandt Peale presented another very important argument in support of his claim that Stuart's portrait of Washington was not the best rendering of the general's features and character. Two years before Washington's death, Lavater's *Essays on Physiognomy* was printed in Lon-

Fig. 10. Unidentified artist, *Portrait of George Washington*, 1797, engraving (from Lavater 1797, vol. 3; facing p. 333).

don in an English translation prepared by C. Moore. At the very end of the book, a crude engraving of Washington (fig. 10) is inserted with the following description.

It is already known that I mistrust the accuracy of resemblance in all engraved portraits, and I believe I have before said, that, in general, I look upon the representations of celebrated men, as so many carricatures. I am not acquainted with the original of this print, but he has performed great and astonishing things, such as not one in ten thousand would have undertaken—and can we refuse the character of grandeur to him whose actions bear the imprint of that character? Let us suppose that an individual should aspire to decide an event attracting the admiration of the age in which he lived, and the execution of it not seeming to lie within the scope of possibility, would not the physionomist be anxious to know the traits of the mortal appointed by fortune to be the instrument of so memorable a revolution. Here I see the same oblong form which [in] the other portraits of *Mr. Washington* is still more exaggerated. Such a form, when it is not too angulous, always indicates phlegm and firmness. This is the character of the physiognomy we are now examining, which besides equally recommends

itself by its great sereneness, by its intrepidity, and its expression of probity, wisdom and goodness. Without being so seducing as Julius Caesar or Newton, it is in the number of those physiognomies which improve upon the spectators, upon more close examination; and this portrait would have appeared to more advantage had the strokes been made with more boldness and vigour. I will say further, that if strength and sweetness united in a just proportion and in perfect harmony form that character of a great soul, this countenance represents that character to a certain degree— but I must at the same time acknowledge, that if the expression of the original is not still more animated, if from the vivacity and dignity of the traits it is not superior to the copy, it must impose silence upon the physiognomy. The forehead denotes much perspicuity, but it has not enough of profundity, and though it is happily formed, it seems to exclude penetration; the eyes are full of good temper and mildness, but they have neither the benevolence, prudence, nor the energy of heroism which are inseparable from true grandeur. The whole of this face announces a man of integrity, consistent, sincere, firm, deliberative and generous; and these different properties taken together, are capable of forming a personage of the first rank in merit, though neither of them may surpass another in an eminent degree. I persist, then in saying, that if *Washington* is the author of the revolution, which we have been witness to his undertaking and effecting with so much success, the designer must inevitably have suffered some of the most prominent traits of the original to have escaped him. Every man has ideas beyond the reach of his action, and no one is able to concenter all his faculties, all his capacities in what he performs or what he produces—and for this strong reason the physiognomy of a celebrated man must always be superior to the best portraits of him that can be produced.[43]

A few years later, a new translation of Lavater's *Physiognomy* was published by Hunter and for which Halloway had prepared illustrations. It is to this edition that Rembrandt Peale directs his reader. The earlier engraving of Washington's portrait has been reworked and is now combined with a rendering of Washington at Yorktown (fig. 11). Also added were a rough portrait sketch (fig. 12) at the end of the description and a full page copy of Stuart's Vaughan-Sinclair portrait (fig. 13). Due to this addition the text of Lavater's analysis has been augmented by the following paragraph:

Fig. 11. Unidentified artist, *Portrait of George Washington*, 1794, engraving after Peale. National Portrait Gallery, Smithsonian Institution, Washington, D.C.

traits, which Stuart's was intended to replace, represented the real Washington? Did those who preferred Stuart's portrait (see fig. 5)—Rembrandt Peale directed their attention to Lavater's discussion—prefer a rendering that projected the wrong image? We will never know.

If Stuart attempted to render Washington's character by eliminating details and avoiding precise rendering of his features, then Rembrandt Peale attempted to show Washington in a much more clearly defined way (see fig. 1). It is as if a veil before Stuart's painting had been removed; but there is more. Especially in the portrait offered to Congress and purchased by the Senate, Washington's face is placed in a frame, actually and symbolically, which to the generations of John Quincy Adams and Webster, a generation familiar with the classics, was replete with allusions.

The "Porthole Portrait" is distinguished from the many copies by some very specific features (see fig. 1). The porthole is surrounded by a wreath of oak leaves, has a face painted on the keystone, and bears at its bottom the inscription "Patriae Pater." Of these attributes the inscription is most easily understood. It recalls a passage in Cicero's *Republic* (I, vii, 13): "For there is really no other occupation in which human virtue approaches more closely that august function of the gods than that of

The sketch which terminates this Addition, pleases me infinitely more than the large Print [fig. 13]. I say so without the least partiality, for I know not which is the greatest likeness. I wish, however, it may be the sketch, in which I discern most delicacy, most penetration, something which commands respect, and the sentiment which results from a man's being perfectly at peace with himself. The valour depicted in this face seems at the same time, moderated by wisdom, and by a modesty exempt from pretension. It is a noble boldness; it does not suffer itself to be carried down the stream of passion, but is calm, because it has the consciousness of its own energy.[44]

For Rembrandt Peale this verdict must have been encouraging in his own pursuit. If Washington was the great man Lavater believed him to be, then he just could not look the way Stuart depicted him. It seems ironic that the crude engravings of Lavater's *Essays* are stylistically closer to the many less-accomplished renderings of Washington's features than they are to Stuart's painting, which in the words of Daniel Webster "had formed [his] idea of Washington."[45] Have perhaps those por-

Fig. 12. Unidentified artist, *Portrait of George Washington*, 1798, engraving (from Lavater 1789–1798, vol. 3, pt. 2; p. 437).

Fig. 13. Unidentified artist, *Portrait of George Washington*, 1798, engraving, after Gilbert Stuart's Vaughan-Sinclair portrait, 1795 (from Lavater 1789–1798, vol. 3, pt. 2; following p. 434).

founding new states or preserving those already in existence." Hardly any other characterization could better describe Washington's achievements. In this context it is most likely that the face on the keystone does indeed represent a god, and its features point most decidedly to the traditional image of Jupiter. The oak tree symbolizes strength of mind. It was the tree of the golden age, when law and faith ruled, and of its branches was made the *corona civilis*, awarded for merits in battle, especially for saving lives. The Porthole Portrait is not just a portrait of Washington but a portrait full of classical allusions and close to an apotheosis. Emerging from the dark lower part, the head is placed against the light, which is associated with the Jupiterlike image on the keystone in the same way, just as the dark part of the portrait is associated with the lower part of the painting, the *patria* on earth.[46] One has only to relate the Roman references contained in the passage to the American scene to recognize how much this allusion to Washington as Augustus has been stressed in Peale's painting. As Augustus had brought peace to an empire and as he had restored law and order so had Washington. There was

another emphasis as well: Patriae Pater did not just mean the father of an established country, one with definite and limited borders. It also was the title awarded to those who founded cities and states. In the history of the United States hardly any other time was more receptive to the idea of expansion and the possibility of linking such actions with the name of Washington. Nowhere has Rembrandt Peale expressed his own ideas about this portrait more clearly than in his little pamphlet:

It is impossible to contemplate the actions and the character of Washington—his early and steady adherence to the cause of liberty, and his devoted patriotism, without feeling an ardent desire to know how so great and excellent a man really appeared, and how far his corporeal features corresponded with his acknowledged mental greatness. This curiosity is of the most laudable kind, as it is associated with the recollection of actions that his example has rendered illustrious; of virtues which he so eminently possessed; and as it is connected with a veneration of the principles for which he struggled, and a love for the institutions that have been secured to his country.

Cities may be founded bearing the name of Washington—columns may be erected—and his memory be cherished in the bosoms of grateful people; there would, nevertheless, be something wanting. Had his features been more ordinary, and his expression less distinguished, the raising generation would still wish to know his own peculiar look. But when it is recollected that his aspect was noble as his character, and that his countenance corresponded with his conduct, it is the more incumbent on us to seek for, and transmit to posterity the true and impressive image of that countenance. Nothing can more powerfully carry back the mind to the glorious period which gave birth to this nation—nothing can be found more capable of exciting the noblest feelings of emulation and patriotism.

After the enlargement of the Capitol, begun in 1850, the House of Representatives and the Senate moved to the newly added wings. Today Rembrandt Peale's portrait hangs high above the restored speaker's chair in the old, deserted Senate Chamber (see fig. 2). In contrast, Vanderlyn's painting, with the head after Stuart, was not left behind when the House of Representatives moved to the new wing. It was taken along and remains a constant reminder of the way in which the nation wants to think of its first president.

NOTES

1. The quotation is from Rembrandt Peale, *Portrait of Washington* (Philadelphia [1824]). Beginning with page 9, Peale published "Letters addressed to Rembrandt Peale, by several distinguished characters, expressing their approbation of his Portrait of Washington." The first letter cited is from Chief Justice Marshall. "I have never seen a portrait of that great man which exhibited so perfect a resemblance of him. The likeness in features is striking, and the character of the whole face is preserved and exhibited with wonderful accuracy. It is more Washington himself than any Portrait of him I have ever seen." Marshall's letter was written 10 March 1824. The second letter is by Judge Washington. "I have examined with attention and pleasure the Portrait you have drawn of General Washington, and I feel no hesitation in pronouncing it, according to my best judgment, the most exact representation of the Original I have ever seen. The features, as well as the character of his countenance, are happily depicted."

2. Denis Diderot, *Correspondance* (Paris, 1965), 12:57.

3. Rembrandt Peale's portrait had already been painted in 1825. At that time Peale unsuccessfully tried to interest members of Congress in his portrait.

4. The responsibility for this kind of recommendation usually rested with the Joint Committee on the Library. Members of various other committees, however, used their positions to promote artists of their choice. An interesting case is that of Julia Plantou.

5. On the early history of the Washington Monument and the activities under the auspices of the Washington Monument Society see Frederick L. Harvey, *History of the Washington National Monument and of the Washington National Monument Society* (Washington, 1903 [57th Cong., 2d session, Senate Document 224]); and Robert B. Freeman, "Design Proposals for the Washington National Monument," *Records of the Columbia Historical Society* (1973–1974), 151–186.

6. *Register of Debates in Congress* (Washington, 1831–1832), 8: pt. 2, cols. 1809, 1824–1827. For a summary of the debate see Kenneth C. Lindsay, *The Works of John Vanderlyn: From Tammany to the Capitol* (Binghamton, N.Y., 1970), 133.

7. When Governor Harrison of Virginia had Charles Willson Peale copy one of his full-length portraits of Washington as a model for Houdon, the sculptor refused that visual aid and preferred to undertake the long voyage to America. Houdon might just have wanted to meet Washington simply because the Peale portrait did not in his opinion grasp the sitter's qualities or because he expected from a visit to the United States more commissions than the one offered by the State of Virginia or the federal government. During the debates of 1832 dealing with the commission of a Washington portrait from Vanderlyn, Representative Dearborn from Massachusetts mentioned that when Chantrey was commissioned the statue for the Boston State House, he was provided with copies of Houdon's bust and Stuart's portrait (most likely the Athenaeum portrait).

8. Vanderlyn had been working with Stuart; already in 1817 he had hoped to be considered for the decoration of the rotunda at the time when Trumbull netted all commissions. Jarvis was clearly trying to help Vanderlyn obtain this job. The way Jarvis proceeded reflects a familiar pattern in early nineteenty-century government patronage. Thus the choice of Stuart's head as model might have been made with Vanderlyn's experience with this portrait in mind. At one point Jarvis even maintained that all that is required from Vanderlyn is a copy, as he is not expected to create an original portrait. Had Jarvis consented to the statement that Peale's portrait was indeed a better likeness of Washington, then he would have deprived himself of the argument in favor of Vanderlyn's employment. Jarvis prevailed; Vanderlyn finally obtained the long-hoped-for commission, and the continuity of the influence of the Stuart portrait was assured.

9. *House Journal*, 19th Cong., 1st sess., 13 January 1826, 146 (U.S. Serial Set No. 130). Van Rensselaer offered the following resolution: "That the Speaker be directed to procure a copy of the most approved portrait of General George Washington, of full length, to be executed by one of the most eminent native artists of the United States."

10. Edward Everett, *Orations and Speeches on Various Occasions*, 2d ed. (Boston, 1850), 1:564–598.

11. For a discussion of nineteenth-century Washington imagery see Mark E. Thistlewhaite, *The Image of George Washington: Studies in Mid-Nineteenth-Century American History Painting* (New York, 1979).

12. William Spohn Baker, *Character Portraits of Washington as Delineated by Historians, Orators, and Divines* (Philadelphia, 1887).

13. See Margaret Brown Klapthor and Howard Alexander Morrison, *G. Washington: A Figure upon the Stage* [exh. cat., National Museum of American History, Smithsonian Institution] (Washington, 1981), for interesting and revealing examples of the use of Washington in a variety of circumstances "beyond his control." Albert T. Reid's poster *Uncle Sam*, 1932, is a prime example of political kitsch (their ill. 60); the photo of the 1939 rally of the German-American Bund and the 1980 poster "Washington for Jesus" are frightening examples for the unscrupulous use of the image of Washington for the sake of political manipulation (their ills. 54–55).

14. For most American painters of the late eighteenth and early nineteenth centuries painting portraits was a main source of income. As Trumbull once noticed most artists hoped for an opportunity to display their skill in history paintings, but there were virtually no chances for lucrative commissions for such paintings. Trumbull, for reasons not entirely related to his artistic accomplishments, was the first to break this barrier and win the commission of four large paintings, each twelve by eighteen feet, for the rotunda of the Capitol for an unprecedented price. Since then Trumbull's success had been the reason for artists seeking government patronage—and the profit connected with it. *Mutatis mutandis*, ever since have members of Congress used their influence to award lucrative contracts to their friends. On Trumbull see Egon Verheyen, "John Trumbull and the U.S. Capitol: Reconsidering the Evidence," in Helen A. Cooper, ed., *John Trumbull: The Hand and Spirit of a Painter* (New Haven, 1982), 260–275.

15. Leon Battista Alberti, *On Painting*, trans. and ed. John R. Spencer (New Haven and London, 1956), 63.

16. On this issue, especially with regard to portraits of Martin Luther, see Martin Warnke, *Cranachs Luther: Entwürfe für ein Image* (Frankfurt, 1984).

17. Physiognomic observations are the basis for caricature, which presents with a few strokes the "characteristic expression and yet transforms the man into an animal" (E. H. Gombrich, "The Cartoonist's Armoury," in *Meditations on a Hobby Horse and Other Essays on the Theory of Art* (London, 1963), 127–142, especially 134–135.

18. Johann Caspar Lavater, *Essays on Physiognomy Calculated to Extend the Knowledge and the Love of Mankind, Translated from the Last Edition by the Rev. C. Moore* (London, 1797). Johann Caspar Lavater, *Essays on Physiognomy Designed to Promote the Knowledge and the Love of Mankind. Illustrated by More than Eighthundred Engravings Accurately Copied; and Some Duplicates Added from Originals. Executed by, or under the Inspection of Thomas Hooloway. Translated from the French by Henry Hunter, D. D.* (London, 1789–1798). Lavater died in 1801. For the purpose of my argument other editions of Lavater need not be quoted here.

19. Lavater preferred engravings over paintings because the clear lines of the engraving were thought to be more precise than the brush of a painter.

20. Lavater 1797, 2:74–75. The quote continues: "If what Goethe has somewhere said be true, and in my opinion nothing can be more true, that—the best text for a commentary on man is his presence, his countenance, his form—how important is then the art of portrait painting; To this observation of Goethe's I will add a passage, on the subject, from Sultzer's excellent dictionary. 'Since no object of knowledge whatever can be more important to us than a thinking and feeling soul, it cannot be denied but that man, considered according to his form, even

though we should neglect what is wonderful in him, is the most important of visible objects.'"

21. The physiognotrace was invented by Gilles-Louis Chrétien and exploited commercially in partnership with Edmé Quenedey. It became fashionable in the United States through the émigré artist Févret de Saint-Mémin, who produced profile portraits of Washington (done in Philadelphia, 1798) and Jefferson (done in Washington, 1804). For some examples see William Howard Adams, ed., *The Eye of Jefferson* [exh. cat., National Gallery of Art, Washington] (Charlottesville, 1976), 147–148.

22. John Hill Morgan and Mantle Fielding, *The Life Portraits of Washington and Their Replicas* (Philadelphia, 1931), 59, no. 1.

23. Morgan and Fielding 1931, 77, no. 6.

24. For illustrations and descriptions of Washington's portraits see Morgan and Fielding 1931. It must suffice to touch only briefly on those renderings in which a portrait is connected with a background battle scene, like Charles Willson Peale's *Washington at Princeton* or his *Washington at Yorktown* or Trumbull's *Washington at Trenton*. In none of these paintings is any effort made to establish a meaningful connection between foreground and background. It is left to each spectator to envision the combat, defeat or victory. Most people of Peale's generation had participated in one or more of these battles. There was no need for a detailed depiction. This concept of visualization of an event by invocation of a name has been a major argument in convincing members of Congress to commission or buy historical paintings from Trumbull. The same concept guided Trumbull to secure portraits of all who had participated in the signing of the Declaration of Independence or any of the battles of the war, as for instance the surrender of Cornwallis or the battle at Trenton. The heads in these paintings had to be as lifelike as possible, but this requirement in turn was one of the foremost reasons why some of the history paintings are such unconvincing renderings. One simply cannot produce a portrait and not endow it with all the passions a given scene calls for.

25. Baker 1887, 9.

26. Baker 1887, 12.

27. Baker 1887, 15.

28. Baker 1887, 18.

29. Baker 1887, 23.

30. Baker 1887, 26.

31. Baker 1887, 27.

32. Baker 1887, 41. Already the Prince de Broglie had commented that "his face is much more agreeable than represented in his portrait."

33. Baker 1887, 51.

34. Jane Stuart, "The Stuart Portraits of Washington," *Scribner's Monthly* (1876), 367–374. Great parts of this account have been incorporated in Charles Merritt Mount, *Gilbert Stuart: A Biography* (New York, 1964).

35. After Stuart had been introduced to Washington, the Peales—Charles Willson, James, Raphael, and Rembrandt—had been granted a sitting during which they painted Washington from different angles. If Jane Stuart's account of the events of 1795 is correct, then the sitting for the Peale clan postdates Stuart's initially unsuccessful attempt and thus must be interpreted as an effort to regain or maintain what Stuart had attempted to assert for himself. In this light we must interpret Stuart's slightly derogatory pun that the president had been "pealed."

36. Stuart 1876, 370. This claim may not be correct. James Sharples' portrait might have been drawn after 1795, and Saint-Mémin's sketch (the original is lost) is said to have been the last one made while Washington was alive.

37. Cited in Stefan Lorant, *The Presidency: A Pictorial History of Presidential Elections from Washington to Truman* (New York, 1951), 38.

38. John Adams to Thomas Jefferson on 3 July 1813: "Gordon's and Marshall's *Histories* were written to make money, and fashioned and finished to sell high in the London market. I should expect to find more truth in a history written by Hutchinson, Oliver or Sewell. And I doubt not, such histories will one day appear. Marshall's is a mau-

soleum, 100 feet square at the base, and 200 feet high. It will be as durable as the monuments of the Washington benevolent Societies." On 3 September 1816, Adams wrote to Jefferson, "Events following the death of Washington were staged to keep in Countenance the Funding and Banking System, and to cast into the background all others who had been concerned in the Service of their Country in the Revolution" (Lester J. Cappon, ed., *The Adams-Jefferson Letters: The Complete Correspondence between Thomas Jefferson and Abigail and John Adams* [Chapel Hill, 1959], 2:487–488).

39. This type of explanatory description of history paintings was used by Trumbull in connection with his paintings of the Revolutionary War; it would also be used by all painters who after Trumbull contributed to the decoration of the rotunda of the Capitol.

40. Peale [1824], 3–8.

41. Peale [1824], 6: "The excellence of this Portrait consists in a peculiar species of pencilling, which in a considerable degree marks the expression of the countenance; but it may be seen, by a comparison with Houdon's Authentic Bust, that the features are inaccurately drawn and the character heavily exaggerated."

42. Peale [1824], 7–8.

43. Lavater 1797, 4:333–334.

44. Lavater 1798, 1:436–437.

45. *Register of Debates*, 22d Cong., 1st sess., 30 January 1832, 1155.

46. On the implications of the title Pater Patriae see Ovid *Fasti* II, 127–144.

Measures of Authenticity: The Detection of Copies in the Early Literature on Connoisseurship

JEFFREY M. MULLER
Brown University

MY PURPOSE IN this essay is to examine the concept of authenticity as it was formulated in the early literature on connoisseurship. The literature I have in mind dates from the mid-sixteenth century to the early eighteenth century. I use the term *authenticity* here in the sense defined by Walter Benjamin, to indicate the perceived uniqueness of the original work of art.[1] This concept was first articulated in what quickly became a central and staple issue of the subject: the distinction between copies and originals. Two opposing attitudes toward copies emerged. One, seeking to isolate the qualities that separate originals from copies, dismissed copies as inferior by nature and gave theoretical substance to the value of authenticity. The other attitude recognized the value of copies and, as a consequence, attempted to differentiate them in type, grade them in quality, and defend the usefulness of their functions. This second attitude challenged the absolute value of authenticity. Because many writers expressed both attitudes, the discussion is characterized by a persistent ambivalence.

The demand for authenticity in works of art is obvious from at least the early sixteenth century. This demand was soon translated into the skills of attribution, and the detection of copies was grouped under the heading of connoisseurship. For example, on 5 January 1532 Marcantonio Michiel visited the house of Antonio Pasqualino in Venice, where among other pictures he noted that "the head of the young man holding an arrow in his hand is by Giorgio da Castelfranco, and was obtained from Messer Giovanni Ram, who possesses a copy of it, which he believes to be the original."[2] One of these versions may be identical with the picture now in the Kunsthistorisches Museum, Vienna.[3] Much is implied in this brief comment. The skills of connoisseurship were already developed to a high degree of refinement. Two points about copies are raised. First, it is suggested that even the owner of an original can be deceived by a good copy substituted for it. Copies were thus perceived as a real threat to the claims of authenticity because they undermined the unique status of the original. Second, a sharp, experienced eye can penetrate the deception and discern the original from the copy. Michiel must have thought that authenticity is marked by certain regular characteristics.

What Michiel implied is stated outright in Enea Vico's *Discorsi* (1555), a work discussing ancient coins.[4] Vico devoted a whole chapter to the detection of forgeries and copies.[5] It is the earliest known methodical treatment of the subject. Every variety of fraud is listed along with the telltale signs accompanying deception. Most trickery involved tampering with partly ruined ancient coins and could be detected by technical analysis.[6] A skillful modern copy, however, presented a potentially more difficult problem. Giovanni dal Cavino's mid-sixteenth-century reproduction of an ancient Roman sesterce with the head of Nero on the obverse offers an example of what Vico had in mind (figs. 1–2).[7] Vico warned that if such a copy was struck with a die, covered with a false patina, and free of anachronistic interpolations, then only the connoisseur's eye, measuring degrees of quality, could arrive at the truth.[8] By drawing qualitative distinctions between originals and copies Vico began to articulate some of the cultural assumptions that supported the increasing value of authenticity. Vico thought that modern copies of ancient coins always will betray themselves by the inferior quality of the figures: "because in the modern figures there is neither the skill nor the comeliness [*venustà*] that one sees in the antique."[9] This difference is most visible in details: "in the master's style [*maniera*] of drawing, and in the execution of hair, eyes, ears, hands, and folds of

Above: Fig. 1. Giovanni dal Cavino, copy of an ancient Roman sesterce with the head of Nero, obverse, mid-sixteenth century. National Gallery of Art, Washington, Samuel H. Kress Collection (A1140.403A).

Below: Fig. 2. Ancient Roman sesterce with the head of Nero, obverse, first century. British Museum, London.

drapery, and similar things."[10] Vico was convinced that the work produced by each individual and historical period possesses unique and inimitable traits.

It is no accident that the first extensive discussion of copies in works of art applied to ancient coins. The critical study of antiquities was already well founded by the time Vico wrote. More important, numismatics was intimately tied to the methods of humanism. Philology and archaeology served as tools to reconstruct the culture of antiquity. In this endeavor the most pressing need was the ability to recognize what is authentically ancient, to refine standards of judgment for placing texts and monuments in history.[11] Vico, when he classified the original according to historical and personal styles that can be distinguished by levels of quality, depended for support on the most deeply held humanist articles of faith.

The moral and then economic value of authenticity founded on the veneration of antiquity was transferred to the work of modern artists through the rising cult of individual genius. Take, for example, Felipe de Guevara's sharply drawn distinction between originals by and imitations after Hieronymus Bosch. In his *Comentarios de la pintura* (1560 [?]) de Guevara advised the reader to beware of the countless forgeries "which are signed with the name of Hieronymus Bosch but are in fact fraudulently inscribed: pictures to which he would never have thought of putting his hand but which are in reality the work of smoke and the short-sighted fools who smoked them in fireplaces in order to lend them credibility."[12] What separates Bosch's work from that of his imitators is the superior intellect evident in the originals: "That which Hieronymus Bosch did with wisdom and decorum others did, and still do, without any discretion and good judgment."[13] The imitators latched onto a superficial characteristic of Bosch's art, his monsters and imaginary creatures, without understanding the context in which Bosch used them. De Guevara defined authenticity purely in terms of the individual cast of the artist's intellect as expressed by invention. He ignored the question of handling as an element of authenticity and consequently did not address the problem of literal copies.

Giulio Mancini was the first to discuss the problem of literal copies as it concerns painting. In his *Considerazioni* (c. 1620) Mancini cautioned prospective buyers that it is most important to determine whether a painting is an original or a copy.[14] Like Vico, Mancini directed the search for authenticity to the examination of characteristic details. A collector first had to ask whether a picture was executed at the level of perfection customary to the master under whose name the picture was being sold.

He could decide this best by looking for the "boldness" (*franchezza*) of the master's touch:

especially in those parts which demand resolution and cannot be well executed in the process of imitation, as is true in particular for hair, beards, and eyes. Ringlets of hair, if imitated, will betray the laborious effort of the copy and if the copyist does not want to imitate them, then they will in that case lack the perfection of the master. These elements of painting are like the strokes and groups of letters in handwriting which require a master's boldness and resolution. The same can be observed in those spirited passages and scattered highlights that a master renders with one stroke and with a touch of the brush that is inimitably resolute; as in the folds and highlights of drapery, which depend more on the fantasy and resolution of the master than on the verisimilitude of the thing represented.[15]

Mancini's critique rests on the premise that copies are inherently inferior. This deeply ingrained conviction has its roots in ancient philosophy and in the theory of rhetoric. Plato, of course, attacked painting as the imitation of an imitation.[16] In a hierarchy leading from truth to mere appearances, the copy is always at the bottom. Abraham Bosse, writing in 1649, echoed Plato when he maintained that, just as a painter who imitates nature never approaches the perfection of his model, "ainsi le copiste ne rend jamais sa copie à la perfection de son original" ("so the copyist never brings his copy to the perfection of its original").[17] According to Bosse, everything in a copy—relief, delineation of contours, color—will be vitiated; a pale reflection of the original.

Franciscus Junius observed in his *Painting of the Ancients* (1638) that "Lovers of art" display their skill above all in "that they doe most readily discerne originall pictures from the other that are copied; finding a perfect and natural force of grace in the originalls, whereas in the copies they can see nothing but an unperfect and borrowed comelinesse."[18] Junius supported this view of copies with a string of quotations taken from ancient authors. Dionysius of Halicarnassus is representative: "Originals have in themselves a naturall grace and vigor, . . . but Copies, though they attaine to the height of imitation, have alwayes something, which being studied, doth not proceed out of nature: and Rhetoricians doe not onely discerne Rhetoricians by this precept, but painters doe also by this rule distinguish *Apelles* his works from their works that imitate him." Junius quoted Cicero, Quintilian, and Pliny the Younger to the same effect.[19]

One can assume that these ancient writers supplied an important critical principle to Renaissance theorists like Mancini, who sought to define the characteristics of authenticity.

Mancini, the sharp-eyed collector, indicated more precisely than Junius where the force and grace of the original were to be found. Mancini focused attention on the passages in a picture that allow for a fluid and spontaneous handling of the brush. He looked for boldness and resolution. He thought these qualities to be inimitable because they assume the condition of license that is available to the original artist but denied to the copyist. The slavish repetition of a model, be it an object of nature or a work of art, inhibits the free play of the brush. Giorgio Vasari had already put together the same complex of ideas when he noted with disdain the reaction of Florentine painters to *grotteschi* by Giovanni da Udine. Vasari praised Giovanni's work for its "vivacity and marvelous practice" and for its capricious invention.[20] The painters to which he referred could not fully approve because their own work was tied to the literal representation of objects drawn from life. This produced a style marked by laborious effort and absence of resolution, exactly the weaknesses Mancini saw in copies.[21] Elsewhere Vasari observed that the late work of Titian, executed in broad, bold strokes and patches of color, is extremely difficult to imitate. Titian's apparent freedom of practice disguised his consummate mastery of art.[22] The demand for authenticity seems to have placed greater emphasis on styles that made the master's touch more evident and difficult to reproduce.

Taking into account that Mancini isolated the marks of authenticity in passages of open brushwork, one can understand the logic of Peter Paul Rubens' remarks to Sir Dudley Carleton concerning originals and copies. In 1618 Rubens had offered Carleton a group of pictures that included student copies that he had retouched.[23] When Carleton insisted on originals only, Rubens reassured him that the other pictures were not "mere copies, but so well retouched by my hand that it would be difficult to distinguish them from originals."[24] The implication is that free and open brushwork, executed in lightninglike strokes of drapery and highlight, is inimitable. The rest could be reproduced mechanically and, therefore, made less of a difference in regard to authenticity.

What Mancini and Rubens implied was made explicit by Bosse in his *Sentimens* (1649). Bosse, like Mancini, drew an analogy between handwriting and painting to clarify the distinction between originals and copies, only Bosse gave the comparison a precise new twist. Legal scribes, he said, must of necessity be able to tell original documents and signatures apart from copies. Everyone knows that large letters and flourishes are more difficult to counterfeit than unornamented script or what he calls the "corps de lettre." This is because the large letters require a free hand.

La grandeur & forme desdites grandes lettres & traits dependent d'ordinaire de la volonté de ceux qui les font, le contraire est à ceux qui les veulent imiter car ils se trouent contraints & gesnez, & ainsi lon reconnoist que ce qu'ils en ont fait est d'ordinaire tremblant & corrompu en ses formes ("The size and form of these large letters and strokes usually depend on the will of those who make them, while the opposite is true of those who want to imitate them because they find themselves constrained and cramped, and so one recognizes that what they have made of it is usually trembling and corrupted in its forms").[25]

Bosse argued that the same is true of paintings and drawings.

Bosse, himself an artist, supported the theoretical distinctions with practical explanations. The painter of a freely worked original will often break in brushes for special jobs. He will trim and soften them and give them varied points and irregular bristles in order to fluidly compose details such as wisps, tufts, and curls of hair. One stroke with this kind of brush will force a copyist to make one hundred. Highly finished pictures are, by contrast, easier to copy because they are painted with the kind of pointed brush that is standard equipment for all artists.[26] What we call a painterly style came to be associated ever more closely with the signs of authenticity.

By the end of the seventeenth century the equation between freedom of touch and authenticity was invested with the authority of a hard-and-fast law. Filippo Baldinucci was skeptical about the reliability of every other principle of connoisseurship. In his letter on painting addressed in 1681 to the Marchese Capponi, however, Baldinucci subscribed to what he termed the "universal rule of more or less boldness in handling" by which one can tell originals from copies.[27] Jonathan Richardson senior in his essay *The Connoisseur* (1719) methodically synthesized the theoretical tradition as if it were given truth. Copies are different from originals for three reasons. First, they are one step removed from nature—the echo of an echo; second, copyists will be unfamiliar with and at pains to imitate convincingly the customary styles of original artists; third, copies are made under the con-

straint of their models, whereas originals are executed with license. Keeping these distinctions in mind, Richardson was confident that "the best counterfeiter of hands cannot do it so well as to deceive a good connoisseur."[28]

Authenticity was identified with the free play of the artist's hand and mind. Caprice, fantasy, will, boldness, resolution, and spirit characterized an original. Laborious effort, fatigue, trembling, and hesitation were the marks of a copy. The original was exalted because it embodied the qualities that were taken since the early sixteenth century as proof of mastery.[29] The new critical values that separated artists from artisans and the premium on authenticity were thought to be mutually supportive. The unique existence of the original and what Benjamin calls the aura of the original were confirmed.[30] Carlo Ginzburg is correct in maintaining that this confirmation was at heart a cultural and historical choice.[31] Once the choice was made there were theoretical arguments and empirical evidence to support it.

The same writers who armed themselves with universal rules for the detection of copies also interjected edges of skepticism that opened the way to a different approach toward the value of authenticity. What of those copies, it was asked, that fool even the keenest eye? Mancini, despite the separation he made between originals and copies, warned that sometimes "a copy is executed so well that it deceives, even though the artist and the buyer are in on the secret. Rather, what is more, having the original and the copy they cannot distinguish between them."[32] In such cases, where there are two arts combined, that of the original master and that of the copyist, the copy is to be preferred over the original as a jewel of painting.

It may be that Mancini had in mind a story recounted by Vasari. This concerns Andrea del Sarto's copy, now in Naples, after Raphael's *Portrait of Pope Leo X with Cardinals Giulio de' Medici and Luigi Rossi* (copy, 1525; original, c. 1517; figs. 3–4). The copy was secretly painted and given to Federigo Gonzaga, duke of Mantua, who thought he was getting the original as a gift from Pope Clement VII. Vasari, who had seen Andrea make the copy, later visited Mantua where Giulio Romano displayed the picture to him as the treasure of the Gonzaga collection. Giulio, Raphael's former assistant, was sure that this was his master's work. He was especially confident because he himself had a hand in the original; nor would Giulio believe otherwise until Vasari showed him Andrea's mark on the panel. Giulio's response was to shrug and say that he valued the copy more than the original "because it is extraordinary that one great artist should

144

Fig. 3. Andrea del Sarto, after Raphael, *Portrait of Pope Leo X with Cardinals Giulio de' Medici and Luigi Rossi*, 1525, oil on canvas. Museo e Gallerie Nazionale di Capodimonte, Naples.

Fig. 4. Raphael, *Portrait of Pope Leo X with Cardinals Giulio de' Medici and Luigi Rossi*, c. 1517, oil on canvas. Palazzo Pitti, Florence.

be able to imitate so well the style of another."[33] Giulio's wonder was aroused by Andrea's ability to reproduce the individual qualities, the *maniera* of Raphael's art.

Perhaps because it must be true in gist and concerns famous pictures by eminent artists and the dupe was more qualified than anyone to see through the ruse, Vasari's story became the classic example of the power of copies to deceive. Baldinucci, Roger de Piles, and Jean-Baptiste Du Bos all repeated it.[34] Similar anecdotes about copies by Rubens after Titian and by Pierre Mignard after Guido Reni were used to the same effect.[35] First, the stories eroded confidence in the criteria established for the recognition of authenticity. De Piles concluded from Vasari's example that "la verité se peut quelquefois cacher à la science la plus profonde ("the truth can sometimes hide itself from the most profound science").[36] Du Bos, writing in 1719, reversed the thrust of the analogy

between painting and handwriting previously used by Mancini and Bosse. If testimony from the more exact art of handwriting analysis is not admitted as evidence in courts of law, then, Du Bos asked, "Que penser de l'art qui suppose hardiment qu'on ne puisse pas si bien contrefaire la touche de Raphël & du Poussin qu'il y puisse être trompé ("What to think of an art which rashly supposes that one could not so well counterfeit the touch of Raphael or of Poussin that it could be deceived therein").[37]

The second effect of these stories was to reassert the power of the artist at the expense of the connoisseur. This can be illustrated with an example that, although involving an imitation rather than a literal copy, deals with the same issue. I am referring to Hendrick Goltzius' *Circumcision of Christ*, 1594 (fig. 5).[38] This engraving is one of six in a series depicting the life of the Virgin.

Each print is executed in the style of a different old master, and together they form one of the major variations from the sixteenth century on the theme of imitation. Among the six engravings, the *Circumcision*, Goltzius' homage to Albrecht Dürer, is special. Karel van Mander, Goltzius' friend and colleague, reported in his biography of the artist that Goltzius played a trick with his engraving. He burned out his identifying self-portrait and monogram, treated the print to make it look old, and then passed it off as an original by Dürer: "artists and experienced connoisseurs saw it with great wonderment and pleasure; some paid a high price for it, delighted to have secured such a completely unknown print by the great Nuremberger."[39] Van Mander added that "together, all these things prove that Goltzius is a strange Proteus or Vertumnus in his art."[40]

Like Proteus, Goltzius changed form to avoid being caught. Goltzius had to free himself from Dürer's ghost. Connoisseurship had constructed an image of authenticity that exalted the dead at the expense of the living. Goltzius had to destroy the certainty of that classification. The value of authenticity that had begun by affirming the freedom of the individual artist paradoxically came to limit that freedom. Goltzius' deception and the stories about deceptive copies that it resembled asserted the power of art to take any form it wished.

The third effect of these stories was to affirm the value of copies as works of art. Marco Boschini wrote in 1674 that if copies are truly deceptive then "they are laudable deceptions and worthy of envy."[41] As an example he pointed to Giovanni Battista Zampezzi, who "when it comes to transforming himself into Bassano, surpasses all others, so that his copies appear to be the twins of the originals, and this is the most difficult style to imitate because it is executed with so bold a touch."[42] Freedom of handling, which had been perceived as the most reliable mark of authenticity, was now a sign of the copyist's virtuosity.

All the stories I have cited involve exceptions that could be said to prove the rule. Nevertheless, the paradox that a convincing copy deserves more praise than its original suggests that copies come in different grades of quality. Indeed, Walter Benjamin has observed that the gradation of levels of authenticity was a major function of the art market. The early literature on connoisseurship, serving as a kind of consumer's guide to pictures, rationalized and confirmed this gradation. I do not agree with Benjamin's assumption that degrees of authenticity were primarily graded in response to the introduction of reproductive printing processes, which he thinks struck at the

Fig. 5. Hendrick Goltzius, *The Circumcision of Christ*, 1594, engraving. The Metropolitan Museum of Art, New York, Gift of Henry Walters, 1917 (17.37.36).

root of the quality of authenticity by placing in doubt the uniqueness of the original.[43] I think that the workshop production of replicas and flood of good copies raised the problem independently of prints.

Baldinucci, in his letter of 1681, was the first to develop at length the idea that copies come in different grades of quality. He dismissed from serious consideration "every rag of canvas or bit of panel smeared rather than painted."[44] He also alerted connoisseurs to the variety of good copies they might encounter. There are student copies retouched by the master and sold as originals, study pieces by great painters like the Carracci, which equal the beauty of their originals, and copies by artists who have a special knack for this line of work.[45] De Piles later agreed that mediocre copies do not merit attention and that only good ones present difficulties for the skilled connoisseur. He classified copies into three kinds: faithful but slavish, unfaithful and free, faithful and free.[46] The last kind will obviously cause the most trouble because it approaches the condition of spontaneity thought to be typical of authenticity.

Richardson attempted to differentiate levels of authenticity according to what he believed to be a rational standard. Following John Locke's method, he insisted on precise definitions of terms and on a logical demonstration of classifications proceeding from the terms.[47] "A copy," he stated, "is the repetition of a work already done when the artist endeavours to follow that; as he that works by invention, or the life endeavouring to copy nature, seen, or conceived makes an original."[48] Richardson divided originality into components of thought and handling. He thus was able to conclude that a painting made from a drawing or sketch by another artist "cannot be said to be a copy: the thought indeed is partly borrowed, but the work is original."[49] According to Richardson's definition, Sebastiano del Piombo's *Flagellation of Christ*, c. 1520, in San Pietro in Montorio, although painted after Michelangelo's design, is Sebastiano's original. Richardson's logic also led him to conclude that some works are part copy and part original: "A copy retouched in some places by invention, or the life is of this equivocal kind. I have several drawings first copied after old masters . . . and endeavoured to be improved by Rubens; so far as his hand has gone is therefore original, the rest remains pure copy."[50] Rubens' famous drawing in the Louvre after Leonardo's *Battle of Anghiari* fits this classification since it has been shown that the center is a literal copy by an anonymous artist freely retouched by Rubens.[51] Richardson defined his terms, noted hybrids, and then asked a series of questions calculated to include every conceivable permutation.[52] After the progressively more complex classifications of Baldinucci, De Piles, and Richardson the value of copies must have been evident and the connoisseur's job more complicated. It was no longer enough to tell a copy from an original. One was now expected to distinguish as well among many kinds of copies.

The most positive and forceful defense of the value of copies was made in a remarkable section at the end of Baldinucci's letter of 1681. The prevailing view, he said, is that copies are to be shunned like the plague. He argued, however, that they serve many important functions. First, as Cardinal Federico Borromeo had already observed in his *Musaeum* (1625), copies often preserve the appearance of lost originals.[53] Second, good copies afford us pleasure through the sheer feat of imitation in which we take instinctive delight. Third, copies augment the small and often inaccessible supply of excellent pictures. This is vital to aspiring artists who need the guidance of good models. Baldinucci cited the beneficial effect of copies made after Raphael by the artist's students. They are supposed to have spread Raphael's style throughout Europe "like the rays of a new light."[54] The infinite number of copies distributed through engravings expanded and expedited the dissemination of ideas. As proof, Baldinucci observed that the art of sculpture lagged behind the development of painting because it took so long to invent an effective technique for making three-dimensional copies. This, however, has been remedied with the spread of casts all over the continent. Tintoretto, for example, owned casts after Michelangelo's *Twilight* and *Dawn*. Rubens had casts made of the antiquities that he sold to the duke of Buckingham. Painters also avidly collected copies of paintings.[55]

Baldinucci was the first to record a historical development that challenged the quality of authenticity. If the power of the original could be distributed so effectively through copies, then the importance of the original was necessarily diminished.

Ambivalence toward the value of authenticity in works of art actually solved some difficult problems. First, it acknowledged the simple fact that, according to the measures we apply, most originals are better than copies. There are, nevertheless, some excellent copies and many that are good. Second, arguments were provided to give everyone satisfaction with what he or she could afford in an art market where prices were set with increasing regularity on a scale of authenticity.[56] Third, the dual purposes of art as a system of illusion and expression of individual character were confirmed. Behind these easy combinations of opposites there stands the more difficult problem of human identity.

NOTES

A different version of the present essay will appear as section 4 of a forthcoming article in which I discuss the early literature of connoisseurship: "An Outline of the Early Theory of Connoisseurship: From Mancini to Richardson."

1.   See Walter Benjamin, "The Work of Art in the Age of Mechanical Reproduction (1936)," in *Illuminations,* trans. Harry Zohn, ed. Hannah Arendt (New York, 1969), 220–222.

2.   Marcantonio Michiel, *Der Anonimo Morelliano (Marcantonio Michiel's notizie d'opere del disegno)*, trans. and ed. Theodor Frimmel (Vienna, 1896), 78: "La testa del gargione che tiene in mano la frezza, fu de man de Zorzi da Castelfranco, hauuta da M. Zuan Ram, della quale esso M. Zuan ne ha un ritratto, benche egli creda che sii el proprio." The translation is from *The Anonimo: Notes on Pictures and Works of Art in Italy Made by an Anonymous Writer in the Sixteenth Century,* trans. P. Mussi, ed. G. C. Williamson (London, 1903), 93. Williamson reads the date as 15 January.

3. On this picture see Kunsthistorisches Museum, *Katalog der Gemäldegalerie. I. Teil. Italiener, Spanier, Franzosen, Engländer* (Vienna, 1960), 61, no. 553.

4. Enea Vico, *Discorsi di M. Enea Vico Parmigiano, sopra le medaglie de gli antichi* (Venice, 1555).

5. Vico 1555, 61–67: "Delle fravdi che si fanno intorno alle medaglie moderne per farle parere antiche, e delle Patine diuerse di colori. Cap. XXII."

6. Vico 1555, 61–62.

7. For Giovanni dal Cavino's copy see George F. Hill, *Renaissance Medals from the Samuel H. Kress Collection at the National Gallery of Art,* revised and enlarged by Graham Pollard (London, 1967), 75, no. 403. For the type of the original see Harold Mattingly, *Augustus to Vitellius,* vol. 1 of *Coins of the Roman Empire in the British Museum* (London, 1923), 260–261 and pl. 45: no. 19. Vico 1555, 67, included dal Cavino in his list of the best imitators of ancient coins.

8. Vico 1555, 62.

9. Vico 1555, 62: "perche nelle figure moderne, non è quella pratica di fare, ne quella uenustà ne' corpi, che nelle antiche figure si ueggono."

10. Vico 1555, 62: "per la maniera del maestro nel disegno, e per fare de' capegli, de gli occhi, dell'orecchi, delle mani, delle pieghe de' panni, e simil cose."

11. On the place of numismatics see Roberto Weiss, *The Renaissance Discovery of Classical Antiquity* (Oxford, 1973), 206–207; Peter Burke, *The Renaissance Sense of the Past* (London, 1969), 69, where the skeptical approach to evidence taken by Vico is equated with the criticism of documents in the Renaissance; on the critical study of antiquities see Erna Mandowsky and Charles Mitchell, eds., *Pirro Ligorio's Roman Antiquities: The Drawings in MS XIII. B.7 in the National Library in Naples* (London, 1963), 26, 30.

12. Felipe de Guevara, *Comentarios de la pintura que escribió Don Felipe de Guevara* (1560 [?]), in F. J. Sánchez Cantón, ed., *Fuentes literarias para la historia del arte español,* 5 vols. [Madrid, 1923–1941], 1:159–160: "Ansi vienen a ser infinitas las pinturas de este género, selladas con el nombre de Hyerónimo Bosco, falsamente inscripto; en las quales a él nunca le pasó por el pensamiento poner las manos, sino el humo y cortos igenios, ahumándolas a las chimeneas para dalles autoridad y antigüedad." The translation is from Wolfgang Stechow, ed. and trans., *Northern Renaissance Art, 1400–1600: Sources and Documents* (Englewood Cliffs, N.J., 1966), 19.

13. De Guevara 1560 (?) in Cantón 1923–1941, 1:159: "Esto que Hyerónimo Bosco hizo con prudencia y decoro, han hecho y hacen otros sin discreción y juicio ninguno." The translation is from Stechow 1966, 19.

14. Giulio Mancini, *Considerazioni sulla pittura* (c. 1620), ed. Adriana Marucchi, with preface by Lionello Venturi and commentary by Luigi Salerno, 2 vols., Accademia Nazionale dei Lincei, Fonti e Documenti inediti per la storia dell'arte (Rome, 1956–1957), 1:134.

15. Mancini [c. 1620] 1956–1957, 1:134: "di più se vi si veda quella franchezza del mastro, et in particolare in quelle parti che di necessità si fanno di resolutione nè si posson ben condurre con l'immitatione, come sono in particolare i capelli, la barba, gl'occhi. Che l'anellar de' capelli, quando si han da imitare, si fanno con stento, che nella copia poi apparisce, et, se il copiatore non li vuol imitare, allhora non hanno la perfettione di mastro. E queste parti nella pittura sono come i tratti e gruppi nella scrittura, che voglion quella franchezza e resolutione di mastro. Il medesimo ancor si deve osservare in alcuni spiriti e botte di lumi a luogo a luogo, che dal mastro vengon posti a un tratto e con resolution d'una pennellata non immitabile; così nelle pieghe di panni e lor lume, quali pendono più dalla fantasia e resolution del mastro che della verità della cosa posta in essere."

16. Plato *Republic* X: 595–603.

17. Abraham Bosse, *Sentimens sur la distinction des manieres de peinture dessin, et graveure, et des originaux et coppies, &c.* (Paris, 1649), 56–57.

18. Franciscus Junius, *The Painting of the Ancients* (1638; Westmead, 1972), 348.

19. Junius [1638] 1972, 348 (quote), 349.

20. Giorgio Vasari, *Le Opere di Giorgio Vasari* (1550), ed. Gaetano Milanesi, 9 vols. (Florence, 1906), 6:557: The *grotteschi* were painted "con fierezza e pratica maravigliosa."

21. Gianlorenzo Bernini's practice exactly responded to this conception of originals and copies. Paul Fréart de Chantelou reported that Bernini, in executing his bust of Louis XIV, claimed to work mainly from his imagination and rarely from the life drawings he made of the king: "qu'autrement, s'il avait travaillé d'après ses dessins, au lieu d'un original il ne ferait qu'une copie; que même, s'il lui fallait copier les bustes lorsqu'il l'aura achevé, il ne lui serait pas possible de le faire tout semblable; que la noblesse de l'idée n'y serait plus à cause de la servitude de l'imitation" (see Paul Fréart de Chantelou, *Journal du voyage en France du Cavalier Bernin,* with preface by G. Charensol [Paris, 1930], 92).

22. Vasari [1550] 1906, 7:452.

23. For the list of pictures sent by Peter Paul Rubens to Sir Dudley Carleton on 28 April 1618 see Ch. Ruelens and Max Rooses, eds., *Correspondance de Rubens et documents épistolaires concernant sa vie et ses oeuvres,* 6 vols. (1887–1909; Soest, n.d.), 2:135–137.

24. Ruelens and Rooses [1887–1909] n.d., 2:149: Rubens to Carleton, 12 May 1618: speaking of Carleton's desire for originals: "pur non pensi V. E. che le altre siano copie semplici ma si ben ritocce de mia mano che difficilmente si distinguerrebbono dalli originali."

25. Bosse 1649, 67–68.

26. Bosse 1649, 60.

27. Filippo Baldinucci, *Lettera di Filippo Baldinucci Fiorentino Nella quale risponde ad alcuni quesiti in materie di pittura* (1681), in Giovanni Gaetano Bottari and Stefano Ticozzi, eds., *Raccolta di lettere sulla pittura, scultura, ed architettura Scritte da' più celebri personaggi dei secoli XV, XVI, e XVII,* 8 vols. [Milan, 1822–1825], 2:509–510: It is easiest to spot copies in sketchy drawings where the free execution of the original is hardest to imitate: "Questa universal regola della maggiore o minor franchezza nell'operare, ha luogo ancora nelle cose colorite."

28. Jonathan Richardson [senior], *Two Discourses. I. An Essay on the Whole Art of Criticism as it relates to painting shewing how to judge I. Of the Goodness of a Picture; II. Of the Hand of the Master; and III. Whether 'tis an Original or a Copy. II. An Argument in Behalf of the Science of a Connoisseur; Wherein Is Shewn the Dignity, Certainty, Pleasure, and Advantage of It* (1719), in Jonathan Richardson [senior], *The Works of Jonathan Richardson* (London, 1792), 159, 162 (quote).

29. Vasari [1550] 1906, 4:9–11, observed that painters discussed in the second part of his book lacked the following qualities possessed by painters of the third part: "una licenzia che, non essendo di regola, fosse ordinata nella regola. . . ." "quella facilità graziosa e dolce, che apparisce fra 'l vedi e non vedi. . . . quelle minuzie dei fini, che sono la perfezione ed il fiore dell'arte. . . . una gagliardezza risoluta. . . . uno spirito di prontezza."

30. Benjamin [1936] 1969, 221.

31. Carlo Ginzburg, "Clues: Morelli, Freud, and Sherlock Holmes," in *The Sign of Three: Dupin, Holmes, Peirce,* ed. Umberto Eco and Thomas A. Seboek (Bloomington, 1983), 93.

32. Mancini [c. 1620] 1956–1957, 1:134–135: "alle volte avviene che la copia sia tanto ben fatta che inganni, ancorchè l'artefice e chi compra sia intelligente, anzi, quello che è più, havendo la copia et l'originale, non sappia destinguere."

33. Vasari [1530] 1906, 5:41–43 (anecdote), 42 (quote): "perchè è cosa fuor di natura, che un uomo eccellente imiti sì bene la maniera d'un altro." On Andrea's copy and for a correction of Vasari's facts see Sidney J. Freedberg, *Andrea del Sarto: Catalogue Raisonné* (Cambridge, Mass., 1963), 131–133; John Shearman, *Andrea del Sarto,* 2 vols. (Oxford, 1965), 2:265–267.

34. Baldinucci 1681 in Bottari and Ticozzi 1822–1825, 2:506–507; Roger de Piles, *Abrégé de la vie des peintres avec des réflexions sur leurs ouvrages et un traité du peintre parfait, de la connoissance des desseins, & de l'utilité des estampes*, 2d ed. (1699; Paris, 1715), 99–102; Jean-Baptiste Du Bos, *Réflexions critiques sur la poësie et sur la peinture*, 3 vols. (1719; Dresden, 1760), 2:373.

35. On Rubens see Marco Boschini, *La carta del navegar pitoresco*, ed. Anna Palluchini (1660; Venice, 1966), 82–83. On Pierre Mignard see Christoph Martin Wieland, "Etwas aus den Anecdotes des Beaux-Arts," in *Wieland's Werke*, 40 vols., ed. H. Düntzer (Berlin, 1879), 35:397–399. Ernst Kris and Otto Kurz, *Legend, Myth, and Magic in the Image of the Artist*, trans. Alastair Lang and Lottie M. Newman, with preface by E. H. Gombrich (New Haven, 1979), 97–98, place these kinds of stories in a category that demonstrates the artist's virtuosity.

36. De Piles [1699] 1715, 102.

37. Du Bos 1719, 2:375.

38. On this print see Otto Hirschmann, *Hendrick Goltzius; Meister der Graphik* (Leipzig, 1919), 7:77–79.

39. Karel van Mander, *Het Schilder-Boeck* (1604; Utrecht, 1969), fol. 284v; fol. 284v: the engraving "was by den Constenaren en verstandighe Liefhebbers met groot verwonderen en behaghen geern ghesien / oock van eenighe om grooten prijs ghecocht / wesende verblijdt te hebben becomen van den constighen Norenbergher sulck stuck / darmen noyt meer ghesien hadde." The translation is from Stechow 1966, 54–55.

40. Van Mander [1604] 1969, fol. 285r: "Al dees verhaelde dinghen t'samen bewi jsen/ *Goltzium* eene seldsame *Proteus* oft *Vertumnus* te wesen in de Const." The translation is from Stechow 1966, 55.

41. Marco Boschini, "Breve instrvzione per intender in qualche modo le maniere de gli Auttori Veneziani," in *Le ricche minere della pittura Veneziana*, 2d ed. (Venice, 1674), 3: "e questi, tutto che siano veramente inganni, sono inganni lodeuoli, e degni d'inuidia."

42. Boschini 1674, 3: "Giouanni Battista Zampezzi, che per trasformarsi nel Bassano, non vi è che vi si possi auuicinare à segno, che le coppie di questo paion con l'originali gemelle, ed è la più difficile maniera da imitare; perche è d'vn colpo cosi franco."

43. Benjamin [1936] 1969, 243 n. 2.

44. Baldinucci 1681 in Bottari and Ticozzi 1822–1825, 2:526–527: "noi non intendiamo di parlare d'ogni straccio di tela, o pezzo di tavola che per imitare qualche pittura abbia piuttosto imbrattato, che dipinto qualche fanciullo o principiante."

45. Baldinucci 1681 in Bottari and Ticozzi 1822–1825, 2:504–506.

46. De Piles [1699] 1715, 97–98.

47. For an account of Richardson's dependence on John Locke see Carol Gibson-Wood, "Jonathan Richardson and the Rationalization of Connoisseurship," *Art History* 7 (1984), 38–56.

48. Richardson 1719 [1792], 157.

49. Richardson 1719 [1792], 157–158.

50. Richardson 1719 [1792], 158.

51. On this drawing see Anne-Marie Logan, "Rubens Exhibitions 1977," *Master Drawings* 15 (1977), 408–409.

52. Richardson 1719 [1792], 156–165.

53. For Federico Borromeo see *Il museo del Cardinale Federico Borromeo*, trans. Luigi Grasselli, ed. Luca Beltrami (Milan, 1909), 12–13 (Latin text), 50–51 (Italian translation).

54. Baldinucci 1681 in Bottari and Ticozzi 1822–1825, 2:527–530: "le copie come gioie rarissime eran mandate per tutta l'Europa, fino agli ultimi confini della quale, mediante le medesime, in un subito raggi di nuova luce si sparsero in queste belle arti."

55. Baldinucci 1681 in Bottari and Ticozzi 1822–1825, 2:530–533.

56. See, for example, John Michael Montias, *Artists and Artisans in Delft: A Socio-Economic Study of the Seventeenth Century* (Princeton, 1982), 233–235.

You Irreplaceable You

ROSALIND E. KRAUSS
*Hunter College and the Graduate Center,
City University of New York*

Embrace Me, You Sweet Embraceable You

AGAIN AND AGAIN, in his various essays on the Paris Salons, Charles Baudelaire attempts to characterize the nature of the critical act, declaring that "criticism should be partial, passionate and political" ("The Salon of 1846"). Perhaps his most endearing description is the one that uses Honoré de Balzac as its exemplar and comes from Baudelaire's account of the 1855 *Exposition Universelle*.

> The story [Baudelaire writes] is told of Balzac (and who would not listen with respect to any anecdote, no matter how trivial, concerning that great genius?) that one day he found himself in front of a beautiful picture—a melancholy winter-scene, heavy with hoar-frost and thinly sprinkled with cottages and mean-looking peasants; and that after gazing at a little house from which a thin wisp of smoke was rising, 'How beautiful it is!' he cried. 'But what are they doing in that cottage? What are their thoughts? What are their sorrows? Has it been a good harvest? No doubt they have bills to pay!'[1]

Leaving aside the fact that Balzac's thoughts have a certain cruel relevance to the present, in 1855 Baudelaire was quite aware that some readers would find such a response ridiculously far from the regulative processes of aesthetic judgment, and so he counters:

> Laugh if you will at M. de Balzac. I do not know the name of the painter whose honour it was to set the great novelist's soul a-quiver with anxiety and conjecture; but I think that in his way, with his delectable *naïveté*, he has given us an excellent lesson in criticism. You will often find me appraising a picture exclusively for the sum of ideas or of dreams that it suggests to my mind.

Although Baudelaire tries to recover within this paragraph the active, "appraising" voice of the critic—partial, passionate, and political—the essential passivity of the scene of criticism closes over the rest of his sentence. Something is done to the critic by the ideas or dreams that are suggested to his mind. The critic is invaded, possessed by these thoughts; he is embraced by them.

The nature of this embrace—as it concerns the hero of his example, Balzac—Baudelaire would no doubt refer back to the activity of the real, memories of real farmers and of their real distress observed by the novelist on the spot and reinvoked by this depicted image. But the banality of that "No doubt they have bills to pay!" creates a certain closure between Baudelaire's Balzac and a much later one, the Balzac of *S/Z*, the Balzac to whom Roland Barthes denies even the status of copyist of the real, designating him instead as its *pasticheur*. For this Balzac is forever resorting to the codes of the already written, the already known, the codes by which society constructs what it then turns around and calls Nature.

"To depict," says Barthes, "is to unroll the carpet of the codes, to refer not from language to a referent but from one code to another."[2] Therefore, Barthes would maintain, as we listen to Balzac's invocation of those peasants' humble thoughts and sorrows, it is not clear who is speaking, for

> in the classic text, always haunted by the appropriation of speech, the single voice gets lost, as though it had leaked out through a hole in the discourse. The best way to conceive the classical plural [of voices] is then to listen to the text as an iridescent exchange carried on by multiple voices, on different wavelengths and subject from time to time to a sudden *dissolve*, leaving a gap which enables the utterance to shift from one point of view to another, without warning: the writing is set up across this tonal instability . . . which makes it a glistening texture of ephemeral origins."[3]

Through Balzac's "No doubt they have bills to pay!" we hear echoing the voice of the cultural code, which never opens its stereotypic essence to question. This voice, "whose origin" Barthes reminds us "is 'lost' in the vast perspective of the *already-written*," acts to "de-originate the utterance."[4] That is why, even as Balzac utters it, it speaks through him, embraces him in its insistent banality, in its stupendously unquestioning staleness.

Now, in speaking of the nature of criticism, Baudelaire is always careful to set up the analogical relation between the critical and the creative act. So that, in 1846, just before erecting that busy machine of the partial, passionate, and political, he had stipulated that "insofar as a fine picture is nature reflected by an artist, the criticism which I approve will be that picture reflected by an intelligent and sensitive mind. Thus the best account of a picture may well be a sonnet or an elegy."[5]

The parallel Baudelaire constructs between the picture and its analysis, between the operations of the painter and those of his critic, is then played out in the *Exposition Universelle* text as Baudelaire turns from Balzac to Jean-Auguste-Dominique Ingres. Indeed, this text is one of the most spectacular analyses of Ingres' work that we possess. Baudelaire depicts Ingres as constantly veering between the active construction of a classicizing system and the passive submission to nature, describing this

Fig. 1. Ingres, *Raphael and La Fornarina*, c. 1850–1865, oil on canvas. The Chrysler Museum, Norfolk, Virginia, on loan from Walter P. Chrysler, Jr.

oscillation as "the antique ideal, to which he has added the frills and furbelows of modern art." Inevitably speaking of this ambivalence in Ingres in terms one reserves for the erotically obsessed, Baudelaire describes him as "thus smitten with an ideal which is an enticingly adulterous union between Raphael's calm solidity and the gewgaws of a *petite-maîtresse*."[6] Ingres is for Baudelaire someone who cannot resist the appeal of the observed moment, and thus he writes, "Sometimes it happens that the eye falls upon charming details, irreproachably alive; but at once the wicked notion flashes across the mind, that it is not M. Ingres who has been seeking nature, but Nature that has *ravished* M. Ingres—that that high and mighty dame has overpowered him by her irresistible ascendancy."[7] In this passage it is the verb *violer* that has been rendered as "ravished." Embrace me, we might think, you sweet embraceable you.

152

Embrace Me, You Irreplaceable You

Of the many famous Ingres embraces there are two on which I will focus: Paolo's timorous, but fateful caress of his sister-in-law, Francesca, and Raphael's strangely distracted fondling of his mistress, the Fornarina. There are a variety of reasons for choosing these examples, but perhaps the first is that of their status within the representation of famous couples and thus of the assumed value of the beloved as irreplaceable, unique. Perhaps Ingres has never achieved outside his *Paolo and Francesca* so great a sense of this ardor focused on a single point, an achievement that caused one of his contemporaries, visiting the Ingres section of the 1855 *Exposition Universelle* to comment on this picture, "Paolo is not a man; he is a kiss."[8]

Another reason for my interest in these examples stems from the degree to which each picture was, precisely, replaced by Ingres over the course of his almost endless career. Speaking late in life of the *Raphael and La Fornarina* (fig. 1), the first example of which had issued from

Fig. 2. Ingres, *Paolo and Francesca*, 1814, oil on panel. Musée Condé, Chantilly.

his brush in 1814, Ingres explained his decision in 1860 to undertake yet a fourth version in oils by saying, "I am taking up again the picture of *Raphael and La Fornarina*, my last edition of this subject, which will, I hope, cause the others to be forgotten."[9]

This explanation of the master's desire to replicate his own work, to issue it in multiple copies—which in the case of *Paolo and Francesca* resulted in no fewer than eighteen versions—is referred to as "The Pursuit of Perfection" in the recent exhibition examining the fascinating question of Ingres' creation of what the curators describe as "original replicas."[10] What the relationship might be between the serial elaboration of an image, multiplying and reproducing it in a potentially endless chain, and a notion of perfection in which each last member of the series is thought of as subsuming, and, therefore, effacing all earlier versions—Ingres' project of causing "the others to be forgotten"—is the theoretical problem I wish to address.

Some idea of the actual course of this process might be obtained by following the multiple reworkings of Ingres' *Paolo and Francesca*, for which he executed over the course of nearly forty years seven paintings and eleven drawings of the identical moment in the couple's story. An initial drawing with the apposite verse from Dante inscribed below the image sets the tone of an appropriately primitive quattrocentrism, which is then carried out in the first oil version, dated 1814 (fig. 2). An exact oil copy of this version was made by Ingres for the engraver Jean-Alexandre Coraboeuf. Two drawings of the subject were then made in 1816. In 1819 Ingres executed another, larger oil version for the Société des Arts, this canvas employing far more decorative detail. A 1820 scaled-down drawing then shifts Paolo from the right to the left side of the composition, and Ingres made a tracing of this new conception. In 1834 a lithograph of the Société des Arts version established a similar reversal of direction. Following this print, Ingres did another painted variant of his subject, reducing its scale and refocusing its space (fig. 3). Two other late versions in oil maintain this heightened concentration on the pair, although both reintroduce the figure of Francesca's husband.

In 1850 a firm of engravers mounted a campaign to publish the complete works of Ingres to date, a project in which Ingres himself became deeply involved, insisting that the style of the reproductive image be the at-that-time outmoded form of outline engraving, dear to Ingres from his early experience of the work of, for example, John Flaxman, and dear to him as well from his own addiction to tracings, the form in which he in-

Fig. 3. Ingres, *Paolo and Francesca*, c. 1845, oil on canvas. The Hyde Collection, Glens Falls, New York.

gested the world of art to which he exposed himself—Greek vase painting, Byzantine ivories, medieval manuscripts, and endless prints of old master paintings. It was Achille Réveil, a former producer of volumes after John Flaxman and Antonio Canova, who finally produced these strangely reductive versions of the master's works, using etching on steel. Réveil's 1851 outline rendition of the Société des Arts version of the picture (fig. 4) led Ingres to produce three more drawings—in his customary attempt to aid and elaborate the engraving project. The new possibilities of experiencing the subject led to yet one more oil version, the smallest in the entire series and from the point of view of doubled light sources and complex interior the most assimilable to the form of the miniature illumination (fig. 5). The appearance of this version, undertaken some forty years after the first rendering of the idea, is entirely congruent with Ingres' conduct of his late career, for after 1850 (which is to say for the last seventeen years of his life) he undertook no new compositions, spending his time instead redoing through replicas and variants the contents of his published catalogue: the 1851 *Works of J.-A.-D. Ingres*.

Ingres' compulsion to redo was not, however, restricted to this last phase of his career. It had happened throughout his work, leading his most loyal student, Eugène Amaury-Duval, to attribute the limited repertory of Ingres' compositional output to his compulsion to rework his pictures.[11] Less-sympathetic critics of the master simply accused him of auto-plagiarism as when Théophile Silvestre responded to the *Exposition Universelle* installation by writing, "M. Ingres has passed his life as much in repeating the same forms as in insidiously combining the most famous traditional types with the living models."[12] As hostile as he was to criticism of any kind, even Ingres is recorded as saying that perhaps "I reproduce my own compositions too often."[13] In this confession, in which that perfection that will "cause the others to be forgotten" is not mentioned, irreplaceability is corrupted by seriality; it is thoroughly implicated in a need to repeat.

Just One Look at You, My Heart Grows Tipsy in Me

We have, then, one kind of series that elaborated itself within Ingres' career, moving with a kind of inexorability away from the studio conditions of the oil replica and toward the technology of mechanical reproduction. For Ingres moved steadily toward a definitive edition of his ideas that increasingly took the form of the reproductive engraving, whose natural milieu was not the wall of a gallery but the page of a book. Multiple, schematic, reductive—shorn of color, texture, modeling, touch—this outline rendering became the pure "idea" of the image, its naturally most "perfect" form. The trajectory of Ingres' painted replications, indeed, moves in this direction. The replications become ever smaller, ever more involved in the minute additions and subtractions made technically possible by the constant use of tracing paper. Thus Ingres' addiction, begun as a student, to the technique of tracing created, within his personal artistic comportment, the medium within which this movement toward the multiple unfolded. As the catalogue text for the exhibition *The Pursuit of Perfection* states it, "The process of tracing is the technical epitome of Ingres's method."[14]

There is, however, another series involved in the two embraces Ingres pursues in the examples I am discussing. This is the series of narrative scenes through which a story might unfold and which indeed Ingres had every intention of pursuing when he first undertook *Raphael and La Fornarina* and *Paolo and Francesca*. Paolo and Francesca's story was to be developed in four separate ta-

Fig. 4. Ingres, *Paolo and Francesca*, as etched by Achille Réveil, in *Works of J.-A.-D. Ingres* (1851).

bleaux: first, the moment of their kiss; second, the husband standing over his slain victims; third, the encrypted bodies; and fourth, the souls of the couple caught in the whirlwind of the inferno. Ingres, however, never passed beyond that first moment. This is similar in the case of the Raphael double portrait. There as well Ingres wished to elaborate a cycle based on the life of his great artist-hero; yet only *Raphael and La Fornarina* and the *Betrothal of Raphael* were undertaken, the first more than four times.

That the narrative cycle was open to the painter within the classical tradition had become a commonplace of late eighteenth- and early nineteenth-century thinking, an extension strangely enough of the great lesson of the *Laocoön*. Thus we hear Flaxman repeating, "First, a poet speaks by words. The painter and sculptor by action. Action singly, or in series . . . thus the story of Laocoön is told by the agony of the father and sons, inextricably wound about in the folds of serpents. . . . And every action is more perfect as it comprehends an indication of the past, with a certainty of the end, in the moment chosen."[15] This is, of course, Gotthold Lessing's notion

of the "most pregnant moment . . . the one most suggestive of what has gone before and what is to follow."[16] In setting out the conditions for which moment to choose for the pictorial representation Lessing is clear that it should be one that will allow for maximum imaginative dilation, within which a kind of narrative temporality will open and expand; and that for this reason it must on no account be the final instant of the tale. "No moment," he writes, "in the whole course of an action is so disadvantageous in this respect as that of its culmination."[17]

The *opening* moment, however, is no less disadvantaged, for it could be argued that it is not quite "pregnant" enough; there are not yet enough layers of implication to allow for an imaginative projection into the future, while the retrospective pleasures of reviewing the narrative chain are cut off from the start. Thus, within the theoretical ambience he inhabited, Ingres' choice of moment would make sense only within a developing narrative cycle, Flaxman's "series." Yet instead of pursuing that development, Ingres, like a frantic stutterer, repeated the initial, excessively static vocable of his tale.

Fig. 5. Ingres, *Paolo and Francesca*, c. 1850, oil on canvas. Musée Bonnat, Bayonne.

Fig. 6. Ingres, *Raphael and La Fornarina*, 1814, oil on canvas. Fogg Art Museum, Cambridge, Massachusetts, Grenville L. Winthrop Bequest.

It would seem too quick, however, to say that there is no expansion, no movement backward and forward along a sequential chain in the choice Ingres places before us. It would seem simply more accurate to qualify that expansion as not narrative but rather what we might call semio-psychological.

For the passion of Paolo and Francesca has an anterior moment, not in terms of story but in terms of model: a precedent that it copies by repeating. Paolo and Francesca are recognizable in relation to the book Francesca holds, a book in which their love has already been written. *S/Z* will obviously remark on this, and indeed Barthes writes, "Without the—always anterior—Book and Code, no desire, no jealousy: Pygmalion is in love with a link in the code of statuary; Paolo and Francesca love each other *according to* the passion of Lancelot and Guinevere (Dante *Inferno* V): itself a lost origin, writing becomes the origin of emotion."[18] "We read of the smile," Francesca says in Canto V, "desired of lips long-thwarted, such smile, by such a lover kissed away." She herself calls the book in which they read of it, Galleot—the go-between for Lancelot and Guinevere: "The book

was Galleot," she says, "Galleot the complying Ribald who wrote; we read no more that day."

In *Raphael and La Fornarina* (figs. 1, 6–8) we find a similar positioning right on the fold of replication and thus a similarly satisfying dilation along the chain—backward and forward—of serial, repetitive expansion. For the artist embraces what he does not look at. Ingres' Raphael has eyes only for what is on his easel, which is to say, the model *in representation* of what will educate his heart. In each version the Fornarina is held only after she has been beheld in what Ingres himself depicts, even more so in the later versions, as a burgeoning system of aesthetic instances. For Raphael: from the *Madonna della Sedia* to the Fornarina nude; and then if modern scholarly hypothesis is right, on to the education of Ingres' heart as well, as—remaining tipsy for more than fifty years—Ingres was to repeat the swiveled image of this nude, seen as though from the back of Raphael's canvas, in his own obsessionally beautiful *Bather of Valpinçon*, 1808 (Paris, Musée du Louvre).[19]

You and You Alone Bring Out the Gypsy in Me

The freakishness of Ingres' procedures calls for explanation. In looking for one, the curators of *The Pursuit of Perfection* refer us to Ingres' own: his stated desire to achieve an ideal, true, and perfect version of his aesthetic intentions—to say, finally, in pictorial form, what he means. Perfection would be the ultimate form of what he means, and it would in its ideality, its truth, be irrefutable and thus not only end the series but annihilate it, for all the preceding versions would be thereby demonstrated to be "wrong." Interestingly enough the curators of *The Pursuit of Perfection* make use of a move from the game of connoisseurship to add force to their—and Ingres'—argument, for the very late replicas are far more securely autographic than the earlier versions, which in large part were executed by Ingres' students and assistants.[20] Thus Ingres' hand, his touch, the index of his intentions, the surest, most physical, most personal registration of what he "meant," will be found in these tiny pictures made sometimes more than half a century later than their opening essays, made by a man who had, against the rising tide of public indifference, barricaded himself behind the definitive book, *The Works of J.-A.-D. Ingres*.

What does it mean to take Ingres' stated intentions seriously, to subscribe to an idealist position that can summon "perfection" to its side in order to transform seriality into singularity, in order to outflank repetition by transcending it?

Fig. 7. Ingres, *Raphael and La Fornarina*, as etched by Achille Réveil, in *Works of J.-A.-D. Ingres* (1851).

Fig. 8. Ingres, *Raphael and La Fornarina*, as etched by Achille Réveil, in *Works of J.-A.-D. Ingres* (1851), pl. 99.

Is this dream of perfection, of fulfillment, not a dream of pure and absolute presence—one which would end the repetitive cycle through the obviousness of its truth, the absoluteness of its beauty, to which everyone would thereafter subscribe, thus referring only to it? Would this not be a beauty that would obtain the universality of accord that Immanuel Kant insists is the logical condition of aesthetic judgment? With this notion before us of truth, of presence, of perfection, would we not be churlish to deny Ingres the logical, theoretical possibility of achieving his intentions?

The theoretical roadblock in the way of Ingres' intentions is precisely the degree to which a universal truth can only be repeated. Its status as model is that it is repeatable; and thus by virtue of this structural repeatability it is always in fission, divided, split, never wholly present to itself. Through this movement of repeatability its "perfection" has been breeched in advance. Because—and this was precisely Ingres' practice if not his "intention"—each repetition is always a recontextualization of the model—a change in scale, medium, site. Each repetition thus as well involves a change in meaning. This

is a change to which the model itself has always, and in advance, been open. The model's "truth," its absoluteness, its indivisible self-presence, has never, theoretically, been possible.

This is obviously the argument made by Jacques Derrida with regard to the iterative nature of language, an analysis probing the relation of this structural necessity for repetition to the very idea of both intention and meaning.[21] That the mark is structurally multiple and thus cut off from itself in advance, forms the thrust of a philosophical argument that has great resonance within any discussion of models and multiples, whether textual or plastic.

Indeed, this experience of the beautiful as always multiple empirically constituted the very atmosphere that artists like Ingres breathed in the late eighteenth and early nineteenth centuries. The antique existed in and through its copies, its endlessly proliferated third- and fourth-hand Roman versions, its re-creations in the Renaissance, its nineteenth-century plaster-cast versions that crowded the studios and no doubt the minds. Antoine Chrysostome Quatremère de Quincy addresses the paradox of this experience of the antique as always already self-divided. Speaking in 1821 in the context of the discovery of the Venus de Milo, he refers to the "ever growing numbers of statues, continually excavated in Rome," but far from dismissing these he says, "the immense majority of these works are probably degenerate productions, copies or copies of copies, whose influence, interest, and utility in many ways we are still far from presuming to contest."[22] If these "degenerate productions" have utility it is because, he writes, "The multiplicity of the antique products has propagated the taste for them throughout all the countries, and this taste has also contributed to making the discoveries more and more numerous in Italy."[23]

Quatremère de Quincy thus describes the logic of dissemination. The beautiful is what must be propagated. This propagation is in turn, structurally, logically, a function of multiplicity. Speaking of the Venus de Milo—that dazzlingly, uncontested Greek original—Quatremère de Quincy acknowledges, "Regarding the impression that the view of that work produced upon me, I must admit that it was similar to that made by every fragment of superior style within a given type. To develop the reasons for this impression would be to try to analyze the cause of the effect of beauty in general."[24]

Striving toward "beauty in general," Ingres progressed backward, toward the ever simpler outline engraving, which, one might say, he invested with a certain originary status. Schematic, it would seem the purified version of the idea, its primitive statement, its origin. But it was also, biographically speaking, Ingres' origin, his beginning as a student for whom the outline copy constituted both his model—in the admired works of Flaxman—and his medium—in his assiduous tracings from multiple models that ranged from black-figure vases to engravings of the Vatican Stanze. In this double regression toward an origin that is an origin-in-repetition we begin to see the logic of Ingres' practice of seriality. For that repeated moment at the very outset of Paolo and Francesca's story, in which a beginning is possible only by virtue of its imitation of a model, that is Ingres' own story toward the resolution of which he incessantly worked. It was a resolution that could only end in a book, *The Work of J.-A.-D. Ingres*, a book of engravings through which the chain of dissemination would never be broken, for these images would be "perfect" in their absolute divisibility.

This series of reflections will end with a parable, a story that concerns Ingres' relation to one of his most elaborated works, the 1827 *Apotheosis of Homer*, commissioned as a ceiling painting for the sequence of rooms that made up the Musée Charles X. The opening of this suite of rooms, consecrated by the royal inspection of the decorations, had been an enormous disappointment to Ingres, for his great painting was in the very last of the rooms and the king, weary of wandering around and craning his neck, never even looked at this final object. Ingres told his students afterward, "Well, gentlemen, the king stopped in every room of the Musée Charles X, except mine." Amaury-Duval adds, "Like the king, the public was extremely indifferent to this masterpiece."

Sometime after 1864, during his obsessional period of replication of earlier works, Ingres turned to a drawing he had made in the 1840s for the engraving of his 1827 ceiling. Grumbling that the ceiling painting had been but "a *première pensée* vividly expressed but only half rendered," Ingres got busy reworking the 1840s drawing. This drawing, completed, perfected, was then, due to the marvels of modern technology, able to be maximally disseminated. Ingres issued a limited edition of mammoth-plate photographic prints of this work, which he distributed to a restricted circle of admirers and friends.

And could we say that at last, in this photographic version of *The Apotheosis of Homer*—through this medium on which the great Museum without Walls is constructed, the medium that would make possible the whole discipline of art history—could we not say that in this version, Ingres' debt to Raphael's Stanze, the *School of Athens*, the adored *Mass of Bolsena*, is made maximally visible? Do we not see here the degree to which Raphael brought out the gypsy in Ingres, just as Lancelot and Guinevere had done it for Paolo and Francesca, or English romanticism had stirred up the gypsy in Baudelaire's Balzac?

NOTES

1. Charles Baudelaire [1855], *Art in Paris, 1845–1862*, trans. and ed. Jonathan Mayne (London, 1965), 125.
2. Roland Barthes, *S/Z*, trans. Richard Miller (New York, 1974), 55.
3. Barthes 1974, 41–42.
4. Barthes 1974, 21.
5. Baudelaire [1846] 1965, 44.
6. Baudelaire [1855] 1965, 132.
7. Baudelaire [1855] 1965, 133.
8. Edmont About, *Voyage à travers l'exposition des beaux-arts* (Paris, 1855), 130, in Hans Naef, "Paolo and Francesca," *Zeitschrift für Kunstwissenschaft* 10, no. 1 (1956), 108.
9. Henri Delaborde, *Ingres: Sa vie, ses travaux, sa doctrine, d'après les notes manuscrites et les lettres du maître* (Paris, 1870), 226.
10. Patricia Condon, *In Pursuit of Perfection: The Art of J.-A.-D. Ingres* [exh. cat., J. B. Speed Art Museum] (Louisville, 1983). The extraordinary data on Ingres' practice of copying organized by this exhibition, particularly in the rich introductory essay by Marjorie B. Cohn, has

provided me the foundation on which the present reflections rest.

11.   Eugène Amaury-Duval, *L'atelier d'Ingres* (Paris, 1924), 32.

12.   Cited in Pierre Courthion, *Ingres racontè par lui-même et par ses amis* (Geneva, 1948), 2:48.

13.   Cited in Delaborde 1870, 108.

14.   Condon 1983, 14.

15.   John Flaxman, *Lectures on Sculpture* (London, 1892), 150.

16.   Gotthold Ephraim Lessing, *Laocoon* (1766), trans. Ellen Frothingham (New York, 1957), 92.

17.   Lessing [1766] 1957, 17.

18.   Barthes 1974, 73.

19.   Eldon van Liere ("Ingres' 'Raphael and the Fornarina': Reverence and Testimony," *Arts* 56 [December 1981], 108–115) has put forward the extremely convincing hypothesis that Ingres' *Bather of Valpinçon* is based on Raphael's *La Fornarina* as though seen from behind. Another, recent discussion of this work, to my mind, misses the point of the picture and its relation to the anterior model by characterizing the scene as one in which the model "is represented in the process of being represented" (Richard Schiff, "Representation, Copying, and the Technique of Originality," *New Literary History* 15 [Winter 1984], 334).

20.   Condon 1983, 30.

21.   Jacques Derrida, "Signature, Event, Context," *Glyph*, no. 1 (1977), 172–197; Jacques Derrida, "Limited Inc.," *Glyph*, no. 2 (1977), 162–254.

22.   Antoine Chrysostome Quatremère de Quincy, "A Commentary on an Antique Statue of Venus Found on the Island of Milos (1821)," in Elizabeth Holt, *From the Classicists to the Impressionists* (New York, 1966), 16.

23.   Quatremère de Quincy 1821 in Holt 1966, 17.

24.   Quatremère de Quincy 1821 in Holt 1966, 18.

Phototropism (Figuring the Proper)

RICHARD SHIFF
University of Texas at Austin

THIS ESSAY SUGGESTS a way out of the impasse of recent writing on the nature of photography. Critics and theorists have been wrangling over whether photography is a matter more of art or of documentation, and how it might be either, and why it might be both. For some the debate has focused on the social and institutional discourses in which photographic practice has figured. The various claims that have been advanced, however, could be applied to any mode of representation; painting, just as photography, functions as documentation, has a rhetoric, and is embedded in social events and institutional histories. Why then have so many thinkers selected photography as the area in which to debate the most basic questions of the analysis and critique of images? To reply that photography is the focus because it has become our dominant mode of representation is merely to offer the effect as an explanation of the undefined cause. Why is photography so central?

My essay moves toward three related propositions that reflect not so much on the ontology of photography but on its historical situation. These are the concluding propositions: (1) at any moment in history the value of all representation depends on the existence of some representation that can be regarded as transparent, realistic, or natural; (2) during the modern era photography has provided a kind of fabricated image that can successfully masquerade as a natural one; (3) as such, photography plays the role of a proper (but not literal) term in opposition to painting's figured term. A rhetorician would say that photography plays catachresis to painting's metaphor; photography allows us to see the metaphor in painting without the necessity of our assuming that a photograph, in contradistinction, pictures "true reality." We can accept the photograph as "natural" by comparison with other kinds of images and see how deeply implicated in a system of arbitrary signs it is.

The Figured and the Commonplace

Let our readers fancy the fidelity of the image of nature figured by the camera obscura, and add to it an action of the solar rays which fixes this image (from the announcement of the invention of the daguerreotype, 1839).[1]

Ordinary language is already itself almost entirely composed of figures: one cannot express oneself without using them; and, moreover, the word *figure* is itself a *figured* or metaphoric expression (from Antoine

Chrysostome Quatremère de Quincy's treatise on artistic imitation, 1823).[2]

Is a photograph figured? What is figuration?

The word *figure* as a noun and verb conveys many interrelated meanings. A figure can be any line, shape, diagram, or drawing that is seen as a representation. In very general terms the representation of the form of an object is its figure. A literary form or device, such as metaphor, is also a figure. Thus as a verb *figure* can signify an act of representation by means of drawing or picturing; and the same word also signifies representation by means of a metaphor or any other literary figure. The argument that follows begs the reader to entertain simultaneously these two senses of the verb *figure*. (The first epigraph inscribes *figure* as drawing; the second indicates the word's reference to metaphor and the nature of its own capacity to perform as metaphor.)

It has become commonplace to argue that all representation must be figured. This is not so much to use *figure* in its first sense, to assert that all representation is drawn, whether as a picture or even in the form of handwriting or printing. Rather it is to say that no description or picture can copy its model, its original, without differing from that original; and the difference or distancing is created as if through the deployment of a mode of figuration (*figure* in its second sense).[3] In striving to illustrate or illuminate the original the figured copy cannot become the original, cannot coincide with it, but rather diverges from it by either supplementing its features or effacing them. As a result the effort to expose the truth of the original ironically leads to a kind of falsification or at least to uncertainty. One cannot determine whether features of the copy derive from the original or from the nature of the figuring agent.

What passes for a device of figuration is manifold; we think not only of traditional rhetorical figures such as metaphor and metonymy but also of artistic techniques such as planar projection and contour drawing. These common artistic devices and their variants create divergent characterizations of the same object of representation. (For example, the figuring effect of linear perspective differs from that of aerial perspective; and silhouette does not portray in the same manner as chiaroscuro.) Even when artists resort to the same technical devices, figuration—that is, deviation and difference—results from the inevitable autographic quality of their markings. Although sets of verbal or pictorial signifiers and conventions may be shared, individuals exhibit characteristic styles of representing and so exemplify particular manners of figuration.

Perhaps classicism remedies such rampant diversity. The classic, canonical works of Western art and literature provide an alternative to extremes of individual self-representation to the extent that they become sources of common knowledge. If immediate perceptions and their representations differ, if every representation appears figured, representations of the order and the law of the world nevertheless converge in what is acceptable to all—the commonplace.[4] A commonplace is a representation so acceptable and convincing that one takes it as true to the reality of its model or original; it requires no mediating interpretation. In consequence a commonplace can assume the form of an authoritative interpretation of all (other) figuration—a "right" representation of the truth of other representations. One seeks the "right," classic or proper, representations, however common they may be. Does photography—the fixing and reproducing of a camera image—assume the role of the classic, providing such exemplary and commonplace representation?

The Problem of Original Models and Artistic Copies

Art historians seek out authoritative representation but seldom regard it as common. For the art historian the problem of identifying "right" representation is often linked to that of distinguishing an original from its derivative, inferior copy. There may be innumerable copies but relatively few originals.

In a certain sense all paintings have originality since they are unique, handcrafted images. Nevertheless the study of painting selects out a number of privileged cases. Originality itself becomes a matter either of authenticity or of priority. Often the art historian must determine which of two similar paintings is by a master's hand and which is its spurious double (a question of authenticity); and when similar features are encountered in two works by two undisputed masters, the art historian ascertains which depends on or has been "influenced" by the other (a question of priority). For the painter, however, the problem of original and copy assumes a broader dimension. A painter is likely to be concerned with the individual's originality and consequently struggles to resist the pictorial influence of others; but the true original, the original depicted or copied, is simply the model. This object of representation may be regarded as an external object of vision or as a product of visual imagination. In either case the artist's vision seems to extend, potentially, beyond the confines of antecedent representation.

The issue is still more complicated. Does painting really maintain contact with nature or with some world beyond painting itself? Virtually no one expects a painting to look "exactly" like its model, to mimic its every feature. The degree of resemblance, moreover, is likely to vary as one compares aspects of a given painting to corresponding aspects of its model. Depiction is selective. While indicating the details of a facial contour, a painter may simultaneously eliminate reference to specific facial features, yet the art is said to follow nature. We generally assume that strategies of picture making—aesthetic, expressive, didactic—determine the degree to which a model should be followed literally. When we ask what is the standard for the "literal," however, we look to other representations not to a model in nature. We argue that to copy a model by rendering its likeness is actually to copy a set of preexisting representational models for such depiction—representations must refer to other representations. This accounts for the apparent license to "deviate" from nature; and so the artist's problem seems to collapse back into the art historian's: to relate a painted copy to an original that is itself painted. This is tantamount to relating one manner of figuration to another.

We return to the assertion that representations model themselves on other representations. Why is this claim so commonly made? Do we not believe in an external reality that informs our pictures, at least some of them? Do none of our pictures have their originals in nature, in "reality"? Do none reveal the law and standard that is "reality"?[5]

The fact may seem too obvious and too naively stated, but it is important to note that the existence of photographic representation has liberated painting from any responsibility to a "real" model. Any attempt at a handcrafted correspondence to nature is doomed to failure by comparison with what photography can accomplish.[6] It is not that a photograph must resemble its model in every detail (or even in any detail) but that its image is consistently related to its model throughout. This is true even when parts of the photograph seem distorted. It is as if such distortion resulted from some systematic or specifiable anamorphosis; whatever peculiarities the photograph exhibits can be explained in terms of the working of its mechanism, no matter how complicated (including such variables as lens, exposure, type of film, and development). There are no qualities out of character in a photograph, no willful accidents, no gratuitous acts.[7] In sum, a photographic representation is causally linked to material phenomena in nature, its image is indexical. In photography, however professional the example, we need not presume the action of a skilled artist who has learned from the pictorial representations of other artists—a pattern of reflected light traces out its own image, the image of the model, on the photographic surface.

This, at least, is what the pioneers of photographic practice claimed. It is how they described the significance of their discovery. The model would figure its own image with its own reflected light. The photographic image was conceived as an impression or imprinting, dependent on the "real" presence of its "subject," the object it represented. Was the photographic process active or passive? The earliest accounts are ambiguous. L.-J.-M. Daguerre spoke of a surface being prepared by a human agent "to receive the image of nature" but also of "a chemical and physical process which gives Nature the ability to reproduce herself."[8] William Henry Fox Talbot referred to the subject of a photograph as having "drawn its own picture," and he called photographs "self-representations."[9] It would seem that such self-representation cannot stray far from reality itself. Perhaps we may tentatively say that photography "copies" reality, its "original."

Two Words: Phototropism *and* Proper

In what sense is the photographic copy true to its original, its model? Does the photograph actually deviate, turn from, or trope a more proper representation? Can we speak of photography's mechanism, however passive, as a kind of active movement, a "phototropism"?

The word *phototropism* has remained within the boundaries of the biological discourse that gave birth to it around 1900; it signifies a turning toward or away from light. More specifically phototropism is the turning of an organism, induced by the presence of light. The organism appears to "seek" light only when light is there to be found. The turn or deviation of biological phototropism is thus always an involuntary or passive movement, even as this phenomenon occurs among intelligent and willful animals.

Unlike the compound word *phototropism*, the root word *trope* has no semantic commitment to passivity. To trope is to turn, often with willful determination. A trope is a turn from the straight, the proper, the true. If any such deviance marks a departure from the "true," is there then something false about a trope? Perhaps. Truth, indeed, is associated with the straight and regular. We "true" a line or edge in making it straight; our testimony is "true" when it does not deviate from a straightforward presentation, when it is faithful to the facts of the case, to reality.

By definition figured language, language that turns, is neither literal nor proper. A further distinction is implicit, for the concept of the literal is not quite the same as the concept of the proper. The word *proper* bears a hint of the mannered—one has proper manners, not literal or true ones—and hence this term connotes conventionality. A proper use of language, language seemingly free of tropes and figuration, is not necessarily more "true"; it is simply sanctioned by convention and therefore appears more acceptable, less problematic. Its manner of speaking is commonplace. Tropes and figures do not render a statement false or misleading (turning from the "literal truth") but merely identify that statement as improper, unorthodox, or deviant.[10]

Capitalizing on the rhetorical connotations of the word *trope* (trope as figuration in linguistic or pictorial representation), we can extend the concept of phototropism to photography. The movement of phototropism now becomes active rather than passive. The camera "exposes" its interior light-sensitive surface; it seems purposefully to turn that surface toward a source of light, an illuminated object or scene. A human agent is involved even if only to activate the mechanism at a certain moment. This calculated exposure—determined not by the presence of the light but by the adjustable mechanism of the camera—creates the photographic picture, the figured pattern of reflected illumination. This image is "figured" in its having been traced or "drawn" by the action of light; all pictorial representations, even the products of automatism, are figures in this sense. Is the photograph also figured in the rhetorical sense, in the sense of a trope, a turning from the proper? When the camera turns (or is turned) into the light, does the resultant image become a figure of the "literal truth"? Does the photograph provide a proper picture of reality, one to be accepted as if by convention, no matter how unique? Or is the phototropism of photography a rhetorical turn, a deviation from the straight truth of light even as light itself creates the photograph?

I will argue that the photograph is neither quite proper representation (unequivocally "true") nor is it properly figured representation (figured in the way that other representations are). To this end, I will view photography in relation to a rival mode of representation, painting, and will regard painting as itself appearing in two forms, classical and modernist. If we assume a modernist perspective, classicism will seem to be the obvious antecedent mode, but the precise location of its appearance will depend on how we have defined modernism. The classical and the modernist are interdependent. Thus, my conception of periodization—the passage from classical to modernist art—is not chronologically specific; and indeed I prefer to conceive of a classical syndrome in tacit opposition to and even in collusion with modernist practice throughout the period of modernism's ascendance and domination.[11] For convenience, however, I assume that the "transition" from an era characterized by classicism to one characterized by modernism is most visible during the early years of the nineteenth century, with the most critical period corresponding to the time of photography's emergence as a viable medium, the decades of the 1820s and 1830s, when coincidentally the romantic movement coalesced. Intellectual historians have marked these same decades as a time when classical rhetoric ceased to be a subject of preeminent concern. It has been argued that such phenomena of intellectual history correspond to presumably more fundamental shifts in class structure, including a general decline of aristocratic social hierarchies accompanying the rise of a bourgeoisie—a "classic" society giving way to a "modern" one.[12]

I do not seek to identify the transition from classic to modern chronologically nor do I claim that modernist concerns cannot be found in the classic period or that classical concerns are not expressed in the modern period. My only firm claim is that from our perspective today classicism and modernism are both seen as features of a past that we no longer live through. The classicism that I will discuss is the classicism that modernism conceived as its antecedent, and it does not necessarily accord with a classicism that we might imagine a Renaissance artist to have experienced. My classicism is the classicism that we know only now, because we do not have it. It is the phantasmic creation of the modern period, visible in the commonplaces of criticism and a very real force in our inherited culture. One warning: if, in the following discussion, modernism and classicism sometimes seem to converge, so much the better. Their opposition is not absolute.

The Originality of Classicism

In a set of notes traditionally dated about 1813 to 1827, Jean-Auguste-Dominique Ingres wrote that "Raphael, in imitating endlessly, was always himself."[13] Ingres was not the most original of thinkers. Perhaps his statement par-

Left: Fig. 1. Masaccio, *Expulsion from Paradise*, c. 1427, fresco. Brancacci Chapel, Santa Maria del Carmine, Florence.

Above: Fig. 2. Assistants of Raphael, *Expulsion of Adam and Eve from Paradise*, 1516–1519, fresco. Vatican Palace, Logge, Rome.

aphrases one he had read; perhaps it is even a copy of another's statement, a quotation not indicated as such. Ingres' thought surely is a commonplace of his time and of thinking within the classical tradition.[14] For a classicist, however, to repeat a commonplace does not necessarily interfere with a search for the original.

Consider the statement itself, whether Ingres authored it or merely disseminated it: "Raphael, in imitating endlessly, was always himself." According to historians of Ingres' own time, Raphael had imitated the effects of antique art and had also on occasion imitated a great modern predecessor, Masaccio. In doing so how could he remain "himself"? Since Masaccio belonged to a recent past and was a very specific historical personality both for Raphael and later generations of artists and

critics, the younger painter's apparent dependence on the antecedent master might well suggest a failure of originality. It is one thing to imitate a collective body of anonymous works, antique art in its totality, and another to imitate the renderings of a named master whose works exhibit a personal style. In addition, as the scholar Johann David Passavant stated in 1839, Raphael had been born into an environment charged with an appreciation of antiquities. Antique art and literature had awakened his intellectual faculties at a very tender age. Only later would he seek out Masaccio.[15] Masaccio had an identifying style like a signature, and Raphael appropriated it.

Supporters of the classical tradition looked favorably on this relationship, among them Sir Joshua Reynolds. Reynolds argued that a painter became great only by assimilating the greatness of past masters.[16] Accordingly he could write in 1774 that Raphael had "taken so many models, that he became himself a model for all succeeding painters; always imitating, and always original."[17] The echo of Reynolds' classicism in Ingres is obvious: "always imitating, and always original." A decade later, in 1784, Reynolds invoked a feature of the notion of the commonplace—that which is available to all—to spare Raphael from the charge of plagiarism: everyone knew Masaccio's work, it was in the public domain.[18] Thus its theft would always be apparent and could not be a stealthy act; to choose to imitate Masaccio did not damage one's artistic integrity but rather demonstrated one's sound artistic judgment. Masaccio's figure inventions and compositional principles should be regarded as common property yet distinguished and rare commodities. Raphael's imitation merely spread the wealth around, disseminated it.

In a monograph on Raphael first published in 1824, Quatremère de Quincy (who was *secrétaire perpétuel* of the Académie des Beaux-Arts and a strong opponent of the romantic movement) repeated Reynolds' argument in another form. Referring again to Raphael's use of Masaccio's figures, Quatremère de Quincy wrote: "Once a beautiful thought has been struck with the mark of genius, there is also genius in refraining from giving it a new imprint, and there is more merit in thus proclaiming one's indebtedness than in hiding the debt beneath deceptive variations."[19] Raphael, in other words, acted properly in not attempting to alter substantially or improve on Masaccio's mark of genius. Quatremère de Quincy had in mind the two masters' similar conceptions of the Expulsion from Paradise (Masaccio in the Brancacci Chapel, c. 1427; Raphael in the Vatican Logge, c. 1516–1519; figs. 1–2).

One is reminded of a commonplace: it takes genius to recognize genius. Raphael had the genius and good sense to borrow from Masaccio with minimal alteration. Such a direct form of reproductive representation surely is not the only mode of transmission within the classical tradition. Indeed since the scenes that adorn the Vatican Logge are not attributed to Raphael's hand but to assistants, we have here the possibility of a distinction between generative mind (Raphael) and executive hand (Giulio Romano, Gianfrancesco Penni, and others), aided by Raphael's own drawings "influenced" by Masaccio.[20] Despite such complex mediation in the transmission of the "mark of genius" from one *Expulsion from Paradise* to another, there are close formal correspondences, at least by Quatremère de Quincy's standard of similarity.

How does that standard operate? We surmise that for Quatremère de Quincy similarity of invention dominates similarity of handling or personal style just as Raphael, the prime inventor, dominates his assistants, who perform the execution of the painting. What counts as formal correspondence largely depends on choice of pose and composition, the gross features of a painting that are most readily visible and most easily copied. When genius speaks to genius, however, even these obvious statements need not be repeated. Quatremère de Quincy discusses a form of borrowing that allows genius to pass from one master to another without such clearly reproductive results. He states—again in his monograph on Raphael—that Raphael borrowed from Michelangelo, taking neither his style nor his devices, for these were so idiosyncratic as to be inimitable. Raphael instead assimilated something of Michelangelo's spiritual force. He borrowed "what one might call [Michelangelo's] virtue and the direction of his talent"; Raphael's act, according to Quatremère de Quincy, resembled "the way in which one borrows from a fire, taking its heat, but without taking anything from the hearth that produces it."[21] In such a transaction nothing material moves, only the spiritual.

Quatremère de Quincy spoke of this second form of transmission from master to follower (or from original to copy) as a borrowing. Perhaps that was something of a euphemism. The case of Michelangelo and Raphael had been (and continues to be) discussed in terms of brute influence. This conception of the transmission renders the earlier or original party in the relationship active, while the act of borrowing becomes rather passive, perhaps necessitated by the overwhelming force of the more original presence. Art historians today are particularly sensitive to previous abuses of the concept of influence that were motivated by an obsession with originality. It seems now to have become common to speak not of influence and borrowing but of a selective, deliberate referencing. If we note that Raphael created a figure that recalls one of Masaccio's, we hesitate to conclude that Masaccio influenced Raphael; we say instead that Raphael "quoted" or—more accurately but more awkwardly—that Raphael "referenced" Masaccio. The sentiment here is commendable if not the phrasing.[22]

The issue, however, does not end in this reversal of active and passive roles. Spirituality is fundamental to the evaluation of photographic as well as handcrafted copies. The possibility of spiritual influence of the Michelangelo-Raphael sort allowed nineteenth-century theorists to dismiss the reproductive powers of the camera just as the purely material copy could be dismissed in favor of the spiritually informed imitation. If the classical tradition merely were a matter of the reproductive copying of proper models, photography could take part in it. It was instead a matter of the spirit. This was spirit engaged with body, for the spiritual force of human genius showed itself only in the active mark of the hand. Curiously the body had to act for either mind or soul to assert itself. Art was material and spiritual, but photography—regarded essentially as a mechanism—exhibited neither quality in quite the right way.

Two academicians of particular importance employed this argument, Charles Blanc and Henri Delaborde. Blanc did so when he reported in 1863 on the publication of photographic reproductions of Marcantonio Raimondi's engravings after Raphael, which were themselves reproductions of a kind. (Delaborde was at the same moment preparing a monographic study and catalogue of Marcantonio's oeuvre.) Blanc stressed the engraver's capacity to interpret the genius of Raphael and other masters and to convey genius selectively through a different medium: "Marcantonio conceived engraving as a concise translation that spotlighted the essential, that could indicate all without saying all." Most importantly, Marcantonio, through personal experience in Raphael's studio, was imbued with Raphael's own spirit as he worked. Whatever features might distinguish Marcantonio's images from Raphael's were proper ones that remained faithful to the effect of the original. However excellent, photographic reproduction could never match the hand engraving's power of translation, its "proper" (or appropriate—and appropriating) figuration. To photograph Raphael's art would reproduce less of its essence. Yet, given that Marcantonio had already performed the artistic task of translating Raphael into a medium of multiple replication, what could be more suited to disseminating the engraver's images than the medium of replication par excellence, photography? With photography, Blanc stated, "for a few francs [collectors] will acquire not a copy or an imitation, but, so to speak, the thing itself.[23] Is it not, in effect, the thing itself, repeated in a mirror and certified true by a ray of the sun?" Once Marcantonio had supplied the mind and the hand the photographic mechanism could render innumerable faithful copies. Photography would nevertheless fail whenever it copied something raw and unassimilated, something alive: "Whatever thinks and lives can only be seen by a being that itself lives and thinks. The eye of photography, so clearsighted in the material world, is blind when it regards the spiritual [esprit]."[24]

Blanc's remarks reproduced the substance of an argument Delaborde had made in 1856 (with this exception: in his extremism Delaborde concluded that photography failed even at copying engravings). Delaborde stated that the successful engraver must "have assimilated the spirit [esprit] of his model" while having "modified the letter." The engraving "copies and comments on painting simultaneously," whereas the photograph "begins and ends" with material facts, never extending beyond "blind fidelity." It was Delaborde's position that engraving thinks through its act of representation, both figuring and assimilating its copy, whereas photography merely performs a mechanism. In photography "we feel that the hand, or rather the spirit [âme], is absent."[25] Delaborde implied that the material mark of the hand was to be taken as the sign of immaterial spirit (either mind [esprit] or soul [âme]). Photography exhibited no such material handiwork and hence could attain no spirituality.

Blanc and Delaborde were themselves the spiritual descendants of Quatremère de Quincy and, like him, admirers of Ingres. They championed the handcrafted copy as a device for revealing both the genius of the copied and that of the copyist.[26] They conceived of the spiritual force of the classic master as transferred to canvas through the modern master's hand in an act of consummate assimilation. This was the kind of "handling" that would assure the vitality of the classical tradition.[27] It would preserve the past without denying the present. It could even assert the present through the distinguishing marks that any modern master would bring to his figured, individualized copies.

Consider another commonplace, one related to these thoughts about spiritual transmission and individual hands: the inimitability of genius. Quatremère de Quincy and many others spoke, for example, of the inimitability of Michelangelo's genius.[28] Raphael could not directly imitate Michelangelo because Michelangelo's manner of representation was simply not proper.[29] It was irregular and unassimilable. Was it then more original than Raphael's or Masaccio's? The question suggests a distinction between the proper and the original. Such a distinction is a feature of modernism that undermines traditional classicism.

According to the nineteenth-century account, Raphael could appropriate Masaccio's figures quite naturally and quite literally, but he could do little with Michelangelo's. Having imitated Masaccio, Raphael resembled Masaccio. Consequently, barring any special metaphorical sense to the comparison, one would have to say that Masaccio resembled Raphael. Classicism entails such commutability to a great extent.[30] For modernists it became possible to denigrate the classical tradition and, in particular, its reincarnation in academic form by arguing that all members of this tradition, having a common view of what was proper, resembled one another; they, therefore, lacked any true marks of originality and selfhood. There would, of course, be one exception to this damaging rule: the first member of the repetitive series would be the original master and hence the master with originality.

Here each of the terms *original* and *originality* is used in two different senses, indicating that the first or original member of a generative sequence can be credited with a marked individuality or originality despite the fact that all other members of the sequence may resemble this master of masters. Chronological priority becomes one of the keys to originality for modernist critics. We are familiar with how important it was for art historians of the recent past to discover which artist could claim priority for a visual invention and to locate what in a work might be ascribed to "influence."[31] It is difficult to determine whether the art historian's concern for influence represents a continual reassertion of the force of classicism or whether in contrast it signifies the modernist anxiety over originality in the sense of singularity. The two concerns, one classicist and the other modernist, converge in the ambivalence of an art-historical evaluation that seeks out novelty and the instituting examples of a style while simultaneously concentrating its most detailed study on identifying a work's imitative features (stylistic and iconographical "borrowings" and references). Such features are ascribed to outside influences.

Critical viewers of a more purely classical orientation do not express such ambivalence. Within the critical framework that I have designated as classical Raphael's literal borrowing from Masaccio will be as valid as his figurative borrowing from Michelangelo. In addition, the need to distinguish first from last in a series will be far less compelling. Raphael and Masaccio can share the same originality. Theirs is the originality of the classic, commonplace, and proper.

We return to Ingres and his statement concerning Raphael's classic originality: "Raphael, in imitating endlessly, was always himself." How can Raphael be himself if he also imitates others to the point of being very much like them, resembling them with regard to the features he chooses to imitate? Raphael must already share these features with his predecessors. They must be native to him as well as being acquired or made manifest through his acts of imitation. Another commonplace of art crit-

Fig. 3. Ingres, *Raphael and La Fornarina*, 1814, oil on canvas. Fogg Art Museum, Cambridge, Massachusetts, Grenville L. Winthrop Bequest.

icism is suggested: not only does genius recognize genius but genius recognizes genius of its own kind. Ingres, like Reynolds, refers to the common property of the classic works and states that each modern master is free to take whatever is personally appealing.[32] To say that Raphael imitated and yet remained himself might mean that he always added something new to his copies. Within the classical tradition, however, the statement can also mean that Raphael imitated just those classic works that together constituted his own character.[33] He *was* those classic works in the same sense that Ingres and others would argue that the classic works were themselves nature. Ingres once wrote, perhaps following Johann Winckelmann and Quatremère de Quincy: "You will learn from the ancient works to see nature, because they are themselves nature."[34] The entirety of this classical claim to nature is represented visually in one of Ingres' own depictions and pastiches of Raphael, the painting of 1814 known as *Raphael and La Fornarina* (fig. 3).

The type of scene that this painting depicts is by no means unusual within the history of art. A painter is shown in a studio working from a model (compare, for example, images of Saint Luke). The specific narrative situation makes this painting somewhat distinct but still not unexpected—there appears to be an amorous relationship between artist (Raphael) and model (La Fornarina). This raises familiar questions about the relationship of vision, representation, and desire.[35] Consider instead a seemingly simpler matter: Why within the painting does the woman sketched in on the canvas on the easel resemble as much as she does her presumably real-life counterpart? Why has the depicted painter's style not transformed that model to a greater degree? Are we to assume that the depicted painter, Raphael, is a realist?[36] One conclusion is that Ingres not only depicts Raphael during a process of depiction, but imitates Raphael to find his, Ingres', own classic style. The net result is an image of Raphael's realism as well as idealism, a picture in which an ideal of feminine beauty appears in "real" nature as well as in art, and in "real" portraiture as well as in a depiction of an ideal type (the same figure appears on the easel and in the image of Raphael's own *Madonna della Sedia*, painted into the background of *Raphael and La Fornarina*). In turn one views—as if reflected by the art of Raphael—Ingres' own realism and idealizing classic manner, his native preference. Ingres is drawn to Raphael as if the two masters shared a single mind and hand. Ingres' painting collapses time and tradition, making classicism seem whole, while it also demonstrates how close a classic vision is to nature, both external nature and the nature of a proper artist (either Raphael or Ingres).

Ingres' nineteenth-century critics sometimes complained that he remained too close to the details of nature, and sometimes they carped that he indulged in idiosyncrasy and mannerism. Some also accused him of plagiarism because of his borrowings from Raphael. But when one classic master imitates another there can be no plagiarism, for both are merely doing things properly, in the proper classic manner. Ingres' style looks like Raphael's style, which looks like classic style, which looks like nature. We know that nature must look as it does when represented by a classic master because there is no competing manner of proper representation. This is the beauty of the classical system, the authorized beauty that directs us all to view the world in like manner. Photography threatens classicism's beautiful hegemony with the unselective ugliness of its own version of proper visual representation.

Classicism and Modernism

To equate art and nature, as Ingres' painting *Raphael and La Fornarina* seems to, is to deny the figuration of painting or at least of classic painting; it is to depict classic painting as the proper, or even the literal, representation of reality. Art historians may be more in the habit of regarding classical art as idealization, but such art always laid claim to the real. We encounter the residue of that claim to the real whenever we or our less-critical contemporaries recognize that a Renaissance, baroque, or academic painting somehow offers a more convincing picture of the real than does a painting by Wassily Kandinsky, Pablo Picasso, or even Paul Cézanne. The modernist works appear distorted and as a result perhaps more original. They appear deviant, figured, or metaphorical, at least with regard to antecedent classic and academic works that serve by comparison as examples of proper, conventional, or commonplace representation. Certainly the modernist works appear figured or metaphorical when placed beside most photographs.

We can conceive then of three familiar modes of two-dimensional pictorial representation, all of which claim to represent the real. They do so in different ways. First, there is the mode of painting that I have referred to as classical. It equates art and nature and valorizes an originality of sameness rather than of difference; it seeks out first principles, original truths, and disseminates them through repetition. Second, there is modernist painting, which valorizes the originality of difference. It stresses individual style and discredits plagiarism wherever it can be discerned. If classic style is conventional or proper, the modernist manner is metaphorical or deviant. Third, there is photography. To most viewers the photograph will appear more literal, more realistically proper, than even classical painting. It seems, however, to lack the distinction of painting, painting's handcrafted, autographic features. The photograph, by comparison with even a hack academic painting, might appear quite commonplace. Is a photographic image really a commonplace, a representation that stands unquestioned, one that convinces without any supporting evidence?

To determine the status of the photograph and its impact on our sense of representation the distinction between classic and modernist painting must be elaborated in terms of one of photography's own finest features, its capacity to index. If we refer to a photograph as indexing its model because the model seems to be a physical cause of its representational image (as any object can be linked causally to its own shadow, reflection, or other product of its interaction with light), then we must refer to the capacity of a painting to index in a more distanced or metaphorical manner. If painting indexes objects of vision, it does so only indirectly, through the medium of the hand. The practice of painting inserts the hand between object and representation, distancing the one from the other.

Precisely how and to what extent is the handmade painting indexical? Seen as a physical trace, the painter's brushmark becomes the indexical sign of the brush that imprinted the mark. As if following a chain of physical evidence, the viewer reaches the hand that grasped and manipulated the brush; that hand too is signified indexically by the painter's brushmark. But to pass beyond this hand to an eye and a brain, to an act of vision, is problematic; to do so we must enter the body. The causal connection or mechanism operating between hand and eye or brain remains obscure. If the interplay of brushwork and vision, mediated by the human organism, was as well formulated as the mechanism of photography, the hand might seem little more than an element of a machine operated by a brain systematically responding to stimuli in visual form. This clearly is not the case. Moreover, the appearance of irregularities and missing links in the putative causal sequence—from external object, to vision, to mind, to hand, to painting—lends to each element a certain autonomy. (As much as Quatremère de Quincy and others wished to subordinate hand to mind, they had to admit the hand's essential and irreplaceable action.) It appears that if painting indexes something beyond a hand moving a brush, if it indexes an object viewed, it does so only *figuratively*.[37] We presume some connection between visual image and painted image by way of the hand but subject its precise nature to the vagaries of interpretation. Like figured language, painting describes by distanced indirection.

Despite the distance of figuration that painting introduces between original model and imitative representation, it nevertheless asserts contact with the real whenever we regard it as if reliable evidence. The nature of this contact with "reality" is itself figurative. Painting indexes its model figuratively since the causal link between model and representation has no determinate reality. It is as if painting's capacity to index was itself merely depicted or connoted rather than exercised. Instead of the physical trace of light (as in a shadow or a photograph), we see in painting evidence of a bodily action calculated to represent the appearance of such a trace. Painting thus demands faith in the artist's capacity to master the technique (the device, the figuration) of

indexing and to regularize whatever distortions such technique might impose. Whenever the viewer has faith in the process, an act of classic painting may indeed be seen to index, as if authorized by some law of nature or of vision. In concept classic painting can succeed in indexing both a collective, traditional manner of vision and the external reality that falls under its gaze. One accordingly assumes that the world really looks the way a classic painting depicts it, given the transformative conventions of this medium. A modernist painting, in contrast, indexes a self, an individual and internalized vision, not a collective one.

This distinction between classic and modernist can be drawn from a painting by Henri Matisse of 1917 (fig. 4), one that shares the theme of artist and model with Ingres' *Raphael and La Fornarina* of a century earlier. Here, as in Ingres' painting, the depicted artist's representation of his model closely resembles the model herself, at least

Fig. 4. Matisse, *The Painter and His Model*, 1917, oil on canvas. Centre nationale d'art et de culture Georges Pompidou, Paris.

as she is depicted. But now neither the model in the picture nor her representation on the canvas on the easel seems proper. Because of the license taken in rendering contour and color, we can assume relatively little as to how the model might have appeared in real life. It is not so much that we presume that a representation and its model must offer the same visual qualities to our eye but that we lack the code of transformation to convert the one image into the other. What this idiosyncratic depiction unequivocally reveals is that Matisse painted the picture—it is a picture in his style and of his style. The rhetoric of this image indicates that there can be no question of plagiarism nor of any collective authorship. This modernist painting indexes its author singularly, as if independent of any tradition of masters who might share a similar spirit.[38]

The photograph, of course, because of its mechanism, can be said to index external reality and nothing else. As a result it seems to eliminate the mediating artistic personality and hand, thereby returning the history of representation to its primitive and magical sources, back to a time when an image was considered an organic part or true analog of its originating object.[39] Photography does other things too, but what it excels at is appearing to be without an author, to picture without the direction of an artist's hand.[40] It naturalizes and objectifies reality in rendering it as a picture, that is, as an artificial or made thing. This made thing has the capacity to assert the living reality of what made it—not the author-photographer but whatever the photograph pictures.

In sum, we see that the classic painting can refer to an external reality and a collective ideality, whereas the modernist painting refers first and foremost to a singular or individual ideal. The modernist work is "original" in that it displays the mark of a unique "genius." In contrast the photograph primarily refers to external effects, as if without the vagaries of a personally motivated vision. The modernist painting and the photograph, taken together, thus reconstitute the functions of the classical painting, which was at once "ideal" and "real."

Photography and Catachresis

I have been referring to classic art as proper in several related senses. Classic art, and indeed anything that is classic, serves as a model. The classic image that is proper is a commonplace and a common property; it belongs to you and to me. What is proper becomes your own (proper to you) as you model yourself on the classics; for instance, as you model your use of language on the

language of the classic texts. This is the process through which the word *classic* acquires its present meaning. In ancient Rome the term was used to identify the highest ranking group of citizens, those who enjoyed certain privileges, including the right to bear arms. Members of this class were both different from others (in part because of a distinguished lineage) and better than others. Because they embodied all that was right and proper, they were worthy of emulation. If one were seeking a noble and wholly proper manner of discourse, one would imitate the speech and writing of those classics who happened to be orators and authors. Highlighting distinction in linguistic skills, we come to speak of a select group of classic authors, perhaps forgetting whether their nobility stems from birth, genius, or acquired education. Eventually, we come to speak of classic painters.[41]

The social and cultural hierarchy reveals its circularity since classics are born to be proper, but one can acquire the status of the classic by imitating what is already taken to be proper. Consequently the proper is subject to falsification or improper imitation, just as an academic tradition may falsify its classic models through an unthinking, mechanistic process of copying. This argument against academicism is a commonplace even among academics. One would be accusing Ingres of the false consciousness of academicism were one to claim that he displayed the surface effects of Raphael's style without the depth of his understanding. Similarly when deviance from the proper is to be valued, as it is in Matisse's modernist painting, one can falsify the mark of stylistic idiosyncrasy, the technical look of sincerity that makes a work seem self-expressive. Recognizing this possibility of fraudulent figuration, modernist criticism often investigates artistic biography, seeking evidence of struggle and sincerity in a developmental sequence of works or even outside the work itself.

Can a photograph falsify? Can it belie its origins? (The matter of montage and other so-called trick photographs does not alter the argument and need not be investigated here; nor is it necessary to consider procedures of "mechanical" or "automatic" figuration other than photography.)[42] If the photograph can directly refer to reality, without manipulation, without handling of any kind, is it not necessarily more proper than modernist and even classic painting? Does it not set the standard for the representation of the real?

One can argue that the format and many of the visual features of the photograph were calculated to imitate the look of traditional paintings and graphic works.[43] The crucial difference—what separates the photograph from tradition—is its mechanism, its automatism. As Walter Benjamin succinctly stated, "photography freed the hand."[44] This is the foundation of an unrewarding debate over whether photography is a matter of art or documentation. The debate runs the entire course of photography's history, with photographers as well as critics and theorists appearing on both sides of the issue.[45] Why the debate has occurred may be far more significant than how it has been conducted. The basic dispute is whether the photographic image is found or made. Do photographers simply find and record the presence of light-reflecting objects with a mechanical device that facilitates the use of a kind of light-sensitive tracing paper? Or is the essence of photography as in painting an act of choice, an aesthetic or rhetorical choice of view that the photographer can fashion through selection of lens, focusing, developing and printing techniques, cropping and the like? The majority of those who have carefully thought about the problem have argued that the photograph is both found and made. This clever answer ultimately is unilluminating. It was offered even by those such as Charles Blanc who held the photograph in low esteem. Blanc rather reluctantly admitted that a photograph revealed the typical preferences for pose, lighting, and focus that the photographer brought to his model.[46] A more considered and generalized version of the double solution to the art/documentation problem was given by Hans Tietze in a 1936 essay on forgery. Tietze wrote:

> Every copy, whether made by an artist or by mechanical means, has two kinds of value, one documentary and one creative. Even the freest transcription, a copy by Rubens after Titian or by Cézanne after a book illustration, has a certain documentary value with regard to its original. This value, however, is trifling in comparison with that of the copyist's creative power. On the other hand, even a mechanical photographic reproduction is a kind of interpretation of its model, just as every restoration is.[47]

By comparing the "mechanical" photograph to the handcrafted restoration Tietze restored to the photograph a certain handled, tradition-laden, and interpretive quality, which in turn would allow the photograph to assume an element of spirituality. Recall that nineteenth-century theorists claimed that genius became visible in the mark of the hand and that the activity of the hand signified the engagement of the mind, a spirituality modernism transformed into self-expression. The tendency to join mind or self to hand or body was itself especially marked after the advent of photography. Before that time it was often argued that any apparant signs of handicraft might indicate an unhealthy concern for material qualities. Ingres had made such a statement, and one can relate the polished finish of his paintings to this premodern suspicion of the hand.[48] In offering a finished representation more free of handicraft than Ingres' paintings could ever be photography mooted the case to be made against the hand and the body. Today Ingres' concern for polish and finish seems oddly old-fashioned, perhaps because modernist painting, in opposing itself to a mechanistic photographic practice, unproblematically reunites body and mind. Needless to say, paintings of the modern period that seem too mechanical or detailed in their handling are often labeled "photographic."[49]

To save photography from its inhumanity, hand and mind had to be reintroduced within its practice—both in its documentation and in its art. Photography became the art of documentation, and those who excelled at this art were attributed a genius for documentation. This, for example, is the argument that emerges from Lincoln Kirstein's poetic essay on Walker Evans, published in 1938. Kirstein dramatically distinguished photography's mechanism from painting's handicraft: "Brush, paint and palette can scarcely be considered a machine—the camera can never have been thought of anything else." Yet art enters into the camera's productions: "Although the camera is a machine and photography a science, a large element of human judgment comes into the process, amounting to creative selection." Some selections may be better than others, especially when the "truth" of documentation is at stake; Kirstein noted that a candid-camera style had replaced "artistic" soft focus as the documentary manner of the day. Nevertheless the improvement in "realism" was negligible: "The candid-camera . . . drugs the eye into believing it has witnessed a significant fact when it has only caught a flicker not clear enough to indicate a *psychological* image, however solid the material one." Having dispensed with one style of candidness, Kirstein affirmed another, that of Walker Evans. He praised the truth of Evans' pictures, a truth that depended not only on recording the "disparate chaos" of American material culture but on eliminating artifice from documentary style—Evans took his photographs straight on and never used the device of the angle shot: "All through the pictures in this book, you will search in vain for an angle-shot. Every object is regarded head on with the unsparing frankness of a Russian ikon or a Flemish portrait. The facts pile up with the prints." It

Above left: Fig. 5. Walker Evans, *42nd Street*, 1929, gelatin-silver print. Collection, The Museum of Modern Art, New York Purchase.

Above right: Fig. 6. Robert Frank, *Movie Premiere, Hollywood*, c. 1955, gelatin-silver print. Collection, The Museum of Modern Art, New York Purchase. Copyright Robert Frank, from *The Americans*, 1958.

Below left: Fig. 7. Lee Friedlander, *New York*, 1968, gelatin-silver print. Collection, The Museum of Modern Art, New York Purchase.

seems that Evans' primitive genius for documentation allowed him to attain the status of the classic as his own documentary style became the proper one, the one to be imitated by others. In fact, for Kirstein, such a style had already appeared elsewhere, in all representations that exhibited equally classic candor.[50]

Without much elaboration the ironies of Evans' canonical documentation become evident; and we realize that the documentary must itself be a recognizable genre even when mixed with other genres. Nevertheless photography holds a spell on the modernist imagination that longs to document itself through self-expression. Its power generates the apparent ironies of the following statement, taken from the International Center of Photography's *Encyclopedia of Photography* (1984): "The basic ex-

pressive nature of photography is defined as springing from the photographer's ability—unique among visual artists—to record his immediate perceptions and reactions without particular technical skills or reliance on visual conventions."[51] Here all dreams of individual liberty come true in visual representation. Photography provides a proper documentation of personal expression, a kind of canonical singularity—bound to appear as commonplace as a snapshot—yet free not only of the hand but of any sense of what was proper to the past, free of visual convention.

When we compare Walker Evans' straight-on shots and compressed spaces (fig. 5) to Robert Frank's angles and blurs (fig. 6) or Lee Friedlander's partially and pointedly obstructed views (fig. 7), we recognize that styles of documentation change. One of the impetuses to change may simply be the conventionality that comes to be ascribed to a documentary manner that has become communally proper.[52] Diane Arbus found it necessary to return to the straight-on style and even to return ragged edges to her prints, imperfections normally avoided by a neatly registered and slightly cropped printing. Arbus' style indicates that her approach is hands off, pure documentation, no cropping at all. The silent, sometimes imperceptible irony of her pictures makes Friedlander's irony seem contrived, even boisterous, by comparison. Yet Arbus' pictures reek of irony as her subject matter plays one sense of fashion against another and her format plays one photographic manner against another.[53] I will leave aside the complex ironies conceived by the photographer and those brought to the picture by its viewers to draw a simple and obvious conclusion. At any given moment in the history of representation something, some kind of image, will stand as a proper representation of the real. It will appear as a norm against which all other representation will appear deviant, figured, or metaphorical. It need only momentarily resist a viewer's tendency to establish an ironic, interpretive distance.

Our most naive as well as our more sophisticated thoughts tell us that since the advent of photography some kind of photographic image must hold the title to the real. Just as styles of documentation may change from Evans to Frank to Arbus, the particular type of photograph that most obviously connotes the real also changes from time to time. At all times the title is held by photography (or by some other mode that is perceived as indexical, such as holography). Why then do theorists seem to doubt photography's claim against painting as the more proper mode of representation? Why have so many good thinkers weighted their ontological arguments toward photography as rhetorical art rather than as faithful documentation? My answer is that phototropism—photography's peculiar turn or manner of figuring—subverts the sense of proper representation. The photograph is neither proper nor figured, neither properly documentary nor properly art; the photograph is a catachresis.

What is catachresis? Many rhetorics list it as false metaphor or simply misuse of metaphor. A more reasoned definition is given by Pierre Fontanier in the last great rhetoric published in France. (Composed between 1821 and 1830, the work was completed at the time of the advent of modern photography.) Fontanier defines catachresis as the case when "a sign, already attached to a first idea [or image], is attached also to a new idea, which itself had no sign or has none that is proper within the language." Fontanier as well as many others offers as an example of catachresis the locution "arm of a chair." This cannot be a metaphor because there is no proper or unfigured way of referring to the arm of a chair; no comparison is available; the figure if there is one is incomplete.[54] Such catachresis operates by extension of what is assumed to be the most primitive use of the word, in this case, *arm* as a human limb. There are more interesting and more problematic examples of catachresis, such as most of the common words that refer to the operation of mental faculties. Do experiences, properly speaking, leave impressions on the memory? How does the word *on* function in "on the memory"? Impressions are marks, imprints, traces. Is the memory to be regarded as a planar surface on which figures are drawn? Do we grasp this point? In what sense does our intelligence ever "grasp" a point? To replace *grasp* with *comprehend* will not solve the problem since the Latin etymology only refers back to grasping. Trying to substitute for the word *point* may be even more difficult. Both *grasp* and *point* can be construed as examples of catachresis.[55]

One might object that this is all only a matter of dead metaphors, ordinary commonplaces. This thought leads us to classic images of any kind. They go unchallenged because they are so proper, so expected, so satisfying, just like dead metaphors. To members of a classical tradition, however, such images live. How does one articulate their rhetorical mode? Among theorists educated at a time when rhetoric was a most fundamental study, when its hierarchical distinctions seemed in agreement with a desired social structure, the standard rhetorical figures could be applied quite naturally to the theory of the visual arts. Accordingly, Quatremère de Quincy associated linguistic metaphor with the desirable transformation and idealization of subjects rendered by visual artists: "Every composition in which an artist proposes to express something other than a servile imitation or a copy of things ['le portrait identique des objets'] is more or less a metaphoric composition."[56] Thus the conventions of the accomplished academic artist, no matter how standardized, effected a metaphorical transformation from the "real" to what Quatremère de Quincy variously named the "fictive," the "poetic," the "figured."[57] One can imagine that the most canonical modes of metaphorical transformation would produce fictions so familiar that they would pass for "reality." Classic art claimed such a propriety, a literal reality that was also an ideality, also a particular, but right, way of seeing the world through ideal, nondeviant figuration. And so Ingres and other supporters of classical doctrine spoke not of dead metaphors but of living classics and of the classical tradition as able to absorb and reflect new personalities—"Raphael, in imitating endlessly, was always himself."

If classic art sought to represent reality with an all-powerful, proper form of figuration (a metaphor that passed for the literal), then photography undermined classic art's claim to this kind of right representation. It did so not because it was itself unfigured, but because it made all other representation look more figured. Figuration is the mark of the hand, not only in that it draws and makes a figure—Raphael's and Ingres' Fornarina, for instance—but in that the hand draws in a manner proper to itself. For the modernist such propriety is unique and most desirable. The figuration of modernist painting asserts the mark of the individual and becomes a metaphor of the self. In contrast, the classical image belongs potentially to all society and history; the mark of classical figuration is made by a master who represents the true vision that ought to come to all, whether through noble birth, genius, or acquired education of mind and hand.

To perceive the photograph as a representation of the "real" depends on an understanding of the camera's mechanism and in most cases on an association of the real with seamless detail. The past history of "realistic" classical painting also comes into play; such painting traditionally offered the viewer all that one expected to see in terms of a proper degree of detail that would define or identify an object. Photography breaks with this past. The viewer of the photograph is shocked by its extension of the standards of proper detail. One faces a representation more real than what the real has been. Nevertheless, the photograph is recognized as a representation, as a picture; and having no tradition, no authority behind it, it can hardly be proper.[58] As both its proponents and detractors note, anyone—whether aristocrat or commoner, educated or not—anyone at all can be a photographer: "Anyone can take the most detailed views in a few minutes."[59] The photographic image does not derive from a collective tradition of genius (it is not classic) nor does it pointedly reflect individual authorship in its figurality (it is not modern). It thus is not a metaphor but a catachresis of the real; it becomes the only available image of the real. It appropriates, instantaneously and forcefully, all claims to the real.

If photography were itself metaphoric or figured representation, it would have to be matched against classic painting as the given proper standard. Representations must be matched against other representations. Indeed, one of classicism's defenses against photography's realism was the assertion that the new medium could not capture a *mental* reality; and this failure was linked not only to an absence of spiritual input but to photography's lack of handicraft. Many argued that if photography triumphed over painting, this conquest involved only the realm of *material* reality—a matter of documentation not art. Yet given the peculiar indexical nature of photography's pictorialism, how telling were (and are) the terms of such comparative evaluations?[60]

The advantage to considering photography as catachresis, once one grasps the concept, is that one understands why the art/documentation debate leads nowhere. A catachresis may appear both proper and figured but is neither. Its status seems to depend on a context of comparative representations, yet that context never becomes sufficiently complete to determine on which side of the distinction the catachresis should lie—figured or proper, art or documentation. The historical circumstances in which photographic practice arose established its products as catachretic representations. They were not improved pictures that merely replaced old ones but a different kind of picture that displaced the order of the old.

One never quite recognizes catachresis for what it is. Thus one struggles to push photography one way or the other. Art historians tend to regard the medium as artistic as if it commanded a tradition like painting, articulated by masters, masterpieces, and acts of imitative emulation of the Raphael-Masaccio and Ingres-Raphael kind. To study a photograph in terms of the artistry or manifested genius of a photographer is not only to convert documentary features into aesthetic ones; it is also to convert a catachresis into a metaphor, into a proper and manageable figure. It is to convert the shocking originality of the photograph into either the repetitive originality of classicism or the self-expressive originality of modernism. By this maneuvre the effect of the third, catachretic term (photography) is annulled and the traditional binary system is retained. Representations remain either proper (classical) or figured (modernist).

The commonplace photograph, with its potential to convince, continually threatens to overpower preexisting figuration and become itself the only proper figure, the figure of the real. This phototropism is strange and magical, and rational minds naturally resist it. Especially in recent years, we have come to speak of a rhetoric of the photograph, thereby reducing it to the product of an art, a figure like any other. We collectively establish a photographic rhetoric in two complementary ways that as individuals we tend to set in opposition. On the one hand we aestheticize the photographic image, withdrawing it from the world of "common" documentary representation. On the other hand we deny such rarefied artistic status and insist that photography is immersed in a world of institutions and practices motivated by a struggle for power.[61] To recognize the complementarity of these two interpretive gestures is to encounter the catachretic force of photography, its phototropism.

NOTES

At the beginning of this volume Rosalind Krauss defines two positions (presumed to be antithetical) under which she classifies all contributions to the symposium "Retaining the Original: Multiple Originals, Copies, and Reproductions"; and she implies that all possible positions must be variants of these two. Whereas one position problematizes the relation of original to copy, the other does not and tends to preserve a traditional sense of authorship. Krauss argues—according to her reading of my commentary on Ingres' *Raphael and La Fornarina*—that my essay engages in "retaining the original," that is, it preserves Ingres' authorial presence by regarding his painting as a unique, finished object that finds its origin and end in his model and in his relation to her. Readers may note that I instead treat Ingres' painting as a *representation* (a depiction) of a much more complex "classical" position (quite like that Krauss attributes to postmodern works). Ingres' painting becomes emblematic of the classical and—with a certain irony—emblematic of the inherent anonymity or lack of fixed authorial identity that classicism entails. In fact I argue that "modernist" works represent (depict) authorship with far less ambiguity or duplicity than do "classical" ones. Yet this is not a simple antithesis; for photography, as a *third* term, further complicates the matter.

Why has my argument been misrepresented or misunderstood by Rosalind Krauss? One answer may be particularly instructive for readers of my essay and for those like myself who feel that our usual critical dichotomies force us into reductive solutions to problems of interpretation. Krauss uses the term "poststructuralism" but actually invokes the dyadic distinctions characteristic of structuralism rather than the fluid indeterminacies of poststructuralism. She may misunderstand my argument because I choose to displace prevailing dichotomies instead of merely restructuring them. I call upon alternative sets of trichotomies: not painting versus photography, but classical painting *and* modernist painting *and* photography; not proper versus figural, but the proper *and* the figural *and* the catachretic. And I ask that oppositional distinctions be suspended or allowed to collapse as my argument progresses. All this may very well present difficulties for the reader, but it has the advantage of opening up interpretations of the "originality" of both painting and photography outside the dualistic boundaries that might be read into the symposium structure of *Retaining the Original*. R.S. August 1988

1. H. Gaucheraud, "The Daguerotype," *Literary Gazette* (London) (12 January 1839), 28, translated from Gaucheraud's article in *Gazette de France* (6 January 1839), 1. The shift from French to English reveals that the word *figure* has a double sense in both languages. The French "Que l'on se figure" becomes in English "Let our readers fancy" (mental figuration), while "nature figured" is used to translate "la nature reproduite" (physical figuration).

2. Antoine Chrysostome Quatremère de Quincy, *Essai sur la nature,*

le but et les moyens de l'imitation dans les beaux-arts (Paris, 1823), 331. (Unless otherwise noted, translations are mine.)

3. Despite the ploy of paraphrase in this sentence ("it is to say") my statement figures its antecedents and enacts the process of "figuration" that I attempt to describe. To dwell on cumulative levels of distance or figuration can fascinate, but an obsessive interest in such ironies immobilizes a text. For the most part I will avoid the further reaches of speculation on the nature of figuration. In recent years many deeply suggestive accounts of representational figuration have appeared; see, for example, Paul de Man, "The Epistemology of Metaphor," in *On Metaphor*, ed. Sheldon Sacks (Chicago, 1979), 11–28; Jacques Derrida, *Of Grammatology*, trans. Gayatri Chakravorty Spivak (Baltimore, 1976), especially 108–112 (on "proper" names). See also Roland Barthes, "Proust and Names," in *New Critical Essays*, trans. Richard Howard (New York, 1980), 55–68. Here Barthes discusses the propriety or apparent naturalness of proper names as a function of the constructive act of the one who writes (or figures) those names. In so doing he reapproaches the apparent paradox of the photograph (as an image both "real" and figured) that he defines in his influential essays "The Photographic Message" and "Rhetoric of the Image," in *Image—Music—Text*, trans. Stephen Heath (New York, 1977), 15–51.

4. For a very succinct account of the traditional concept of the commonplace see Walter J. Ong, "Commonplace Rhapsody: Ravisius Textor, Zwinger and Shakespeare," in *Classical Influences on European Culture, A.D. 1500–1700*, ed. R. R. Bolgar (Cambridge, 1976), 93. The commonplace can be exemplary in both "content" and "form." Orators who practiced by learning commonplace arguments mastered both the logic of the discourse and its rhetorical strategies (the distinction is Aristotelian; today it is often claimed that these two features of argumentation cannot be separated). Children's copybooks are collections of commonplaces (proverbs, for example) presented in the form of samples of model penmanship. Commonplaces so presented are representations doubly suitable for copying. They call attention to the double sense of figuration—verbal (conceptual) and visual (graphic).

5. Recent literature on this matter is voluminous. See, for example, Richard Rorty, *The Mirror of Nature* (Princeton, 1980); Christopher Norris, *The Deconstructive Turn: Essays in the Rhetoric of Philosophy* (London, 1983), especially 144–162.

6. This realization is hardly profound, yet neither is it easy to establish. What cannot be denied is that it operates in our culture. Compare this statement of 1869: "Photography translates and represents external objects with an admirable fidelity; to surpass it, the artist must give interpretation greater importance. . . . In thus forcing the painter to apply more of a personal stamp to his work . . . photography will contribute to the advancement of the fine arts" (Louis Figuier, "La photographie [1869]," in *Les merveilles de la science*, 4 vols. [Paris, 1867–1870], 3:187–188).

7. This argument, which applies even to "trick" photography, has been made numerous times in numerous forms. For a recent example see Kendall L. Walton, "Transparent Pictures: On the Nature of Photographic Realism," *Critical Inquiry* 11 (December 1984), 246–277. For an early statement acknowledging that the photograph rendered some aspects of resemblance far more adequately than other, equally obvious ones, see Figuier [1869] 1867–1870, 3:179–180, 184–185.

8. The quotations are from L.-J.-M. Daguerre, *Description pratique des procédés du daguerréotype* (1839), in Adrien Mentienne, *La découverte de la photographie en 1839* (Paris, 1892), 75; and a broadside published by Daguerre in 1838, cited in Beaumont Newhall, *The History of Photography* (New York, 1964), 17. Daguerre also wrote that the "process consists in the spontaneous reproduction of images of nature received in a camera, not with their colors, but with a very subtly gradated range of tones" (in Mentienne 1892, 73).

9. William Henry Fox Talbot, *The Pencil of Nature* (1844–1846; New York, 1969), note to pl. 15.

10. I am emphasizing the effect of a general history of representa-

tional practice that establishes proper as opposed to literal sense; this history facilitates the perception of local differences between proper and figured (or deviant) uses of specific words or images. There are other ways of opposing the proper to the literal. Paul Ricoeur, for example, regards the proper sense of a word as an originary meaning, whereas the literal sense is that in current usage (*The Rule of Metaphor*, trans. Robert Czerny [Toronto, 1977], 18–19). See also Paul de Man, "Pascal's Allegory of Persuasion," in *Allegory and Representation*, ed. Stephen J. Greenblatt (Baltimore, 1981), 4–5.

11. For instance, aspects of classicism are traditionally seen in the concern for an authoritative, universal language among symbolists and abstractionists (c. 1890–1930).

12. Compare, for example, Tzvetan Todorov, *Theories of the Symbol*, trans. Catherine Porter (Ithaca, N.Y., 1982), 107–110; Nicos Hadjinicolaou, "'La Liberté guidant le peuple' de Delacroix devant son premier public," *Actes de la recherche en sciences sociales*, no. 28 (June 1979), 15. For evidence of a nineteenth-century concern for linking systems of pictorial and social organization see, for example, W. Bürger [Théophile Thoré], *Musées de la Hollande*, 2 vols. (Paris, 1858–1860), 2:xiv–xv.

13. Cited in Henri Delaborde, *Ingres: Sa vie, ses travaux, sa doctrine, d'après les notes manuscrits et les lettres du maître* (Paris, 1870), 140.

14. Compare, for example, Antoine Chrysostome Quatremère de Quincy, *Histoire de la vie et des ouvrages de Raphaël* (1824; Paris, 1835), 340: "One must recognize, with Raphael, an identifying characteristic [*une propriété*], that of being himself . . . of always remaining original, even in the very faithful imitations he made of antique style."

15. Johann David Passavant, *Raphaël d'Urbin et son père Giovanni Santi*, 2 vols. (1839; Paris, 1860), 1:297.

16. Sir Joshua Reynolds, *Discourses on Art*, ed. Robert R. Wark (1797; New Haven, 1975), 217.

17. Reynolds [1797] 1975, 104.

18. Reynolds [1797] 1975, 217.

19. Quatremère de Quincy [1824] 1835, 241–242.

20. There is extensive recent debate regarding the authorship of individual frescoes in the Vatican Logge and their preparatory drawings. See, for example, Nicole Dacos, *Le Logge di Raffaello* (Rome, 1977), especially 158–159. Bernice F. Davidson dismisses such concern by arguing that since the character of the frescoes is remarkably consistent, they may rightfully be collectively regarded as the "creation of Raphael's own imagination" (*Raphael's Bible: A Study of the Vatican Logge* [University Park, Pa., 1985], 30–31). In thus privileging mental figuration over manual figuration Davidson reapproaches the position of Quatremère de Quincy.

21. Quatremère de Quincy [1824] 1835, 77. (Compare Passavant [1839] 1860, 1:314.) The word *virtue* (*vertu*) should here be taken to refer to a desirable or worthy quality found within an individual.

22. Quatremère de Quincy himself expressed the sentiment when he interpreted changes in Raphael's style that some considered signs of Michelangelo's influence. He argued that Raphael was calling public attention to his rivalry and difference from Michelangelo, not to a growing appreciation and indebtedness (see Quatremère de Quincy [1824] 1835, 81).

23. Charles Blanc does not clearly distinguish here between "copy" and "imitation." On both the difference and its absence see Richard Shiff, "The Original, the Imitation, the Copy, and the Spontaneous Classic," *Yale French Studies*, no. 66 (1984), 27–54.

24. Charles Blanc, "L'oeuvre de Marc-Antoine," *Gazette des beaux-arts* 15 (September 1863), 270, 274, 268. On photography's preeminence as a mode of mechanical reproduction compare Alfred Bonnardot, *Histoire artistique et archéologique de la gravure en France* (Paris, 1849), 188: "je me crois obligé . . . de placer *le soleil* au nombre de nos *graveurs*" ("I feel obligated . . . to place *the sun* among our *engravers*"). Figuier (1869), like Blanc, concluded that the role of the photograph in art was "to serve as a document to be consulted" by draftsmen and painters.

(On this compare also the well-known remarks of Charles Baudelaire, "Salon de 1859 (1859)," in Charles Baudelaire, *Oeuvres complètes*, ed. Claude Pichois, 2 vols. [Paris, 1975–1976], 2:618.) With regard to the aesthetic quality of photographic reproductions Figuier was far more enthusiastic than Blanc. Blanc (begrudgingly) and Figuier (readily) noted that individual photographers had recognizable styles; see Charles Blanc, "Grammaire historique des arts du dessin: De l'imitation et du style," *Gazette des beaux-arts* 6 (1 May 1860), 138; and Figuier [1869] 1867–1870, 3:182–188 (these pages include passages from Figuier's *La photographie au Salon de 1859* [Paris, 1860], 4–6). On photography's material capabilities, including its use to reproduce engravings, as well as its spiritual failings, compare also Francis Wey, "Comment le soleil est devenu peintre," *Le Musée des familles* (July 1853), 298–300. Debates over the evolving legal status of the photograph in France as artistic or intellectual property and documentary artifact reveal the same concerns and ambivalences evidenced in the aesthetic debates of the 1860s; see Bernard Edelman, *Ownership of the Image*, trans. Elizabeth Kingdom (London, 1979), 43–52.

25. Henry Delaborde, "La photographie et la gravure (1856)," in Henri Delaborde, *Mélanges sur l'art contemporain* (Paris, 1866), 364–366, 371. Delaborde elaborated on the effect of the absent hand in noting that within a given work the "touch" of the photograph does not vary (373). To remedy the situation Delaborde described, Robert Demachy (among others) would later advocate not only compositional choice but forceful manipulation of negatives to introduce the missing "thumb-mark of the living, thinking, and feeling artist" (Robert Demachy, "On the Strait Print," *Camera Work*, no. 19 [July 1907], 24).

26. See, for example, Henri Delaborde, "Le musée des copies," *Revue des deux mondes*, 2 ser., 105 (1 May 1873), 215.

27. On aspects of "handling" in relation to classic art and photography compare Richard Shiff, "Handling Shocks," *New Observations*, no. 47 (1987), 14–19.

28. See, for example, Quatremère de Quincy [1824] 1835, 76; Eugène Delacroix, "Sur le *Jugement denier* (1837)," in Eugène Delacroix, *Oeuvres littéraires*, ed. Elie Faure, 2 vols. (Paris, 1923), 2:223–224.

29. Quatremère de Quincy implied that Michelangelo's art was doubly improper. First, because it was not in accord with Raphael's conception of the common ground of art, the style of the ancients; second, because it was not in accord with Raphael's own proper manner. See Quatremère de Quincy [1824] 1835, 70–71, 340.

30. Compare Richard Shiff, "Mastercopy," *Iris* (Paris) 1 (September 1983), 113–127, especially 117.

31. See, for example, H. W. Janson, "Originality as a Ground for Judgment of Excellence (1966)," in *Sixteen Studies* (New York, 1973), 151–155.

32. Delaborde 1870, 140. Compare Quatremère de Quincy [1824] 1835, 70.

33. Since Reynolds, Quatremère de Quincy, and others emphasized the broad range of Raphael's imitations drawn from contemporary and antique art, they thereby implied the universality of his character and reconfirmed his status as a "classic" (see Reynolds [1797] 1975, 104; Quatremère de Quincy [1824] 1835, 84, 87).

34. Delaborde 1870, 139.

35. It is significant that Raphael turns his gaze and body toward his emerging painting, while his model and mistress turns toward the undepicted Ingres, whom we may imagine to stand before the painting he is making. In effect the Ingres whom we imagine engaged with his own creation imitates the Raphael whom Ingres imagines in like manner. I find René Girard's concept of "mimetic desire" most useful in probing such representational relationships (see, for example, René Girard, *Violence and the Sacred*, trans. Patrick Gregory [Baltimore, 1977], 145–146).

36. See Richard Shiff, "Representation, Copying, and the Technique of Originality," *New Literary History* 15 (Winter 1984), 333–363, especially 338–344.

37. In other words, we see that the use of the term *index* when applied to painting is figurative and that the indexical image that painting produces is figurative.

38. Compare Shiff, "Representation (1984)," 344–346.

39. As when the tracing of a shadow constitutes an individual's representation or when a proper name itself functions as a true representation of that individual. Compare Ernst Kris and Otto Kurz, *Legend, Myth, and Magic in the Image of the Artist*, trans. Alastair Laing and Lottie M. Newman (New Haven, 1979), 74–75; Derrida 1976, 108–112. On indexing and origins compare also Philippe Dubois, "L'ombre, le miroir, l'index," *Parachute*, no. 26 (Spring 1982), 16–28; and *L'acte photographique* (Brussels, 1983). On the importance of the capacity to index in modern art see, for example, Jean-Claude Lebensztejn, "Esquisse d'une typologie," *Revue de l'art*, no. 26 (1974), 49; Rosalind E. Krauss, "Notes on the Index," *The Originality of the Avant-garde and Other Modernist Myths* (Cambridge, Mass., 1985), 196–219; Stephen Bann, "The Mythical Conception Is the Name: Titles and Names in Modern and Post-modern Painting," *Word & Image* 1 (April–June 1985), 176–190.

40. Even when we recognize that a photograph has been oddly manipulated, the effect carries "reality" along with it. When we view the superimposition of two bodies in a double-exposure photograph, we are inclined to see either real ghostly apparitions or real people appearing as ghosts in this particular view.

41. Compare Ernst Robert Curtius, *European Literature and the Latin Middle Ages*, trans. Willard R. Trask (Princeton, 1973), 250.

42. Those who explain photography's place in our culture by emphasizing the naturalness of its claim to the representation of the real usually summarily dismiss the issue of "trick" photography. I find this strategy justifiable since we seem to have little trouble in dismantling complex modes of photographic production and presentation to distinguish levels of indexing in the image (see, for example, Walton 1984, 267–269).

43. One can additionally argue that photographs require (or used to require) a certain accommodation on the part of their viewers, that photography represents a distortion of what one habitually sees (in pictures or in nature) since it tends to exaggerate effects of perspective and focus. Compare, for example, William M. Ivins, Jr., *Prints and Visual Communication* (Cambridge, Mass., 1953), 138.

44. Walter Benjamin, "The Work of Art in the Age of Mechanical Reproduction (1936)," in *Illuminations*, trans. Harry Zohn, ed. Hannah Arendt (New York, 1969), 219.

45. For indications of the conceptual parameters of the issue, see, for example, Edward Steichen, "Ye Fakers," *Camera Work*, no. 1 (January 1903), 48; and Henri Matisse's statement in George Besson, "Pictorial Photography—A Series of Interviews," *Camera Work*, no. 24 (October 1908), 22. For two distinguished recent contributions to the debate see Christopher Phillips, "The Judgment Seat of Photography," *October*, no. 22 (Fall 1982), 27–63, especially 59; and Joel Snyder, "Documentary without Ontology," *Studies in Visual Communication* 10 (Winter 1984), 78–95. For a brief account and historical overview of a developing social critique of photographic practice as a rhetoric of power see Terry Smith, "Photography for and against the Grain: Leslie Shedden and Allan Sekula," *Afterimage* 13 (Summer 1985), 16–19. Perhaps because of the long history of the debate, categories today are often set in oversimplified, undialectical opposition. For example, critics of the museum as an institution frequently regard the category of the aesthetic (associated with self-expression and genius) as mythical and antithetical to the "real" category of the rhetorical (associated with instrumentality and power). To distinguish a photograph's rhetorical, organizational features from its aesthetic qualities can be deceptive since these categories are interchangeable. All photographs are organized, if not by the producer then by the consumer. When exhibited in the museum or in a photographer's book, the police photo, initially designed to make evident some very specific "fact," is likely to be admired for its novelty, naïveté, or gripping "strangeness." Reciprocally, the artist-photographer's product, examined by the police, immediately becomes evidence, perhaps ingeniously revealing of the essential facts of a case. Seen within the context of a study of visual anthropology, photographs are usually viewed as both aesthetic and evidential.

46. Blanc 1860, 138.

47. Hans Tietze, "The Psychology and Aesthetics of Forgery in Art," *Metropolitan Museum Studies* 5 (1934–1936), 10.

48. Delaborde 1870, 150.

49. Conversely, photographs that seem to eliminate detail and capture a general effect are often said to be "artistic." In this respect the critical framework employed by Delacroix in 1859 is the same as that of many recent commentators (see Achille Piron, *Eugène Delacroix: Sa vie et ses oeuvres* [Paris, 1865], 407).

50. Lincoln Kirstein, "Photographs of America: Walker Evans," in Walker Evans, *American Photographs* (New York, 1938), 183–192. Additionally, Kirstein described Evans' vision as "Middle Western" and "puritanical" and stated that "the sculpture of New Bedford shipbuilders, the face-maps of itinerant portraitists, the fantasy of our popular songsters and anonymous typefounders continue in his camera." That Evans dramatically cropped many of his straight-on shots was not a problematic issue.

51. *International Center of Photography Encyclopedia of Photography*, s.v. "snapshot aesthetic."

52. My examples are works by canonical figures of the recent art history of photography. As photographers with "artistic" ambitions their choice of documentary manner is especially self-conscious and reflects a positioning vis-à-vis the imagery of other professionals as well as in relation to the broader field of images in the culture.

53. One of the best illustrations for this interpretation of the impact of Arbus' oeuvre is her *Two Girls in Matching Bathing Suits* (1967). (The estate of Diane Arbus does not allow reproduction of this photograph; it appears, however, in the Aperture monograph *Diane Arbus* [Millerton, N.Y., 1972].) The photograph pictures two teenagers posing with the natural stiffness associated with a casual, amateur portrait. They wear identical two-piece bathing suits of a particularly loud pattern, which exhibits its own rather comical play on symmetry—the top of each bathing suit opposes solid to stripe from the viewer's left to right, while each bottom displays the same opposition but arranged from right to left. It takes only two who dress in like manner to constitute a fashion. The viewer's own sense of fashion, as well as Arbus' early career as a fashion photographer (if the viewer is aware of it), distances this seemingly matter-of-fact image. It will regain some of its innocence only if we imagine the photograph to have been taken by a third girl, companion of the pictured pair, who was also wearing the same striking bathing suit and who experienced no ironic distance from her subject. Arbus was not such a person. Additionally, *Two Girls* is an example of Arbus' use of irregular print edges, apparently the result of uncorrected irregularities in the negative carrier. (I thank Margaret Olin and Laura Volkerding for information regarding the technical features of Arbus' prints.)

54. Pierre Fontanier, *Les figures du discours* (1821–1830; Paris, 1977), 213, 216. Like Quatremère de Quincy, Fontanier notes that the word *figure* itself is metaphorically used when it refers to the form of discourse or of representation. Its proper reference is to the external form of a physical body, "but," Fontanier adds, "this *metaphor* cannot be regarded as a true *figure*, because we have no other word in the language for the same idea" (63).

55. For related examples see Fontanier [1821–1830] 1977, 216–219. In the tradition of Etienne Bonnot de Condillac, Fontanier conceived of words as signs for preexisting ideas; a catachretic term is to be used when no other word is available, but it does not in itself create the idea or meaning. Today we might prefer to think of the word as giving forth the idea or as indistinguishable from the idea. The catachretic

term would then inscribe the willful as the proper—it would force new meaning on the existing discourse. Hence if photographs are indeed catachretic representations, we understand why they seem so powerful. During the 1970s the potential force of catachresis as a concept caught the imagination of a number of linguists, philosophically oriented critics, and linguistically oriented philosophers. For example, in 1971 Derrida cited Fontanier's definition and noted: "What is interesting to us here, thus, is the production of a proper sense, a new kind of proper sense, by means of the violence of a catachresis whose intermediary status tends to escape the opposition of the primitive [or proper] and the figurative, standing between them as a 'middle.' When the middle of an opposition is not the passageway of a mediation, there is every chance that the opposition is not pertinent. The consequences are boundless" (Jacques Derrida, "White Mythology," in *Margins of Philosophy*, trans. Alan Bass [Chicago, 1982], 256n. Derrida (249) astutely argues that the proper does not adequately represent an essence but is only the proper way of referring to an absent essence.

56. Antoine Chrysostome Quatremère de Quincy, *Essai sur l'idéal dans ses applications pratiques aux oeuvres de l'imitation propre des arts du dessin* (Paris, 1837), 207–208.

57. See Quatremère de Quincy 1823, 268, 323–429. The association with metaphor of an idealized or imaginative art—in Quatremère de Quincy's terms, an art of "imitation"—was so natural that Baudelaire used it also, despite the gulf that separated his theoretical stance from that of the master academician (see Baudelaire [1859] 1975–1976, 2:621). On the factor of metaphoricity as perceived in the painting of the modern period see Shiff "Representation (1984)."

58. Hence the possibility of the countercharge, on behalf of classical painting, that photography's detail is excessive and "ugly."

59. Quotation from Daguerre's advertisement (1838), cited in Newhall 1964, 17. Photography was soon advanced as a medium of representation that undermined the privileged, mannered idealization that academic training promoted (compare Anne McCauley, "Caricature and Photography in Second Empire Paris," *Art Journal* 43 [Winter 1983], 359).

60. Quintilian, 8.6.35, writes that "we must be careful to distinguish between *abuse* [*abusio*, the Latin word for catachresis] and *metaphor*, since the former is employed where there is no proper term available and the latter when there is another term available" (*Institutio oratoria*, trans. E. Butler, 4 vols. [Cambridge, Mass., 1976], 3:321). The photograph might indeed seem a metaphoric representation of what painting already adequately pictures except for the fact that a photograph in comparison with a painting usually appears less distanced from the model. More important, photography's figuration is of a different kind, so a comparison of the two terms, painting and photography, becomes improper. Without a compelling basis for comparison the preexistence of painting is not sufficient to transfer the photograph into the realm of metaphor, that is, to metaphorize it. By Quintilian's standard as well as by Fontanier's the photograph becomes a catachresis. It does so with violence as it robs painting of whatever claim to the proper it may have had. Photography metaphorizes painting as if by comparison, despite the incommensurability of the two terms.

61. The same interpretive controversy characterizes the reception of "primitive" art in the West. What do photography and primitive art have in common? They both undermine interpretive practice because they are perceived as indexical in a rather magical way. They can be integrated into a scientist culture either through a discourse of aesthetics and museology or through a discourse of sociology and anthropology.

PHOTO CREDITS